Process Redesign
for Health Care
Using Lean
Thinking

A Guide for Improving Patient Flow and
the Quality and Safety of Care

Process Redesign for Health Care Using Lean Thinking

A Guide for Improving Patient Flow and the Quality and Safety of Care

David I. Ben-Tovim

CRC Press
Taylor & Francis Group
Boca Raton London New York

CRC Press is an imprint of the
Taylor & Francis Group, an **informa** business
A PRODUCTIVITY PRESS BOOK

CRC Press
Taylor & Francis Group
6000 Broken Sound Parkway NW, Suite 300
Boca Raton, FL 33487-2742

Printed by CPI on sustainably sourced paper

International Standard Book Number-13: 978-1-138-19609-4 (Paperback)

Library of Congress Cataloging-in-Publication Data

Names: Ben-Tovim, D. I., author.
Title: Process redesign for health care using lean thinking : a guide for improving patient flow and the quality and safety of care / David Ben-Tovim.
Description: Boca Raton : Taylor & Francis, 2017.
Identifiers: LCCN 2016044986| ISBN 9781138196094 (pbk. : alk. paper) | ISBN 9781138630864 (hbk : alk. paper) | ISBN 9781315303956 (ebook)
Subjects: | MESH: Delivery of Health Care--organization & administration | Quality Assurance, Health Care--methods | Total Quality Management | Efficiency, Organizational | Organizational Culture | Case Reports
Classification: LCC RA971 | NLM W 84.1 | DDC 362.1068--dc23
LC record available at https://lccn.loc.gov/2016044986

Visit the Taylor & Francis Web site at
http://www.taylorandfrancis.com

and the CRC Press Web site at
http://www.crcpress.com

For Josephine, without her constant support and encouragement, and her enduring belief in the value of the work, none of this would have been possible. With all my love and thanks.

Contents

SECTION II CASE STUDIES: MAKING IT WORK

Chapter 1

Introduction: An Accidental Redesigner

I am an accidental redesigner. Yet, I have spent more than 10 years attempting to redesign the way care is organized and delivered in hospitals and health services.

I am a psychiatrist and clinical epidemiologist by background. The Flinders Medical Centre is a 500-bed teaching general hospital in Adelaide, South Australia. In 2000, I became its Director of Clinical Governance. My job was to oversee safety and quality systems throughout the hospital.

The main problem was apparent. The Emergency Department had become catastrophically congested. Patients were being managed in far-from-optimal settings, and problems that started in the Emergency Department were showing up all over the hospital.

The hospital was not facing an excess patient load, just the work the community had every right to expect the hospital to be able to manage. A variety of efforts had been made to improve things. None had provided lasting relief. Then, my colleague Melissa Lewis came across something called Process Mapping on the Internet. It seemed to involve bringing together the people who worked in a unit and asking them what they did to move the patients through the unit. We thought Process Mapping might help us understand what was going on. Although the senior staff members who worked in the Emergency Department were confident that they had a pretty good handle on how the department worked, they were willing to try anything to get the department working, including Process Mapping.

Process Mapping

One Tuesday morning, about 20 staff from the Emergency Department, Melissa Lewis, and I gathered in the Emergency Department seminar room. Every discipline group working in the department was represented, from the Patient Service Assistants who did the cleaning, fetching, and carrying, to the most senior Emergency Physicians.

Melissa and I decided to ask the participants to describe what they did, step by step, from the moment a patient arrived at the glass doors at the entrance to the department until that patient left the department and went home or was admitted to an in-patient unit.

Over three long sessions, we mapped out the sequences of care the department provided. It was a revelation. As soon as we started, it became clear just how confusing the care processes had become. The Emergency Department staff were as surprised by this as we were.

Every patient who comes to a major Emergency Department in Australia sees a specialized Triage nurse. The Triage nurse is stationed, literally and metaphorically, at the front door. She or he makes a very brief clinical assessment of all the patients and allocates a Triage score to each one. A Triage score is the Triage nurse's assessment of how urgently the rest of the staff in the department need to begin the work of providing definitive care: immediately, within 10 minutes, within 30 minutes, within 60 minutes, or within 2 hours. Many of the problems in the Emergency Department seemed to begin with the way Triage scores were being used. The Triage scores not only described patients but were also used to place patients in queues. Whilst this might seem to make sense, the case study in Chapter 20 makes it clear why this had become a problem.

As we presented our observations to various groups around the hospital, there was widespread agreement that something needed to be done—but what?

The Modernization Agency

A small group of us, including Jane Bassham, at that time the senior nurse in the Emergency Department, and Dr. Di King, the head of the Emergency Department, were able to spend a few days in London as guests of an NHS organization, the Modernization Agency (since then disbanded). We visited Emergency Departments in busy hospitals that had been transformed from war zones into acceptable places for staff and patients alike. Our Modernization Agency hosts, who were very involved in supporting the improvements, gave us copies of the book, *Lean Thinking* (Womack and Jones 2003), telling us that they had found it very useful. They gave us the book on a rather secretive, need-to-know kind of basis. The secrecy surprised us.

Later on, we discovered that there was a concern that if the Modernization Agency talked about learning from industry, it would be taken to mean that the NHS was going to be sold off to private enterprise, which was not the impression the government of the day wanted to make.

Back in Australia, we were also able to spend a few days with Ben Gowland, then a senior staff member of the Modernization Agency. Ben had played an important role in the changes we observed. We kept asking him what we should do. He told us that we were clever people, and we would be able to work things out for ourselves. While this did not feel very supportive, he was right. Under the inspirational leadership of Dr. Di King, we used our experiences in London and our reading of *Lean Thinking* to introduce some dramatic changes in the internal organization of the Emergency Department (King et al. 2006). Overnight, those changes improved our capacity to provide good, timely care. And over the next year, a hospital-wide dramatic decrease in the number of patients seeking redress for serious failures in the safety and quality of care implied that something was having an impact throughout the hospital.

Clearly, there was something to this Lean Thinking business (Ben-Tovim et al. 2007), even though at that time it was not being used in other Australian hospitals and health services.

Ben also said that if we wanted to make a lasting difference, we needed to create a team, with a formal structure and explicit governance, dedicated to improvement work. He said it was as important to think about the team as it was to think about the changes we intended to make. This was very good advice, without which we would not have given much thought to creating a team and a governance structure. The hospital management listened to Ben and set up a small team to "do Lean." I was appointed its Director. Two full time, and one part-time, nurses and a psychologist completed the team. We established both the team (which included Melissa Lewis, Jane Bassham, Denise Bennett, Margaret Martin part time, and later Jackie Sincock and Lauri O'Brien) and a governance structure that brought together the senior hospital leaders. We decided on a name—Redesigning Care—and got started.

Why Redesign?

Why redesign, not design or improve? It is because the hospital already existed, with skillful and committed people already doing their best. We were not beginning with a clean slate. On the contrary, we were trying to improve care processes already in place in an institution that did not have the luxury of closing down until it got things sorted out.

Learning about Lean

Clearly, we needed to learn more about this Lean stuff. The team, plus some senior managers, went on a local university course in Lean Manufacturing. Our fellow students came from a variety of local industries. We learned as much from them as from the formal content of the course. Yes, the contexts differed, but we were all grappling with the same kinds of problems.

Most importantly, during, and after the course, as we set about trying to redesign care across the hospital, the team kept working together to try and make sense of what we were actually doing.

Then and later we were strongly supported by Julia Davidson, Michael Szwarcbord, and Susan O'Neill in various management roles. Paul Hakendorf, Chris Horwood, and John Gray were patient with us and helped us with the key tasks of data retrieval and analysis, as well as provided general and, much needed, support.

Invaluable contributions to both theory and practice have been made by the hundreds of clinical and nonclinical staff with whom we have worked, both at Flinders and across the country, and by the people who worked part time in the Redesigning Care team for longer or shorter periods.

So many people have been important that it is almost invidious to mention specific individuals or groups. But Peter Walsh from Lean Enterprise Australia has been a particular friend and support, as has the Lean community as a whole. Despite their many other responsibilities, Katherine McGrath and Tony O'Connell have provided invaluable support and encouragement. The list could go on but has to include the ever-patient Di Mackintosh and Kylie Thomas whose support and assistance have been crucial.

The Process Redesign for Health Care using Lean Thinking method draws extensively, though not exclusively, on Lean Thinking theory and practice. I begin with a discussion of the origins of Lean Thinking and some of the issues involved in adapting it for Health Care. I then move on to describe Process Redesign methodology in some detail. Brief case material is used to illustrate the principles and the evolution of that methodology. There are then four extended case histories in which I try to provide a more detailed picture of how Process Redesign for Health Care using Lean Thinking (frequently abbreviated to Process Redesign or Process Redesign for Healthcare) works in practice. Almost invariably, the most creative work was done by the staff on the ground. They know the work and, without exception, have been anxious to improve the quality of care they provide. The case studies are not intended to be templates for how to solve certain problems. They cannot be; Health Care problems need solutions that are relevant and specific to their context. The purpose of the case studies is to illustrate the Redesign Process and give a sense of how Redesign actually occurs. To make that possible, the extended case studies are based on the materials produced at the time.

Health Care involves people at their most vulnerable and private moments. To minimize the risk of identifying individuals, details that might identify specific participants, or institutional issues of any sensitivity, have been altered or removed, and if diagrams or figures are presented that are based on materials produced during Redesign programs, they have been altered and redrawn so that anonymity is preserved. Facts or figures that might identify individuals or specific services have also been altered to minimize the risk of inappropriate identifications. However, every effort has been made to faithfully describe the spirit of the Process Redesign programs and not make false claims for program outcomes. However, the case studies have been written up in a format that clearly separates out various phases of the work involved. That was how the work progressed, and where major deviations in the progression of work occurred, they have been discussed; however, case studies are by their nature somewhat simplified representations of a messier reality.

Writing up the case histories has only been possible because of the extensive documentation of the work as it progressed. It is a tribute to the efforts Denise Bennett and the other team members put into reporting to governance groups at each step on the way. Denise was a particular force for good in this area, and much of the credit for the consistency of the documentation must go to her leadership.

Throughout the text, when a personal contribution by a team member has been particularly clear, I have tried to identify that person's contribution to the development of theory or practice, but again, whilst maintaining confidentiality and recognizing the importance of the team as a whole.

A Decade Later

A decade after this work began, there is a growing community of Health Care redesigners using Lean Thinking to redesign and improve Health Care processes, both in Australia and the rest of the world. I am delighted with the role I and my colleagues have been able to play in this development, and with the way the Australasian Lean Health Care Network, which the Flinders group has been part of from the start, has supported that development in Australasia.

Process Redesign for Health Care is for anyone who is trying to improve how their hospital or health service delivers care. I hope there is something in it both for the novice redesigner and the more experienced practitioner curious to learn more. Redesign is never easy. It is hard work. Things never go quite to plan. But it can be done. Process Redesign is a team effort. When faced with the common experience of not quite knowing what you are doing or what to do next, as the Flinders team always said, "have confidence in the method, and don't miss a step."

CONTEXT AND METHOD

Chapter 2

Craft, Flow, Mass

The term *Lean Thinking* first appeared in the book *The Machine that Changed the World* (Womack et al. 1990). The book was a summary of a global research program into car-making around the world. Lean Thinking was the term the authors used to sum up the distinctive production and managerial methods they observed at the Toyota Motor Company.

To understand what excited Womack et al., it's essential to know something about the evolution of methods for making large, complicated objects, such as boats or cars. It is possible to look back in history to fourteenth century Venetian shipyard production or even earlier to the production of terracotta warriors for the tomb of the first Emperor of Qin who died in 221 BCE, but the important period to concentrate on is the end of the nineteenth century. That was when what was commonly described as the British method of manufacturing gave way to the American method, out of which emerged mass production as we know it today.

This short history (Lazonick 1981; Reinstaller 2007) is not simply included to make it clear what Toyota was doing that was different. Modern Health Care makes use of every method of production, from pre-industrial craft work to the most advanced manufacturing techniques. Understanding the differences between the methods helps explain why they do not always fit easily together in the day-to-day work of Health Care.

British Manufacturing: The Extension of the Craft Work System

Britain was at the forefront of the industrial revolution, and the nineteenth century saw a massive expansion in British manufacturing. However, many aspects of the organization of emerging large-scale manufacturing firms stayed locked into pre-existing craft work structures. Groups of workers with a craft inheritance, working in expanding manufacturing firms, gained (or maintained) control over key components of the day-to-day operations of the large-scale manufacturing companies. They retained control over the organization of work, including hiring and firing workers ("no ticket, no start," in the Australian vernacular).

Traditionally, craft work is paid as piece work: you get paid for what you produce. The craft worker controls how he or she does the work and at what pace. By retaining control of the day-to-day management of production, workgroups could determine the tempo of work. They could retain control over rates of pay and influence the extent to which new technology leads to job losses.

Continuity of worker control also provided certain advantages for the firms involved. Only limited amounts of managerial time and energy were spent organizing and coordinating day-to-day work; disruptive strikes were minimized, and continuity of production was guaranteed, which was important in the context of the fierce local competition at the end of the nineteenth century.

The British approach did much to humanize capitalism and contain its excesses. It helped preserve the value and dignity of labor and balance the value of the laborer against the rights of capital. But it also delayed or inhibited the employment of new technologies that lowered the cost of production. And piece-work payments were particularly inappropriate for processes where objects were assembled in a continuous process, so that the tempo of production did not depend on individual effort. All these issues made British manufacturing steadily less competitive.

The American Method of Production

In the late nineteenth century, as people moved westward, the expanding American population and the emergence of the national railroad gave American manufacturers new opportunities for growth and development. In seizing them, manufacturers moved decisively away from the British model, gaining control of production processes using a number of strategies (Reinstaller 2007).

First, they invested in de-skilling technological change. Work was broken down into elementary units designed by production engineers and structured so that unskilled workers needed only brief training before being able to complete their assigned tasks. Sophisticated machinery replaced skilled craft work and craft-trained workers. The machines allowed unskilled or semi-skilled machine operators to replace craftsmen and women. Control over hiring and firing, and control of work tempo, was transferred to managers. A number of important judgments by the American Supreme Court reinforced the rights of managers and restricted the rights of organized labor, and helped the move to hourly rates of pay, rather than piece-work payment.

Work on the shop floor still needed to be coordinated. Large administrative and managerial groups emerged, whose task was to design and coordinate production processes. By the early twentieth century, the new methods provided such competitive advantage that from then on America became the dominant force in manufacturing. However, the American method needed to evolve further before it became mass production–oriented as we know of it today. Many of the early innovations in that evolution are synonymous with the work of Henry Ford.

Henry Ford and Highland Park

Henry Ford's first breakthrough was the Model T car. Model T Fords were assembled at the Highland Park production facility in Detroit, Michigan, using what at that time was a revolutionary moving assembly line production process. Henry Ford's key innovation was to reverse the craft work process where the worker controls the production process. In craft work, the worker literally and metaphorically "goes" to the work. Henry Ford's revolution was to bring the work to the worker.

Ford, together with his assistant Charles Sorenson, developed a continuous belt, moving production line which moved a car chassis past a variety of work stations. At each station, the arrival of the increasingly assembled chassis prompted the worker to add a specific component, using a work sequence developed by a production engineer. As Ford and his colleagues refined the production process, the time taken to assemble a Model T Ford fell from 12 hours to around 93 minutes.

The Model T was both enormously successful and extremely profitable. The Model T Ford was in production from 1909 to 1927. More than 15 million cars were produced in that time. By 1918, probably half of all cars in the United States were Model Ts. Over time, the Model T's sale price fell from $850 to $240 (equivalent to approximately a quarter of the cost of the cheapest new car in today's money).

As competitors caught up and consumers started to demand more choice, Ford needed to move on. Move he did, to the River Rouge complex on the confluence of the Rouge and Detroit rivers, south of Detroit.

The Rouge, Production Villages, and Excess Inventory

At the Rouge, production evolved from flow along a single assembly line to production in a complex a mile and a half wide and a mile long. Production was broken up into large functions—axles, tires, body frames, marketing, purchasing, and so on. The Rouge was so large that each major function was undertaken by a group housed in its own production "village," and each village had its own location: the transmission plant, casting plant, radiator plant, and so on.

Individual models within the range of cars produced at the Rouge were made up from combinations of the output of each production village. The relevant components were mixed, matched, and assembled into actual cars on a limited number of final assembly lines.

Making the parts and components required for modern motor cars, and other elaborately transformed objects, frequently involves using large, expensive, high-precision machines. The settings on such machines are hard to change. So the usual mass production strategy is still to run expensive machines as hard and fast as possible, making large numbers, or job lots, of single parts before changing the machine settings. Then the parts, known in industry as inventory, are stored until they are needed.

It is at this point that the problems of coordination, scheduling, and synchronization in mass production emerge. Discrete groups working in different locations produce their own group of components. Each group strives to maximize the cost-efficiency of what they do by working as fast and hard as possible. Eventually, the different production rhythms and volumes have to be harmonized both with each other and with the varying demands of the marketplace. Harmonization may be difficult to achieve. Complex production schedules have to be devised and, because things do not always go to plan, they will need endless revision and fine-tuning. No sooner are they put out than they need to be changed. Does this remind you of day-to-day life in a hospital—for example, a surgical operating theater list.

Alfred Sloan

Ford was a genius at production; his genius did not extend to organizational design. A common view is that the only way he knew how to make the Rouge work was to make the important decisions himself. Creating an organizational structure that would make large mass production corporations work effectively was the work of Alfred Sloan, who became President of General Motors in the 1920s.

Sloan restructured the sprawling mess that was General Motors into a small corporate headquarters and a series of decentralized divisions that actually produced cars. Sloan managed "by the numbers." Overall business strategy was the province of senior management at the head office. The head office judged the performance of operational units in financial terms. Senior corporate managers did not need to know much about how things were made. That was the responsibility of the divisional managers. What mattered to Sloan was performance against a series of financial metrics. Woe befell the manager who failed to produce good numbers.

Making General Motors, and the other large corporations that followed the General Motors model, work day to day was the responsibility of a group of general managers, and the profitability of the business depended on this managerial hierarchy to coordinate, monitor, and allocate resources as required (Chandler 1988).

Mass production brought about enormous benefits in terms of the capacity to produce large volumes of goods at low cost. There are many aspects of the Sloan model of managing by the numbers that appeal to the current generation of managers of government health departments. But embedded within mass production is the problem of coordination, an excellent example of which is the problems Boeing has had with the production of that most complex of modern elaborately transformed objects, a new passenger jet airplane.

Dreamliner or Bad Dream

The Boeing 787 Dreamliner is Boeing's first all-new aircraft in 15 years. Boeing is a pioneer in the application of Lean production methods in the aircraft industry. But the strategy it adopted for the Dreamliner's production was a radical break from the company's established methods of aircraft production. Previously, Boeing had done much of the work itself. But Dreamliner production was broken down into components that were both designed (at least in part) and produced by suppliers all over the world. By involving suppliers in this way, Boeing intended to reduce the risks associated with the enormous costs of designing a brand-new range of aircrafts. Boeing was essentially becoming an assembler of parts made by risk-sharing suppliers.

Problems began soon after the project started. It was hard to keep production work in sequence, and there were parts shortages and difficulties with software and systems integration that led to years of delay (Terdiman 2011). Most of those problems have now been resolved, and the Dreamliners are rolling off the production line, but at what extra cost?

It was the contrast between the problems of existing mass production methods and the systems Toyota developed in its manufacturing system that interested the authors of *The Machine that Changed the World* (Womack et al. 1990).

Chapter 3

Taiichi Ohno and the Birth of Lean

Toyota describes its systems as "just-in-time" and the "Toyota Production System"; it was Womack et al. (1990), in trying to sum up how the Toyota Production System differed from conventional mass production, who coined the term "Lean Thinking." The "Lean" in Lean Thinking was intended to contrast the processes developed by Toyota with the "Mass" of mass production. Presumably, the "Thinking" in Lean Thinking referred to the driving force behind the development of the Toyota Production System, Taiichi Ohno (1998, 57), who said, "... I want to emphasise the importance of thoroughly understanding production and manpower reduction.... 'Understanding' is my favorite word ... it [is] to approach an objective positively to comprehend its nature."

It is time to acknowledge a bias. In the 1980s, I spent 3 years working in Botswana, then an impoverished, majority-ruled sub-Saharan African country. Shortly after I arrived, the Government of Botswana supplied me with a Toyota Land Cruiser tray top truck. Over the next 3 years, the truck (mostly driven by the incomparable Moffatt Sibanda) and I traveled more than 120,000 kilometers over the appalling corrugated calcrete and deep sand that passed for roads in the Kalahari Desert. The whole time I was in Botswana, the truck started first time, every time. It kept running no matter how much it was put through. So I was already aware of Toyota's capacity to produce reliable vehicles long before I heard about Lean Thinking.

Leaving personal experiences aside, it is possible to make more of Toyota than it warrants. It is a company whose principle business is to make motor cars. In general, those cars are very reliable. Toyota makes them profitably, in large numbers, and with considerable innovation in a number of its lines; but Toyota is certainly fallible. Recent years have seen a string of recalls of Toyota vehicles to correct production problems. But Toyota weathered the global financial crisis without external assistance and is still one of the largest and most successful of all motor manufacturers. It is also a fact that the manufacture of a modern car involves designing and putting together at least 10,000 separate parts, so car-making is not simple.

Why Is Lean Thinking Important for Health Care?

Not because it is a better way to make motor cars. It's because it is a good way to manage, coordinate, and schedule work practices in any industry, including Health Care. Lean Thinking needs some modification before it is "fit for purpose" in Health Care. But the basics of Lean Thinking are relevant and important. There is no better place to understand them than the writings of Taiichi Ohno himself.

Toyota and Taiichi Ohno

The Toyoda family firm started life as a manufacturer of ingenious automatic looms. As the Toyota Motor Company, it started building light trucks before the Second World War. Toyota entered the passenger vehicle market after the Second World War. When it started making passenger cars, it did not have the resources to compete against large American manufacturers, but it had a period of protection from imports, and a workforce on lifetime contracts that needed to be seen as assets, rather than as costs to be minimized. And, its production manager was an extraordinary man.

Taiichi Ohno (1998, 13) was a great admirer of Henry Ford in his Highland Park period and a great critic of mass production as it had evolved. He describes the outcomes of American style mass production using high-performance, high-speed machines in these terms: "… an earlier process forwards products to the later process continuously regardless of the production requirements of that process. Mountains of parts, therefore, might pile up at the later process. At that point, workers spend their time looking for storage space and hunting for parts instead of making progress in the most important part of their jobs, production…."

Waste and Flow

Over and again, Ohno stated that his goal was to eliminate waste. By "waste," he did not mean cutting a sheet of metal in such a way that, when a car body part was pressed out, the minimum amount of metal was wasted as scrap. Ohno emphasized that in conventional mass production, the cost of making a car includes the cost of wasted time and effort looking for things, the cost of making and storing parts before they could be used, and the cost of making good any faulty parts. Those and all the other accumulated costs of doing anything other than designing and producing components and assembling them into a finished vehicle were the wastes that were part and parcel of conventional mass production. Ohno's insight was that if he could minimize the costs associated with such wastes, he could produce cars at a competitive price.

For Ohno, waste and flow were two sides of the same coin. He could just as easily have said that his goal was to maximize flow rather than eliminate waste. Ohno (1998, 4) wrote:

> [T]he basis of the Toyota Production System is the absolute elimination of waste. The two pillars needed to support the system are just-in-time and autonomation. What is just-in-time? Just that in a flow process the right parts are needed in assembly to reach the assembly line at the time they are needed and only in the amount needed. A company establishing this flow throughput can approach zero inventory.

Inventory is the term used in industry to include all the parts, held in stock by a company, that are needed to make the finished product. It does not matter whether the parts are in boxes waiting to be unpacked after delivery by a supplier, or already assembled into components, and stored somewhere in the factory waiting to be used (the latter is commonly known as work-in-progress).

Inventory absorbs time, money, and effort, none of which can be recouped until the final product is delivered to the customer and payment received.

Ohno's goal was to achieve a flow process with minimum inventory. It did not happen overnight. He experimented for many years to develop the innovative production techniques that form the basis of Lean Thinking.

Work and Waste

The heart of this experimentation was working out what was work and what was waste. Ohno defined waste in human terms. For him, waste was needless, repetitive movement that must be eliminated immediately—for example, waiting for or stacking subassemblies, and unnecessary transportation. Work was not one thing. Ohno separated work into nonvalue-adding (but necessary) work and value-adding work. Nonvalue-adding (but necessary) work is work that must be done "under present work conditions," such as removing wrappers from parts purchased from subcontractors, removing parts in small quantities from a pallet full of parts, or walking over to another location to receive parts. For Ohno (1998, 57), value-adding work involves "some kind of processing—changing the shape or character of a product or assembly. The higher this ratio [of value added to necessary but non-value-added work] the greater the working efficiency."

Kanban

How did Ohno set about reaching the seemingly unachievable goal of 100% value-added work with no inventory? Ohno (1998, 33) wrote that "Toyota Production System is the method [of reaching such goals]. Kanban is the way it is managed."

Conventional mass production relies on layer on layer of managers to schedule and supervise production. In the making your-numbers-based systems Sloan pioneered at General Motors, factory managers were judged on their capacity to meet two targets: yield and quality. Yield is the percentage of cars actually produced in relation to the scheduled volumes set by the head office. Quality is the quality of the finished goods at the point they leave the factory. "Moving metal" was all-important because the head office only assessed quality at the final check before the car left the factory. If defects occurred, they were made good at a rework area at the end of the production line.

In conventional mass production, the whole production system revolves around complex scheduling processes devised by humans and computers. Schedules instruct each group on the shop floor what to make and when. Because things never quite go to plan, the schedules have to be constantly rewritten. To make sure that the line never stops, large stocks of components are kept on hand to cover any eventuality.

In a truly inspired change of logic, Ohno realized that all this scheduling by managers was a source of waste in others. Ohno (1998, 28) approached the problem of production coordination in an entirely different way: "Generally, in a business, *what*, *when*, and *how many* are generated by the work planning section in the form of a work start plan, transfer plan, production order or delivery order passed through the plant … 'when' is set arbitrarily and people think it will be all right whether parts arrive on time or early … the word 'just' in 'just-in-time' means exactly that…. If parts arrive any time prior to their need … waste cannot be eliminated."

How to get things just-in-time, at the moment they are needed and in the quantity required? A car (or other kinds of complex goods or services made step-by-step) is produced in a series of defined steps. Let us say a company generally sells around 20 cars per day of a particular model.

Then, ideally the company needs to make 20 such cars each day to replace the ones that have been sold. If the factory works to an 8-hour day (480 minutes), a complete car needs to roll off the line every 24 minutes (480/20). What is the best way to ensure that every component is available at the exact moment it is needed, and that time and energy are not spent making massive stocks of things that have to be stored and moved around?

Ohno's answer was to get the people doing the last step in the assembly to start the day with one or two almost-finished cars, and then inform them how many cars need to be made that day. In our example, the final assembler would set a tempo that revolved around producing a car every 24 minutes. As soon as the final assemblers completed their necessary work on the first cars, taking 24 minutes, they send a signal to the step before to send them the next almost-finished vehicle. And so on down the line, until 20 cars are complete. At each station, the pace of production depends on signals generated at the next step, and passed back to the "feeding" station. Then everyone does enough to start the day with the next day, and goes home. No computers, no schedules, just manufacturing at the rhythm of the market.

In this system, the messages arrive at the individual steps at roughly 24-minute intervals. What happens if something cannot be made in around 24 minutes? Either the production process needs to be changed to make it fit into the 24-minute window, or the component needs to be made at more than one station, so that a needed part can be ready every 24 minutes. As Ohno (1998, 30) wrote: "The first rule of kanban is that the later process goes to the earlier process to pick up products…[when they are needed]."

Kanbans are central to the just-in-time output. The term *kanban* refers to a signal sent from the later process to the earlier process about what and how many the earlier process has to produce, and where it needs to deliver them, so that the later process can happen. The signal can be anything—a piece of paper, an electronic request, a box, a cart, a plastic token—as long as the later process indicates what, how many, and where, it needs from the earlier process. Ohno (1998, 31) states: "To the earlier production process, this means eliminating the production schedule they have relied on for so long. Production workers may have a good deal of psychological resistance to the idea that simply producing as much as possible is no longer a priority." But certainly in hospitals, we have found that people can adjust.

Supermarket

Because no one is perfect and because even in the best developed system there are variations in the time and quality of production of components, Ohno developed a supermarket-type approach to smooth out variations. In many areas, rather than relying on part-by-part signals, the operator at any one step has access to a small store of the parts he or she needs, just as a shopper needing a component for a stew pulls a packet of dried herbs from a shelf in a supermarket. The task of shelf-fillers in supermarkets is to replenish the goods on the shelf to a predetermined level. This keeps the supermarket shelf full (but not overfull) so that there is always enough, but not too many, packets of herbs on display and available for shoppers.

In manufacturing, workers at a particular step may have access to a mini supermarket of the components they need for that step (does this sound a bit like a surgical waiting list?). The operator of the previous step plays the role of shelf filler whose task it is to keep the next step's supermarket shelves filled with the right level of components—not so many as to be wasteful but not so few that there is a danger of a component being unavailable when it is needed. Removing the component/packet is the signal for the previous process to produce a replacement component/packet and make it available on the shelf.

Push and Pull

Conventional mass production (and many hospital processes) is a "push" process. In a push process, I make to my rhythm, and then harass you to take what I have produced. If what I need is not ready, I just have to wait, or keep enough in store to cover all eventualities.

Lean production is a "pull" process. In pull, I seek what I need from the earlier process, making sure that I always have enough, but not too much, of what I need. Many hospital Emergency Departments are filled with patients the Emergency staff have to nag, beg, and threaten staff in the body of the overcrowded hospital to accept. It is hard for staff used to working in this way to imagine how pull can help. But it can. Moving from push to pull has been a crucial strategy in many Health Care Redesign programs.

Workers as Problem Solvers: The Challenge for Managers

Lean Thinkers have tended to downplay Ohno's insistence on the importance of what he, or his translator, called "autonomation." But it was a crucial element in helping to see production line staff as problem solvers and collaborators, not just as a replaceable cost.

The automatic looms the Toyoda Company pioneered had an automated component that stopped the looms when a thread broke. This relieved the loom operator from having to constantly stand over the loom while it was in action. The loom operator only engaged with the loom when a problem occurred. As Ohno (1998, 6) says of the many machines used in Toyota, "… [they are] equipped with a device that could distinguish between normal and abnormal conditions." These devices stopped the machine when a problem occurred, thereby preventing defective products from being passed on. With autonomation, machine operators go from being machine minders to problem solvers. They can look after several machines at once, and solve the problem that caused the machine to stop, rather than mindlessly "minding" the machine.

Seeing workers as problem solvers is very characteristic of Toyota, and of Lean Thinking. Seeing workers as capable of problem-solving, rather than simple-to-replace sources of cost, requires a major shift in management thinking.

The more complex the work at the coal face, the more important that shift becomes. When everyday work is complicated, managers cannot singlehandedly provide all the solutions to problems in the production process. Managers need to acknowledge that the workers may well understand what is needed better than they do. Managers have to become collaborators and facilitators rather than commanders and controllers; not necessarily an easy transition.

As Ohno (1998, 9) wrote: "[T]here is no magic method. Rather a total management system is needed that develops human ability to its fullest capacity to best enhance creativity and fruitfulness, to utilise facilities and machines well, and to eliminate all waste." However, Ohno (1998, 22) did not have a sentimental view of the workforce, arguing that "… it should take no more than 3 days to train new workers in proper work practices."

Chapter 4

The Principles of Lean Thinking

The Process Viewpoint: The Golden Thread of Lean

The process viewpoint is the golden thread that runs through the Lean Thinking principles. Patients seek out Health Care because they are worried about their physical or mental health. Basic to Health Care is the pre-supposition that an abnormal or at-risk physical or mental state(s) or condition(s) may underlie a patient's concerns. The work of Health Care is the step-by-step identification of the abnormal or at-risk physical or mental state(s) and condition(s) and their transformation into a valued health outcome. In industrial terms, the abnormal or at-risk physical or mental state(s) and condition(s) are the raw materials that have to be transformed into a valued health outcome.

How is that transformation achieved? By processes. A general definition of a process is that it is the sequence of knowledge and tasks required to transform a given input (of a raw, or partially processed, material of any kind) into a specified output. The input may be intangible—a set of concerns or emotions. It may be representational—an image on an X-ray plate, a set of numbers from an auto-analyzer, or an equation. It may be material such as human tissue or blood. The process task is the same—to transform an input into a specified form of output.

Health Care is complicated, and it is common for the complete, end-to-end transformation of a patient's concerns into a valued outcome to require a sequence of processes, each with its own particular knowledge base and related transformative methodology.

A good end-to-end sequence of processes is one in which the specific processes link together simply, efficiently, and effectively. By analogy, the end-to-end transformation of a patient's concern may be seen as the product of a chain made up from links of different kinds of materials joined in varying ways. Alternatively, the transformation can be considered as being undertaken via a set of "invisible" Health Care production lines made up from a series of stations where different kinds of processes are undertaken.

As will be discussed in Chapter 11, end-to-end Health Care Processes can often be broken down into a number of procedural chunks where recognizable common intermediate functions such as arrival procedures, initial assessments, diagnostic testing, and so on are undertaken.

The particular actions, or means, required to complete the intermediate function will vary between differing end-to-end processes (a cardiac patient arriving with a possible heart attack will require a very different sequence of procedures from a 4-year-old child with an asthma attack), but the process ends are the same—moving the transformation of the abnormal or at-risk physical or mental state, along its transformative path.

Process Redesign can work at any level, from the improvement of a specific process, through to improving a large or small chunk of processes, up to end-to-end sequences, and groups of sequences. The improvement methodology is the same and is discussed in some detail. However, the focus of Process Redesign for Health Care as a text is mainly at the level of chunks of processes, and end-to-end processes.

Lean Thinking is a process-improvement methodology, and Ohno (1998) and Holweg (2007) provided the basic concepts that Womack and Jones (2003) articulated as Lean Thinking principles which were developed in the context of elaborately transformed goods such as motor cars. It would be easy to reformulate those principles in a language more familiar to Health Care. But language helps shape the way we see the world. A different language helps us see things in a different way, and Health Care Process Redesign is all about seeing Health Care in a different way. So, the Lean Thinking principles are put forward here in the kinds of terms that are in use in manufacturing and service industries.

The Lean Principles

The Lean principles can be stated as follows:

1. Specify value from the viewpoint of the end-customer
2. Identify the value stream for each product family
3. Eliminate waste and make the product flow
4. So that the customer can pull
5. As you manage toward perfection

Principle 1: Specify Value from the Viewpoint of the End-Customer

As it is, it is hard enough for Health Care practitioners to think in terms of customers, let alone end-customers. The late John Long was a Lean Thinking Health Care pioneer who was also a friend and mentor to our group in its early years. John taught us that the customer is the person who uses what you make (Long 2003). John separated out the patient, the Health Care end-customer, from intermediate customers who took possession of the product of one particular process, did a piece of transformative work, and moved the product on to the next process in its step-by-step transformation.

The end-product of Health Care is good-quality patient care. Many people working in Health Care do not interact directly with patients, yet still play an important role in the delivery of care. In a system where value is delivered by a series of processes, each intermediate process has a direct, or immediate, customer who uses what the previous process has made and passes on the product to a customer who uses what has just been made. A pathology laboratory is the customer of a phlebotomist (blood-taking technician). The laboratory subjects the blood sample to a series of procedures and produces an output in the form of a set of readings, printed on paper or delivered electronically. The direct customer for a laboratory will be the physician, but the end-customer is the patient whose samples are being analyzed.

How does all this relate to the issue of value? Value can be thought of, first in relation to the end-customer, and then in relation to the direct, intermediate customers within a process.

Patients: The End-Customer

Patients are the end-customers in Health Care. The primary purpose of any health service is to take the raw materials of patients' abnormal (or at-risk) physical and mental states and conditions and transform them into valued health outcomes. Who can define what is valued? Ultimately, only patients, alone, or in consultation with their families as they interact with the people who provide their care. In that sense, Health Care institutions are like other service industries, except that Health Care institutions cannot use the ultimate test of price and commercial viability to confirm that they are providing what their end-customers value.

When you buy a new car, a car salesperson will use all sorts of tricks to try to get you to spend more than you intended. But at the end of the day, the choice is yours. You know how much benefit you will derive from a heated car seat, split-level air conditioning, and a turbo-charged engine. You can decide to pay the price or walk away. Contrast that with a Health Care scenario. You suddenly develop crushing chest pain. An ambulance takes you to a well-organized hospital. Twenty minutes later you are in a catheter laboratory and a cardiologist is telling you that you need three metal stents inserted into the little arteries that supply blood to the heart. Are you going to try to negotiate over the price of the stents, discuss the virtues of coated or uncoated stents, and ask for some brochures so that you can take them away and see what various manufacturers have to offer? Are you going to shop around before having the stents put in?

In many circumstances, choices are limited for Health Care customers. As Health Care practitioners, we are often the effective monopoly suppliers of biomedical Health Care. It is only too easy for us to assume that we know what patients want. Indeed, some of us justify behaving badly toward patients on the grounds that "I know my work, and my patient gets better—so what if I don't have much of a bedside manner?" The image of the doctor as a temperamental genius is certainly one that TV programs foster. But in the real world of a regulated health system, competency, being able to do a good, professional, job, is surely a basic assumption. Competency is not a virtue but a legitimate customer expectation. In my view at least, it is not enough to use competency as a justification for bad behavior.

Here is a simple thought experiment that I have undertaken with hundreds of health workers. As we work through what value means in relation to Health Care. I ask them "what do you look for when you go into a shop?"

Mostly, the answers are:

- A pleasant environment
- Prompt service
- Clear information
- Respectful treatment
- Choice
- A product that works
- Value for money

I then ask "what do you and I, as patients, look for when *we* go to a hospital or health service?" Mostly, the answers are:

- A pleasant environment
- Prompt service
- Clear information
- Respectful treatment
- Choice
- A product that works
- Value for money

The only thing that separates the Health Care practitioner from his or her patients is time. We will all be patients at some time in our lives. There is nothing particular about what our customers want of health services. It is what we all want from any service provider. With one important addition: the plan.

I live in South Australia. The South Australian government regularly surveys patients, asking large numbers of patients recently treated in South Australian hospitals for their opinions about the care they received. What comes out over and again is the importance of a plan. Patients are terribly concerned that there is a plan for their care. In the survey responses, patients make it clear that they want Health Care workers to make a plan and then discuss it with them. But they are even more concerned that their Health Care providers talk to each other about the plan. Any Health Care worker who is a fairly regular user of health services can bear witness to how frustrating it is to feel that it is up to you, the patient, to keep the doctors, nurses, physiotherapists, pharmacists, and everyone else involved updated about the plan and how it is going. You, the patient, often seem to be the only person who knows the outline of the plan, and what is supposed to be happening when. And experience is that if you are too sick to look after yourself, and you do not have a family member or friend keeping track of the plan and advocating for you, look out.

Value, the Intermediate Process, and the Direct Customer

When I do Process Redesign workshops for Health Care practitioners, the value questions I ask of each attendee are:

- What do you personally make?
- Who uses what you personally make?
- What do these users value?

The only people allowed to answer "better care" are those who provide face-to-face care for patients, and then only in relation to the time they actually spend directly providing that care. For everyone else, the exercise is to think about what your intermediate process actually makes, and what your role is in the making process, to work out who your customers are, and to ask "do you know what they value?."

A Health Care manager who has started to consider "what do the people I manage value about my management" has moved away from a "command and control" viewpoint. If you think of the people you are managing as your customers, you cannot simply rely on telling them what to do. Every service provider knows that simply telling a customer what to buy is a risk. It is just as likely to lead to the customer storming out of the shop, as to making a sale. As the maker of a particular product or service, you need to know if what you are making is useful and valued.

In redesign, we strongly disapprove of mind-reading. The only way to be certain that your customers value what you make is to ask them.

Principle 2: Identify the Value Stream for Each Product Family

A value stream is made up by the processes required to design, produce, and deliver a family of products that pass through related operational processes during the transformation of a raw material into an end-product. Grouping processes into value streams is a way of taking stock of how things are made, as well as what is made.

I am one of three brothers. We range in height from 5 foot 10 inches to 6 foot 1 inch. We have different hair colors, and varying features. We all buy trousers with the same leg length, but different waist measurements. Family members may look quite different and still have much in common. So the tasks and processes involved in generating value within a value stream can look quite different and still be related.

To get the hang of what is meant by a value stream, it's easier to start with other manufacturing and service industries, rather than Health Care, because manufacturing operations and their outcomes are generally more readily available for inspection.

Nowadays, service stations sell much more than petrol. Take a trip to a service station on a hot day. Inside, it is common to see large refrigerated cabinets filled with soft drinks. There are carbonated drinks in a variety of flavors, including colas, fruit-flavored drinks and "energy" drinks; there are fruit juices, water with and without additives, and a variety of flavored milk drinks.

As consumers, we are interested in the taste, texture, color, number of calories, cost, and texture qualities that separate one drink from another, and a great deal of research by the manufacturers will have gone into the development of each drink. But once the drink has been formulated, for the manufacturer the questions are "can or bottle," and "water-based or milk-based." Those are much more important issues than the specifics of what goes into the container.

It is easy to make a wide variety of still and carbonated, water-based drinks using very similar operations. They are all water with various additives. But machines for making and filling cans and machines for making and filling bottles are quite different. Feeding sheets of plastic into machines designed to cut and stamp aluminum sheets would be a disaster, as would trying to put aluminum sheets into machines that convert plastic into bottles. And water-based drink manufacturing companies tend not to make milk-based products, because water and milk need completely different kinds of suppliers, handling, and storage. Manufacturing value streams relate to how water-based and milk-based drinks are put into different kinds of containers, not the flavors of the specific drinks being produced. For soft drinks manufacturers, the value streams revolve around cans, waxed paper containers, and bottles, not Fanta, Coke, or iced coffee.

The value stream concept is equally valid to Health Care but, because the operations involved may not be so obvious or easy to follow, value streams are not self-evident. The operations may have to be made visible.

I was working with the staff of a regulatory agency that provided authorizations for doctors, allowing them to provide ongoing prescriptions for a range of closely regulated drugs. Doctors could start treatment with the regulated drugs but then had to seek permission to go on with the treatment. But the regulator was taking so long to respond to the requests that many doctors were being forced to go beyond the regulations to continue looking after their patients.

It was not a question of being lazy. The staff of the regulation agency was dedicated and hard-working but requests still mounted up. So what was going on?

One morning, I got together with all the staff of the regulator to map out the process of receiving requests and granting permission. All requests came in by fax and the identified faxes were put in a box. When the box was full, it joined an ever-growing pile of boxes on a central work bench. Everyone took a box each day and tried to work through it—except for the staff who took it in turn to man an enquiry line for doctors wanting to know when their request would be approved (for which there was usually no good answer).

The staff thought of the requests in relation to the drugs involved and the specific regulations that governed their use and misuse. And certainly, the operations were slightly different for each drug involved. But about 80% of all requests were straightforward; 10% involved a small amount of extra work, and 10% were very complicated and took half a day or more to resolve.

It became clear that a value stream approach would make sense. It was quite straightforward to predict which requests were likely to be straightforward, and which would take a long time to complete. In which case, the requests could first be divided into "short" (number of operations involved) and "long" (number of operations involved) value streams. Once divided up, the specifics could then be taken into account if need be. By analogy, one value stream could be thought of as water-based drinks, and the other, milk-based drinks, each needing their own sequence of processes. But in this case, one sequence would be short and straightforward (but still needing a lot of skill to get it right) and the other, long and complicated.

After the planning day, the staff experimented with various ways of organizing themselves around short and long value streams, eventually dividing themselves into a new referrals team (which dealt with some short and most of the long requests) and a renewals team (which dealt almost entirely with short work but that needed the sixth sense that comes with experience, to keep an eye out for potential problems). The short work teams could answer short requests quickly and efficiently, while still giving themselves some variety, leaving the new referral team time and space to concentrate on the long work. When I met the group a year later, the boxes had gone and requests were being handled quickly and effectively. No extra resources and no extra staff had been needed, just better organization. The case studies in Chapter 20 onward provide a range of further examples of the value of grouping Health Care operations into value streams.

Thinking in Journeys

The more complicated the overall production process, the harder it is for the different groups that are involved to see themselves as part of the whole. If the participants cannot see how their steps link up with processes further down the line, and what impact poor coordination has on the delivery of care, it will be hard to get the whole process working smoothly.

Seeing journeys end to end is particularly difficult in Health Care. Hospitals are large organizations in which many different functional groups work side by side. Groups may be focused around craft skills (e.g. physicians, surgeons, nurses, physiotherapists), and/or the use of special equipment (e.g. radiology, pathology), and/or location (e.g. ward 1, ward 2), and/or function (e.g. Emergency Department, Operating Theater, Intensive Care, Payroll). Everyone concerned will be trying to do a good job. But it is hard to see past your own particular team boundary (Greenhalgh 2008).

A good way to think about all this is to imagine that individual patients move through these complex structures on invisible production lines. In this context, the raw material of abnormal or at-risk physical or mental states and conditions is worked on in different ways using different procedures at the stations on the invisible lines. A common experience is that, at each station, the people involved find it hard to work on getting what they do right, without spending time worrying about the needs of others further down the line.

When you go into a factory you can see how raw materials are transformed at each step, and whether cans or bottles are being produced. One of the things that make the work of Health Care Process Redesign difficult is that it is not always obvious what people are doing when they are looking at computers, talking to each other, writing things down, or just talking to patients. Considerable efforts are needed to make the invisible knowledge work of Health Care visible so that everyone can understand what is being done, by whom, where, and how their work impacts on the direct and end-customer. When the work becomes visible, it is possible to sort out value-adding activities from waste. The particular methods we developed to see the work are described later on.

Principle 3: Eliminate Waste and Make the Product Flow; the Eight Wastes

The eight wastes are shown in Table 4.1. The first seven wastes were initially identified by Taiichi Ohno and reinforced in Womack and Jones' formulation of Lean Thinking (Womack and Jones 2003).

Wastes 1 and 2: Waiting and Queuing

The distinction between waiting and queuing is not just wordplay. Waiting implies waiting without order. Think of a ward drug store, jammed full of medications of all kinds, stored without regard to when the drugs will go past their expiry date and have to be thrown away. Or consider an Emergency Department, with lots of patients waiting for an in-patient bed in the body of the hospital. The Emergency Department staff has identified that the patients need to be admitted, but each in-patient unit is free to exercise its own priorities. The patients who are waiting are not part of an orderly set of procedures that relate to the length of time they have already waited. They are just waiting to be picked up by a sub-specialty team.

By contrast, a queue implies some kind of time ordering. Patients waiting their turn on a theater list are in a queue. Patients in a waiting room waiting to see a medical officer are in a queue. Whilst patients in a ward may not be able to see it, those patients, patiently waiting for the medical round to reach them, are in a queue of patients, ordered by bed number; and the list goes on. Hospitals are filled with queues of all types.

Table 4.1 The Eight Types of Waste

Types of Waste
1. Waiting
2. Queuing
3. Rework, errors
4. Transportation (of objects)
5. Motion (of people)
6. Overprocessing
7. Overproduction
8. Neglecting the skills and knowledge of the workforce

Waste 3: Rework

Rework and errors are part and parcel of everyday life in hospitals. For many years, it has been known that at least 10% of patients treated in hospitals in countries such as Australia (Wilson et al. 1995), New Zealand (Davis et al. 2002), and the United States (Brennan et al. 1991) experience at least one adverse event during their hospital stay. And the number is probably a lot larger. To name one simple example, think of the amount of time and energy spent managing hospital-acquired infections, and the impact such infections have on staff and patients alike.

Wastes 4 and 5: Transportation and Motion

Transportation is the movement of objects. Motion is the movement of people, staff, or patients. Transportation and motion are common sources of wasted time and energy in hospitals.

Hospitals use a lot of towels. One of our colleagues spent a whole day tracking the journey of a "hospital towel". The journey was as follows.

> Towels arrived in large packs from the laundry; they were unpacked and repacked to fit into packs small enough to fit into the receiving stores; then packed to fit into the trolleys used to transport goods around the hospital; then unpacked and repacked again to fit into storage areas in the ward store room; and unpacked one last time before distribution to patients at the bedside.

Goods are moved. People are in motion. Many hospitals have "take systems." Clinical groups are split up into teams that take turns to be on call for a 24-hour period. A large proportion of emergency admissions will go to the team "on take" that day. Commonly, there are not enough beds on the team's home ward for all the patients needing admission, so the patients get distributed all around the hospital. The morning after being on call, the take team embarks on a "safari" ward round, walking all over the hospital to find their patients, their notes, the nurses who are familiar with the patients, the results of their old tests and X-rays, and so on. Over the next few days, endless hours are taken up with moving patients to get them to the "home wards" of the teams involved. None of these movements add anything to the care of the patients involved.

Wastes 6 and 7: Overprocessing and Overproduction

Overprocessing is easily confused with overproduction. In industry, overprocessing is doing more than that which produces value. Obvious examples are mobile phone apps that have features that are software marvels but are so hard, or irritating, to use, that they decrease, rather than increase, customer value.

Obvious examples of overprocessing in Health Care are when patients are transferred from hospital A to hospital B, and the staff in hospital B redo all the blood tests and X-rays already done in hospital A because they do not trust anyone else to get it right. When this becomes a routine practice, it delays care and wastes resources.

In Lean Thinking, overproduction means making things before they are needed. Overproduction is Ohno's number one waste. Overproduction means goods being made before they are needed that then have to be stored and transported from storage areas to the main assembly lines. This wastes time, energy, and resources that could be better applied to value-adding work.

Overproduction in Health Care may be considered in two ways. When doctors get paid for each procedure they do, they may be encouraged to perform invasive investigations or procedures before they are clinically necessary. Is a knee arthroscopy always the best way to investigate pain in the knee that has only just occurred? The Dartmouth Health Atlas is a long-term project, documenting the massive variations in the frequency with which operations are performed or medical treatments provided across the United States (Goodney et al. 2014). Many of the variations are good examples of overproduction.

At the institutional level, an interesting example occurred during the diagnostic phase of an Emergency Department redesign program. It appeared that one of the common sources of patient delay in getting admitted to the body of the hospital was waiting for a chest X-ray. That seemed odd, as chest X-rays are quick tests to perform. It then emerged that almost every Emergency patient who was going to be admitted had a chest X-ray before they were transferred to an in-patient ward, whether or not there was an obvious need for a chest X-ray at that point in time. Why not wait until the patients were in the wards and then organize for an X-ray? It turned out that the X-ray department had a policy of prioritizing Emergency Department patients. So waiting to order a chest X-ray until after a patient had been admitted would involve a delay before the X-ray could be done. Why? Because the Emergency Department patients took up all the available X-ray slots. Why? Because the ward doctors thought it was better to be on the safe side and ordered a chest X-ray while the patients were still in the Emergency Department. That way the patient got priority. This practice created an artificial demand that took up all the available capacity; and so on round the circle of overproduction leading to restricted supply.

Waste 8: Neglecting Skills and Talents

Neglecting the skills and talents of the workforce is only too common in health systems. Health Care managers get promoted on the basis of their skills as problem solvers. Managers see their role as solution providers, rather than using the expertise of the people who do the work to figure out the best solution. Over the years, we have been more and more impressed by the creativity of staff on the ground. As redesigners, we never worry that we do not know how to solve a problem. We are confident that once all the participants in a redesign program reach a deep and shared understanding of how the work is done, creative solutions for improving work processes will emerge. What is necessary is to allow that creativity to be heard.

Flow

Make the product flow; the concept of "flow" is a natural extension of the notion of a value stream. Flow is about making the patient journey flow from step to step in the value stream as efficiently, and effectively, as possible. Work that flows is work that is well coordinated; where everyone knows, and is working to, the plan; and where the person who uses what you make gets what he or she needs, at the right time, in the right format, and right the first time.

Principle 4: So That the Customer Can Pull

The concept of "pull" was intrinsic to Taiichi Ohno's production strategies. A later process takes what it requires from the earlier process. It takes it when it needs it, rather than when it suits the earlier step to make it.

Health Care is full of "push." The Emergency Department pushes the in-patient units to review patients and move them as quickly as possible. When delays occur, staff members get on the phone, pleading, pushing, and threatening so as to get patients reviewed and moved. Here is a sad paragraph I found in the notes of a patient who had had to wait many hours in an Emergency Department. The patient was an elderly woman with a complex mixture of longstanding heart problems and breathing difficulties, plus a recent history of falls. A medical officer in the Emergency Department wrote:

> Discussed patient with cardiology registrar on call, registrar said problem did not sound cardiac, refer to respiratory. Referred to respiratory on call, refused to see, said falls meant problem not really respiratory, try neurology. Referred to neurology—will not see, falls sound secondary to longstanding medical problems, not neurological in origin. Phoned general medical physician on call, general medicine will review. THANK YOU.

The specialist doctors were all trying to avoid admitting a woman with complex medical problems to their own ward. To avoid this kind of game-playing, many hospitals give responsibility for managing the bedstock to a central bed manager. The bed manager makes the decisions about who goes into what bed. As availability tightens up, the bed manager pushes patients into whatever beds become available. As one after-hours bed manager put it, "At 11 o'clock at night, a bed is a bed. All I want to know is the sex of the patient and whether he or she needs a side room." In many hospitals, 20–30% of patients are cared for as outliers from their home wards, with all the resultant waste of motion and transport involved.

In Health Care, "pull" is wards and teams with particular skills and interests going to the Emergency Department and other areas of the hospital, pulling the patients that they need to fill their beds as vacancies arise. The later process, the in-patient ward, takes the correct patient from the earlier process, the Emergency Department. Sounds impossible? It can be done, and a "ward pull" program in the Flinders Medical Centre cut down the rate of outliers from around 20% of all patients to less than 5%, a rate that has held steady over a number of years.

Principle 5: As You Manage toward Perfection

No one who is trying to make hospitals work better for patients and staff alike should be worried that they will run out of work. The sad truth is that the process-improvement work of Health Care is never done. As you move from the present state of affairs to an improved state, the improved state is merely a platform for the next improvement. Health Care is too complicated and technology moves too quickly to ever reach perfection.

Chapter 5

Health Care Is Not Manufacturing

Studying manufacturing has been enormously important for Health Care's Lean journey. But Health Care is not manufacturing. As Health Care explores Lean Thinking and other related methodologies, its value becomes clear. As does its limitations.

Placing an Order: Customers and Raw Materials

Lean Thinking is increasingly migrating from manufacturing to the services sector. In manufacturing and the majority of service industries, customers place an order. That may be the case for a car, a loaf of bread in a shop, a bank loan, or an insurance policy. The wanted car, the preferred loaf of bread, the sought for personal loan, or the agreed insurance policy is then put together by the service provider using the relevant raw materials, and handed over to the customer. There is a clear distinction between the product and the customer, and Lean Thinking helps streamline production processes and make delivery of the product to the customer faster and more predictable. In Health Care, the customer *is* the "raw material."

The customer, the patient, brings a concern to a health service. The raw material of the (potentially) abnormal or at-risk physical or mental state or condition that has fuelled that concern is within the body or mind of the patient/customer. The combined resources of the health system transform the physical or mental state raw material into a valued health outcome. Those outcomes may include reversing, slowing, or halting, the progression of a disorder and care and reassurance. Whatever the outcome, the raw material being worked on never leaves the patient/customer. The customer is also the raw material.

This has a number of implications. In manufacturing and most service industries, customers take delivery of end-products and are, or are not, satisfied with the products they receive. The owner of a new car is not present while minerals are mined, smelted, refined, and turned into sheets of metal that are delivered to a car maker. The owner of a new car does not feel the heat of the blast furnace or the pressure of a stamping press. By contrast, the patient is a sentient being who is present, observing and experiencing at every stage of the transformation of his or her raw material, except, in the case of some patients, for a brief period of oblivion during an operation.

For the customer seeking a new car, an insurance claim, or a bank loan, the end-product and the quality of service during the process of requesting and obtaining the end-product are what count. For the patient, the experience of the actual process of "manufacturing/transformation" may be as important as the final outcome itself. The patient experience is the experience of care as it is being produced and delivered, and its importance cannot be overlooked.

As Health Care workers, we glimpse this experience when we ourselves become patients. In general, the only way to access this information is to ask the people involved and use their stories to influence the way we shape our services.

Deterioration

It is not only the nature of the patient experience that makes Health Care different from manufacturing or service industries. In many large-scale manufacturing industries, raw materials and components are sourced from different locations and even different countries. Because the materials are inert, they can be transported by land, sea, or air.

Our minds and bodies are not inert. They are volatile and liable to change. As patients, we need to be monitored, observed, and communicated with while we are waiting for the transformative processes to run their course. In hospital, we require washing and feeding, and access to bathrooms and toilets, and care and comfort. With modern Health Care, many of us will recover lost functioning. But the more seriously ill we are, the greater the danger of deterioration, and the greater the need to monitor our health and progress.

Redesign Double Vision

The importance of motion has been discussed in the previous chapters. Motion patterns are different in Health Care from those commonly seen in manufacturing and other service industries. Henry Ford's big idea was to bring the work to the worker stationed along a moving production line. That differentiated mass production from craft work, and in the vast majority of manufacturing and service industries, it remains the norm. The materials being transformed pass from station to station. The material moves to, and through, the relevant machines. This is not the case in Health Care. Once patients have been admitted to hospital and are established in a ward, they change wards infrequently. In general, the "machines"—the doctors, nurses, physiotherapists, social workers, and the host of other disciplines involved—come to the patient rather than the patient going to the machines. There are of course certain exceptions when large X-ray machines, or operating theaters, cannot be moved. But, in hospitals, when the basis of care is a person-to-person encounter, the health worker will usually move to the patient. This is one of the basic differences between hospital and clinic or office care.

But it gets more complicated, and there is a need for what I can best describe as a kind of "redesign double vision." There are aspects of Health Care work that do resemble manufacturing, to the extent that the solution to a technical problem—"what, if anything, is causing the disturbed physical or mental state, and how can the disturbance be corrected?"—moves from knowledge "machine" to knowledge "machine": from doctor to doctor and nurse to nurse, and backward and forward between health professional, patient, and carers. As it moves, the technical challenges of identifying the underlying abnormal or at-risk physical state(s) or condition(s), and transforming them into valued outcomes, are passed between discipline groups who are not physically colocated with each other or with the patient. Gradually, the knowledge work-in-progress is worked on and then assembled into a final treatment plan that can be implemented. Every Health Care worker will have had the experience of taking part in informal or formal review meetings where the strands of evidence are brought together, and a treatment plan is discussed and agreed upon. The participants may be widely separated, with the issues being reviewed over the phone or, nowadays, via the Internet. Night in one continent can be daytime in another, and it is not uncommon for radiologists in Australia to view and review X-rays taken overnight in clinics in the United States and report their findings, all online.

Responding to a patient's needs for personal care and attention requires contact with the patient and has to be provided where the patient is physically located and at the moment it is required. Bringing biomedical knowledge work and caring work together is part and parcel of the redesign double vision that makes up Process Redesign in Health Care.

Health Care Is Complicated

Health Care is extraordinarily complicated. A modern general hospital with a busy Emergency Department is one of the most complicated of all human institutions. Over a number of years, Australia has developed a language system to make the complicated nature of hospital activities more manageable. The Diagnostic-Related Group (DRG) system takes the many thousand specific clinical diagnoses that make up contemporary biomedicine and groups them into roughly 1000 groups that make clinical sense and whose processes of care require similar resources (at least in terms of cost). A general hospital is expected to be able to cope with almost all of those DRGs, 24 hours a day, 7 days a week, 52 weeks a year. Up to half the cases may come with no prior warning, and a wide range of secondary conditions may complicate the primary clinical problems.

Think of this in manufacturing terms. It is like asking a car retailer to provide any one of a thousand different actual models, made up from thousands of basic model types, modified by a mix of options drawn from a catalogue of several thousand options (which range from seat covers to radically different engine configurations). At least half of the cars have to be sourced and delivered with no notice, 24 hours a day, 365 days a year.

Adaptive Problems

Health Care in general, and hospitals in particular, is complicated. There is a current tendency to go from describing hospitals as complicated, to defining them as complex adaptive systems (Plsek and Greenhalg 2001). The concept of complex adaptive systems draws heavily on recent advances in chaos theory and complexity science. It is influenced by mathematical concepts such as phase spaces, strange attractors, sensitivity to initial conditions in recursive iterations of simple variables in continuous interaction, and emergent properties. Yes, there are some areas of hospitals where patient flows become chaotic in the technical, as opposed to the colloquial, manner. In everyday redesign, our experience is that more straightforward ways of thinking are sufficient, and we are particularly concerned with the scheduling and co-ordination required by complicated systems where the parts have to work together to make a whole that is more than the sum of its parts. But the notion of the adaptive is clearly relevant to Health Care, because Health Care institutions, like many other complicated social and technical systems, face two kinds of problems:

1. Technical problems, for which a known solution exists—the task is to get the expert to the problem and support the expert's deployment of the existing solution.
2. Adaptive problems, for which there is no pre-existing solution—here, the system, faced with new realities, has to learn, experiment, and adapt.

Table 5.1 provides a simple contrast between adaptive and technical problems. Table 5.1 draws on the work of Heifitz (1994) and the work published by Demos (Bentley and Wilsdon 2003), a British think tank.

When I do workshops with Health Care practitioners, I always ask them for the major challenges they face at work. Invariably, the challenges are adaptive, not technical. Adaptive problems need learning, and like many knowledge work challenges cannot be solved by command and control methods or by "solution roll-outs."

Table 5.1   Adaptive and Technical Problems

Adaptive Problems	Technical Problems
Cannot be solved with existing packaged solutions	Solutions and experts exist
Assuming that pre-existing expertise will be sufficient to do the job is a limitation	Expertise is the resource
Need learning/innovation	Need knowledge deployment
Need authorization and permission	Need authority and authorization
Always require a change program	May or may not require a change program
The future is uncertain	The future is predictable
No certainty as to how long it will take	Time scale is predictable
Need programs	Solutions are delivered by projects
Need teachers/facilitators	Need project implementers
Need experimentation and learning by doing	Needs sticking to expert advice
Participants need permission to fail and learn	We don't pay experts to get it wrong

Chapter 6

Knowledge Work

In many advanced economies, the transition from small-scale, craft-based industries to large-scale manufacturing occurred in the nineteenth and early twentieth centuries. What is happening in the twenty-first century is the transition from production-based economies to knowledge-based service industries.

Health Care is particularly challenging because, while it is very much a knowledge-based industry, the move from craft to mass production has never happened. The de-skilling of craft workers by sophisticated machinery that took place in the industrial revolution and its aftermath has not occurred. Maybe it will one day, but at present, as Health Care has become more technically complex, the importance of the skills and knowledge of the workforce has increased, not decreased. As I am writing this, the first deaths in cars being driven by autopilot have occurred, and it is clear that a human element will be part and parcel of car driving for some time. And learning to get a Health Care treatment right certainly takes a lot longer than learning to drive.

Yes, healthcare training has evolved. My father was a family doctor. In the 1930s, he got his license to practice from the Society of Apothecaries in London. My father needed to start earning to support his family. He took the LMSSA exam, as the Apothecaries qualifying examination was known, because it was cheaper than the other methods of qualifying to practice medicine. The Society of Apothecaries was an ancient craft guild, given its license to qualify medical practitioners by King James I of England and Scotland (1603–1622). The Society was still granting licenses to practice medicine in England the 1980s. Nowadays, Universities provide the basic medical qualifications, rather than a guild that, according to my father, automatically fast-tracked you to become a Freeman of the City of London (not that he ever availed himself of that privilege). But if a University-qualified doctor wants to become a specialist, he or she has to spend a number of years of further training in programs that are still managed by the relevant craft group, where the new graduate is apprenticed to a group of craft workers (otherwise known as consultants or specialists) whose members both grant access to apprenticeship schemes, and who then set and mark the examinations required to complete specialist training. Craft groups that jealously guard their rights and privileges are not unique to medical practitioners. They are found in all areas of Health Care, including nursing and Allied Health

Within hospitals and health services, there may be jockeying for position between the various craft groups and conflicts between craft groups and generalist managers. But recruitment to specialized positions and the day-to-day organization of Health Care practice remain in the hands of the various craft groups. This is unlikely to change. Whether that is good or bad depends on your point of view. But it is a reality that Process Redesign for Health Care using Lean Thinking recognizes and works within.

The Process Redesign method accepts that craft-based services exist and will remain, and that craft-based skills are vital for safe practice. It does not assume that Health Care workers are akin to briefly trained manufacturing process workers, nor does it expect the methods developed by Alfred Sloan to be easily transplanted to Health Care.

That does not mean there is nothing to learn from modern management techniques. Far from it, there is much to learn from what the late Peter Drucker, a key figure in the evolution of modern management theory and practice, described as "knowledge work" and "the knowledge work economy" (Drucker 1999), and it may be possible that the movement of expertise between other knowledge work service industries and health care may be two-way.

The Nature of Knowledge Work

The work of the knowledge worker is to apply the specialized knowledge of his or her craft to the relevant raw material to create value. Operationally, defining the limits of knowledge work is difficult, as the knowledge involved includes both explicit, formalized, knowledge and the tacit knowledge acquired by experience that is hard to write down and difficult to formally describe. The defining characteristics of the knowledge worker are much easier to define than the limits of knowledge work.

Table 6.1, Knowledge and Manual work contrasts knowledge work (and the knowledge worker) from manufacturing process work (described here as manual work, for convenience) at its most basic. Table 6.1 draws on the insights of Drucker (2008). It clearly caricatures manual work. That is not to undervalue such work but to bring out the particular character of knowledge work.

The table refers to the general characteristics of knowledge workers but is directly applicable to Health Care. It is important to cast the knowledge work net widely. Knowledge work does not apply only to the work of the identified professions (doctors, nurses, etc.) in Health Care. Clerical, administrative and "blue-collar" workers in Health Care are equally highly skilled, and they bring extremely high levels of tacit knowledge and hard won expertise to what they do.

Supervised but Not Subordinated

Knowledge work is specialized. A knowledge worker who does not know more about his or her area of expertise than most other people in the organization is of limited value. The knowledge worker may have a supervisor, but he or she is never supervised in the same way that a manual or process worker is supervised. Knowledge workers are colleagues or associates, never simply subordinates. The supervisor of a manual worker can tell that worker what and when to do, and how to do it (although simply telling people what to do never gets the best out of them). In relation to the knowledge worker's area of special expertise, the knowledge worker's line manager will not get very far by simply telling the knowledge worker what to do or how to do it. In hospitals, the complexity of individual patients, and the mixture of primary and secondary conditions, means that the accredited specialist, working within his or her scope of practice, must be able to make autonomous clinical decisions. When it comes to the application of knowledge worker to a particular patient, it is the knowledge worker who does the talking, not the line manager (unless the line

Table 6.1 Knowledge and Manual Work

Knowledge Work and Worker	*Manual Work and Worker*
The Knowledge Worker programs the work	The Work programs the worker
The Knowledge Worker tells the machine	The Machine tells the worker
Complex machines are tools for knowledge work	Complex machines de-skill and replace workers
Knowledge is the means of production. It is owned by the Knowledge Worker	The employer owns the means of production
The Knowledge Worker forms part of the working capital of the organization	The Manual Worker is a labor cost to the organization
Autonomy is necessary for effective knowledge work	The manual worker is the subordinate of the supervisor
The Knowledge Worker is highly specialized	Manual Workers are members of homogenous workgroups
Independent, mobile	Dependent on employer, limited mobility
The Knowledge Worker defines the work tasks	The system defines manual work tasks
The Knowledge Worker makes the system productive	The system makes Manual Workers productive

manager is a consultant supervising a trainee practitioner). There are a variety of factors that may limit what can be done in any one particular situation, but, as patients, we want the people looking after us to try and take our particular problems and personal needs into account. The counterpart to that is the requirement that the knowledge worker has to be accountable for the outcomes of his or her knowledge-based decisions.

Knowledge Workers Own Their Knowledge Capital

Even more confronting for knowledge-based industries such as health care is the fact that knowledge is the personal capital of the knowledge worker. At the end of the day, fully qualified but dissatisfied knowledge workers are free to move to more sympathetic employers, taking their stash of knowledge with them.

Some years ago, I was an interested spectator to an Australian industrial dispute where the state government of the day (who ran the public hospitals in their state), in a dispute about pay and conditions, hoped to use industrial legislation to prevent groups of specialized medical practitioners withdrawing their labor. The government badly overplayed its hand when faced with groups of doctors who provided their representative organization with dated resignations and proof of excellent offers from other parts of Australia. The state government tried to bluster its way through, stating that they could manage without the medical staff involved, but backed down at the last minute, when it became clear that the doctors were serious about their threat. Resolving the dispute turned out to be a very costly affair.

Machines Extend Knowledge Work, Not Replace It

Knowledge workers may need expensive machines such as computers, CAT scanners, or auto-analyzers. But those machines are of limited or no value without the knowledge of the knowledge worker. They are tools for the knowledge workers to use. They do not replace the knowledge worker; they support them. This is quite different from industrial production, where expensive machines de-skill or replace craft skills.

Take an extreme contrast. Many manufacturing industries make extensive use of industrial robots. The robots are programmed to perform specific tasks such as spot welding, and do so to a high degree of accuracy. They do the work that the manufacturing workforce formerly did. In Health Care, certain machines are commonly described as surgical robots. Currently, they are highly evolved master (the surgeon)–slave (the robot) tools that extend the skills of surgeons operating on hard-to-access parts of the body. The surgeon still controls the machine, and using the machine requires a great deal of training before use. The robot is a surgical aid, not a replacement for the surgeon. The surgeon's capacity to visualize the impact of actions in three dimensions in a hard-to-see, blood-stained field remains difficult, if not impossible, to replicate. The day will come when certain procedures would be undertaken autonomously by robot-like machines. But a human element will remain in place for some time yet.

Design and Redesign

The production worker works in a production engineer–designed environment. The production engineer sets up the line so that it prompts the work. The production-line worker is prompted to fit a wheel on a chassis when the chassis arrives along with the wheel. The questions for the production worker, and the designer of production work, are "How should the manual worker best do the job?" and "How can the work be designed so that the best work is easy to do?" As a result, if the standard work is done as specified, the manual worker cannot be held accountable for the quality of the outcome. The manual worker can however play a crucial role in improving the prescribed standard work for the task in hand.

It is the knowledge worker, and no one else, who best knows what the knowledge task is. In the end, it is only the knowledge worker, alone or in groups with co-workers, and in the case of health care knowledge work, in collaboration with the patient, who can identify what needs to be done. It is only the knowledge worker who can identify what must be done, and whether the way it is being done, under current work conditions, could be better organized. Only knowledge workers can fully improve all aspects of the knowledge work process. So the knowledge worker must take the lion's share of the responsibility for improving the quality of the outcome.

In 2002, our first experiment with Lean Thinking went well. The hospital board was pleased with the extent to which the immediate crisis in our Emergency Department had been resolved. It decided to fund a small Lean team for a limited period. There was enough for a small team of practitioners, and some administrative support. There was no money for external consultants, and anyway, at that time, no other groups had more knowledge of Lean in Health Care than the little we had already got. So we had to be self-sufficient.

We argued about what to call the program of work. Eventually, we decided on Redesigning Care. Design can be used as a verb—to design, plan, purpose, and intend. It can also be used as a noun—a design, a plan of something to be done, a plan for the joining of means to ends.

Redesigning Care summed up what we were trying to do; not imposing a pre-determined plan, but helping practitioners find a better way to join existing means (biomedical skills, knowledge, and experience) to an end, the transformation of abnormal (or at-risk) physical or mental state(s) and condition(s) into valued health outcomes.

Health Care is knowledge work. The deeper we got into redesign, the more we understood that almost everyone in Health Care institutions is a knowledge worker. That is why it is so important to value and access the accumulated skills and expertise of the whole workforce, not just the accredited experts.

Process Redesign for Health Care is not about interfering with the specifics of knowledge work practice. About 99% of us want to do the good work that our patients, and our consciences, demand. The Redesign Task is to make sure that the systems we work with make that possible.

Chapter 7

Redesigning Care: Authorization, Permission, Teams, and Governance

The end-product of a program of redesign is not a plan about what should be done—it is changed behavior on the ground. It is the people, who do the work, getting the work done in a different way: more efficiently, more effectively, and more closely aligned with what their patients define as value.

When we are working simply as redesigners, we are not the people who matter. Our job is to help the people who do the transformation work redesign the way they deliver the services that their customers value. Redesign is about facilitation, rather than command and control. This is for entirely practical reasons. A program of redesign that simply attempts to force the staff who do the work, to work differently, would not be successful.

Maybe, when, as redesigners, we are standing next to a nurse, a doctor, or any one of many disciplines that make up the Health Care community, we can, by force of character, get that person to follow a plan we have devised but about which they were unsure. More likely, no matter how hard we try, nothing will actually happen. Health Care practitioners are masters of passive resistance. If they do not want to do something, they don't necessarily openly refuse to do it—by some strange magic, it just does not happen. As a redesigner, I know this because, as an experienced Health Care practitioner, I have done it myself. I have paid lip service to what is to be changed, and even used the relevant language, while waiting for the whole thing to just go away when the project funds ran out, or for the proposer to move on to another job.

When we started doing redesign work, we instinctively tried to minimize passive resistance. We experimented with finding different ways to ensure that the people who actually did the work owned the ideas and strategies needed to change things on the ground. But when a program of Process Redesign makes a real impact, that impact is likely to be felt outside of the work area being redesigned; there was always a risk of collateral damage, if not collateral impact.

It was during a training workshop that my colleague Sue O'Neill and I were running that we found the right way to describe what needed to be accomplished. Authorization must not be confused with permission. Hospitals and health services are serious places. People have to take responsibility for what happens within them. We realized that the people who ultimately take responsibility when something goes wrong, even if they are not personally responsible (and some of the credit when things go right), have to authorize every related piece of redesign work. But it is just as important to get the permission of the staff on the ground for their particular work to be included in the redesign process.

Having the authority of the chief executive to go in and sort out the Emergency Department is not the same as getting permission from dozens of highly skilled doctors and nurses to examine and improve their work practices. Neither authorization nor permission can be taken for granted. Both have to be built step by step.

Authorization

Health Care decisions have consequences for life and limb. There have to be systems of accountability in institutions whose "customers" are people at their most vulnerable. Consequently, Health Care institutions are structured around formal hierarchies with built-in levels of accountability and control. Redesign programs have to work within those hierarchies. Whatever their inconvenience, they are a necessary part of institutional life. They need to be understood and worked with. The successful Process Redesigner needs to have a good working understanding of the formal institutional organizational structure and the equally important informal systems of influence.

What is necessary is to try and understand the managerial "span of control" within which a potential program is located. I can reorganize my own office using Lean Thinking principles. I do not have to ask anyone else. My office is within my span of control. What if a group of cardiologists want to redesign the way their teams work? Provided the changes have no external impact, their redesign is within their own span of control, and the Head of Cardiology can authorize it. If the proposed reorganization may require the Emergency Department, the Intensive Care Unit, and the General Physicians to also change the way they work, the redesign is not within the Cardiologists' span of control, and if the Head of Cardiology tries to impose it on his or her colleagues, he or she is likely to face all kinds of resistance, no matter how sensible the plan might be. The only people with the span of control necessary to authorize such a wide-ranging program are the senior managers of an institution.

Contrary to the views of some clinicians, senior managers of Health Care institutions are rarely stupid; after all, they are managing some of the largest institutions in their communities. They do have a difficult job. They have to balance the legitimate demands for resources made by the various discipline groups trying to do the best for their patients, against the needs of the institution as a whole (including all the other groups with legitimate claims on extra resources). The senior managers also have to take into account the often complex external funding and political environments within which hospitals work, while doing their best to shield direct care providers from the more disruptive demands of that external environment.

Senior managers hate to be surprised. If the first thing a senior manager hears about a redesign program is when an angry clinician walks into the manager's office and demands to know "who let those b** redesigners loose on my department; they are just making life more difficult," then things will not go well for the redesign program. Redesign programs with any reach need to be properly authorized by whoever will ultimately have to take responsibility for their outcomes if something goes seriously wrong. That authorization cannot be taken for granted and governance structures that work have to be developed for programs of Process Redesign.

Permission

At the heart of the concept of permission are health care workers permitting the way they go about doing their work, to be shared with others. Knowledge can be divided up into explicit knowledge that can be found in lectures, workshops, books, and, increasingly, on the Internet, and tacit knowledge that comes with experience. The hidden or tacit knowledge gained with experience is what binds book knowledge to real-world experience of the enormous variety of human experience. It is a primary resource for the health workforce.

Everyone is proud of their experience, and the expertise that comes with it, and holds it dear. Yet, how little we know of each other's unique capacities? From the first Mapping session in the Emergency Department at the Flinders Medical Centre, it became clear how little people actually knew about how people in other groups and disciplines went about doing what they did; how little doctors understood clerical officers, how little either knew about the nature of nursing work, and so on.

Process Redesign is only possible if, in the context of process analysis and redesign, the workers within a care process give permission, agree to share the way they do their work with others, and those others agree to try and understand it.

Permission relates to sharing how the knowledge work is done at each process step. How does the work come to the worker? What form will it take—verbal, written, digital, direct from the patient, explicit or muddled, and so on? What does the worker do next, and once the work is done, what does the worker need to do, to get the work ready to be passed on to that worker's customers, no matter whether the customers are other Health Care workers or patients?

A free exchange between people who might come from very different levels in formal hierarchies or have varying spheres of influence requires mutual respect. In Process Redesign for Health Care, we assume that people know their own jobs. Knowing what to do is the knowledge workers stock in trade. If redesign is to proceed, what the knowledge workers need to share is how they do it. Not how the policy says they are supposed to do it, but how they actually do it; not "should do" but "do do." In Chapter 12, I describe some specific ways of making that sharing possible that build both Authorization and Permission.

The Redesign Team

It is not possible to stop the operations of a large hospital to redesign its work practices. It is very difficult to ask a frontline Health Care worker to both continue to be a member of a team providing care and simultaneously redesign the processes involved. One role is at risk of being sacrificed for the demands of the other. Whenever possible, the work of Process Redesign for Health Care is best accomplished by creating a small team of redesigners to work alongside the frontline staff, as part of a redesign program that is supported by a well-designed governance structure.

What is the ideal composition of a redesign team? Who should the redesigners be, and what are the roles in the team? Should redesigners be Health Care workers or should we rely on experts from manufacturing and service industries?

There are no scientific studies to draw on here, only experience. It is certainly possible for engineers to learn about Health Care, and we know a number who have made great contributions to Health Care redesign. It is just very difficult. The cultures of engineering and Health Care diverge so much. Engineering is about precision, and bridges do not talk back and argue. It makes sense that the redesign team should largely consist of Health Care practitioners who understand how hospitals and health services work and who then skill themselves up with process redesign skills. This is not an easy adaption, as new team members have to be open-minded and prepared to learn. It can be hard to go from being an expert to a teacher and facilitator, but it is a transition that has to be made.

If Process Redesign is a genuinely novel activity (which I think it is) and not just ordinary common sense, it is likely that the wider Health Care community will take time to understand it and see where it might be of value. Once established, people within the institution will seek out the Redesign Team. But there will be times when someone from the redesign team will need to be a bit entrepreneurial and say "this is the kind of problem that redesign can help with." Otherwise, neither the redesign team nor the Health Care institutions they work within will maximize the value of redesign.

Once the redesign work begins, the redesign team needs members who develop a strong knowledge base in redesign and improvement techniques in Health Care. They are the skilled pairs of hands who know how to get work done. They are crucial to the success of the redesign team, but they need to be cultivated; they do not come knocking, ready and equipped with all they need to know. Once grown and developed, they have to be protected from the many managers who would like to take them away to implement those managers' pet projects!

Hopefully, books like this, local training by Redesign groups, and the ever-present Internet can help develop Redesign Competency. But nothing works better than on-the-job training, getting involved in a Process Redesign program, and giving it a go.

Governance

Once a team has been assembled, it is important to work on matters of governance and access. If a redesign program is going to reach across clinical teams and units, and follow patient journeys as they wend their way through a whole institution, the team needs to report to the people whose sphere of influence spans the whole organization. Otherwise, that redesign program will never be able to take on system-wide improvement. If large-scale system change is envisaged, the chief executive or general manager will have to be a key member of the governance group. If the chief executive chooses not to participate because he or she is too busy, or is waiting to see how things go before committing himself or herself, our advice to the redesigner is simple: "be careful. Don't accept responsibility for system level change without system level authorisation. It will end in tears."

So far, we have been talking about the work of the redesigners. But Process Redesign for Health Care is not done in design studios. Its products are not drawings or prototypes. Process Redesign takes place in the real world of patients and the people who look after them. The most important members of the redesign team are the people who do the work and who will have to make the redesigned processes a reality.

There are many different ways to involve people in the work of redesign. One strategy is to hold a series of kaizen events (also known as "kaizen blitzes" or "rapid improvement events").

Kaizen is the Japanese word for "improvement," and as such, this whole text is about kaizen or improvement. The terms "kaizen blitz" and "rapid improvement event" are commonly applied to a multi-day (usually 5-day) event, in which a team comprising all the people who touch a process is assembled to work through a problem. The purpose of such events is to agree on a new work process and decide how to implement it, and, ideally, rehearse it, so that the new process can begin straight away. Rapid improvement events are major investments of time and energy, and work best with the support of a Process Redesign team of some sort.

There is no doubt that rapid improvement events have their place, and the common experience is that as Redesign Teams become more experienced, they learn to use them more effectively. In public sector Health Care, getting authorization to take staff off-line for 5 days is very hard, and it is often necessary to adapt to shorter time frames.

For many of the things that need redesigning, a single event does not make sense. The more ambitious the Redesign program, the less likely it is that it will be accomplished in one event. It takes time to understand the current state of what is going on, and time to work out how best to proceed. A preferred strategy is to develop a workgroup, or workgroups, of the staff who touch processes and their direct supervisors, and work together with them over the life of a Process Redesign program. For projects of any size, that program will need a governance or leadership group of key stakeholders with excellent links to key authorizers. The governance group should have a clear identity, and governance meeting need to separate from workgroups. The governance group is the link between the workgroups who are working out what needs to be done, and how to do it, and the institutional structures that come into play whenever substantial changes are put on the table.

Health Care practitioners are practical people. They just want to get on with doing the best they can to make things better. Authorization and permission, the specifics of Redesign teams, and a structure of governance are the key ingredients for building the strong foundations necessary to sustain Process Redesign for Health Care using Lean Thinking. With the foundation in place, it is time to start on the work of Process Redesign itself.

Chapter 8

The Virtuous Circle of Process Redesign and the Health Care A3

The basic structure of a Process Redesign for Healthcare using Lean Thinking program of work is shown in Figure 8.1. It is a virtuous circle because each step builds on the preceding step, reinforcing and sustaining gains as they are made, and it is a circle because improvement never ends. At the center of the circle is a set of principles, the Lean Thinking principles described in Chapter 4. Those principles are a kind of North Star that guides redesign programs as they are implemented. Wrapped around those principles are the concepts of gaining authorization and building permission, discussed in Chapter 7.

Turning principles into Process Redesign practice requires a series of steps that influence the structure of the following chapters. The steps are as follows:

- Identify a problem (Chapter 9).
- Define the scope (Chapter 10).
- Undertake a detailed diagnostic phase to ensure that the current state-of-work processes are well understood (Chapters 11 and 12).
- Use the results of that diagnostic process to re-examine whether the problem identified initially was the real problem (Chapters 13–15).
- Develop and implement relevant redesign experiment(s) using a plan–do–study–act cycle(s) (Chapters 16–18).
- Evaluate the outcome of the program of redesign experimentation (Chapter 19).
- Find a way to embed and sustain the gains, to make the new way "the way we do it round here" (Chapter 19). Then the improvement cycle starts again, as every improvement provides a platform for the next round (Chapter 19).

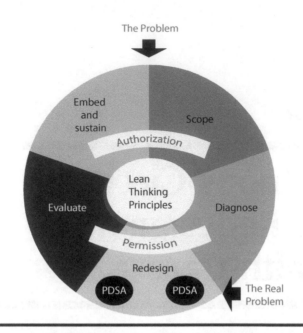

Figure 8.1   The virtuous circle of health care process redesign using lean thinking.

It is important that every stage in the redesign process is open to scrutiny. You cannot build authorization or permission by surprising people. The program of work needs to be clear and documented; easier said than done.

Anyone who has spent any time trying to influence the way Health Care organizations go about changing things will have struck a major problem. Health Care institutions are necessarily conservative. Lean Thinking circles are full of stories about Taichii Ohno whose work was described in some detail in Chapter 3. It is reputed that a reservoir near the Toyota factory was full of his manufacturing failures as he experimented with new ways of organizing the production of motor cars. No doubt those stories have little or no basis in fact. But the point is that if a Redesign program goes wrong, real people are involved, not inert objects. Managers are right to be cautious about rushing too quickly into innovations and change. They need to be kept informed and involved. But when we started the Redesigning Care program at Flinders, it became clear that there was a gap in the standard managerial tool box.

At the level of innovation and change in clinical practice, there are well-developed systems for developing, testing, and publishing new treatments and protocols, and submitting them for agreements to proceed. Indeed, there is a whole branch of Health Care labeled evidence-based practice. At the upper levels of management, there are established ways of developing, resourcing, and implementing policies and programs. But tools such as business-case proposals, and other business-based methodologies, are based on the assumption that a solution has been already been developed to resolve a particular problem or issue.

Process Redesign is at its most effective when everyone facing a problem knows they have to do something ("things just cannot go on like this"), but they do not know what that is. That is the moment when real change is possible; that is the moment when a Redesign program may generate enough momentum to cut across the web of vested interests and embedded assumptions that surround most Health Care acts and activities, and change the way things are done around here.

How to reassure everyone involved that they will not be subject to a short-term, off-the-shelf, solution that will in the end be just another problem to work around? By insisting that what is needed is a program of learning and innovation whose starting premise is the need to base remedial action on a deep and shared understanding of the problem. And that that understanding does not yet exist; if it did, the consequences of the problem would not be as severe as they are.

The title of manager comes with a set of assumptions that are commonly held by you, the manager, and the people you manage. That they can knock on your door, state a problem, and leave with, if not a solution, a plan of action that you have agreed to. How do you as a manager manage a program whose starting premise is that no one understands the problem, let alone knows the answer. Health services do not thrive on anarchy, so a management strategy is necessary, no matter how intractable the problem.

We were fortunate, in the early years of the Redesigner Care program at Flinders to be introduced by John Shook, to the A3, a tool developed by Toyota to manage just the situation we found ourselves in: that of having to do something, but not being sure what, and still having to manage the next steps (Figure 8.2). Basically, it is a "flattened out" version of the

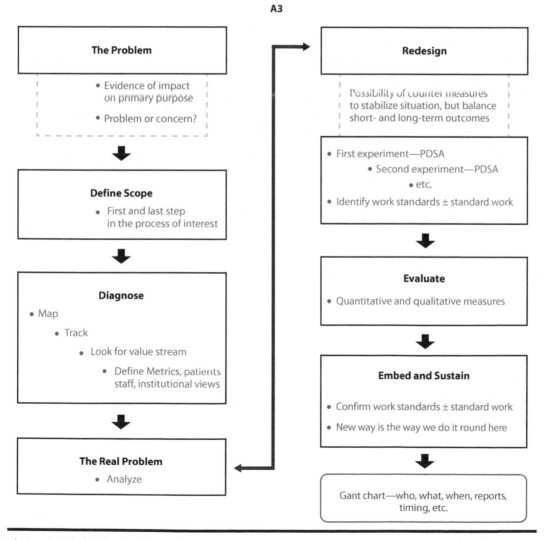

Figure 8.2   The Health Care A3.

Virtuous Circle. Each box describes both the major Process step and some of the important elements in that step.

In my experience, all that anyone ever reads of a lengthy business-case document is the summary on the first page. To avoid the waste of overprocessing, the Health Care A3 is always just one page that sets out the steps of a Process Redesign for Health Care program of work in an orderly and easy to follow fashion. It does not imply that any one step is easy, merely that there is a clear sequence that needs to be followed.

The Health Care A3 is a working document. Its boxes are progressively filled in as the Redesign program proceeds. If you start by assuming you know what the real problem is, you are not doing a Process Redesign program; you are "rolling out" a pre-packaged solution that wastes the skills and expertise of the people who do the work. In total, the Health Care A3 should use no more than one side of an A4 sheet of paper (the Toyota version was handwritten, so needed a larger sheet). It is a tool to communicate and gain authorization at each step on the Redesign path, because it makes it clear what a Process Redesign program consists of, where the program begins, and where it has to go.

It is very common for a redesigner to say to an authorizer: "Yes, there is a problem. If you know how to solve it, just go ahead and do it—you do not need a Redesign program for that. If however you do not know what to do, authorise me and a Redesign group or team, to try and understand what is going on using the Process Redesign Techniques"; in other words, you the Redesigner seek and receive authorization to complete a Health Care A3 up to and including the diagnosis, but no further. Say to the authorizer, "If what emerges makes sense, we can go on to the next step. But we do not yet know what that will be, so we will make sure we get your authorization at every step along the way."

Discussing the finer points of a Health Care A3 and its many uses would take another book. But by the end of Chapter 19, each element of the A3 will have been explored is some detail.

Compressing program documentation onto one sheet of paper requires clear thinking. When I have to prepare reports in a hurry, I will sometimes say, "I am sorry this is so long. I did not have time to make it shorter." The Health Care A3 is an accessible resource for thinking and communicating clearly, and for planning and review, both within the redesign team, and with authorizers and permission granters. To use a phrase beloved of software engineers, the Health Care A3 manages the visible architecture of Process Redesign. It manages the process of Process Redesign.

Chapter 9

Identifying the Problem

Process Redesign for Health Care begins if and when:

- It is possible to identify a problem.
- The problem is having an impact on the primary purpose of the services of concern.
- It is not yet clear what to do.

Primary Purpose, Problems, and Concerns

Health Care organizations play many different roles in the communities they serve. They provide a livelihood and a sense of self-worth for their staff. If they are for-profit organizations, hospitals and health services may provide substantial returns for investors and shareholders. But the primary purpose of Health Care organizations is to improve the physical and mental well-being of the patients they care for.

David Meier, a former Toyota manager who consults on Lean improvement, provided us with a very valuable distinction. If something is interfering with the primary purpose of delivering care, it is a problem and must be solved. If something is causing the organization to lose money, interfering with staff satisfaction, making the job of a manager harder to do, or threatening the career of the minister, but does *not* interfere with the delivery of care, it is a concern. Concerns need to be addressed. Problems have to be solved.

Demonstrating that a problem is interfering with the delivery of care requires evidence. It is evidence that allows us to assess the urgency of both concerns and problems.

It is easy to get overfussy about the exact wording of a problem. Simple and straightforward is best. Problem statements should be open ended, beginning with a statement of the problem, not a solution dressed up as a problem. For example, the statement, "The hospital is failing to meet its discharge by 11 a.m. target" is not a problem in its own right. It is a statement about one possible solution to a primary problem: the Emergency Department is overcrowded. Start with the problem and the evidence that it is a problem. In 2016, the United Kingdom held a referendum on whether to stay in the European Union, or leave it. As the campaign progressed, it became obvious that there was no agreement as to what would be solved by leaving the European Union—was the problem economic, cultural, or essentially political?

What Kind of Problem and Where to Start?

The evidence is that, all over the world, at least one in 16 patients, and probably closer to one in 10, leave hospitals having suffered an adverse event during their stay there. The events are not trivial. They cause distress, discomfort, ongoing disability, and, for a disturbingly large number of patients, death.

This must mean that there are plenty of problems to get started on. Where to start? Should redesign start in a small way, in a safe setting, well away from sensitive clinical services? Or should it start where the problems are most intense, wherever that may be?

The end-product of a program of redesign is changed behavior; people on the ground organize and deliver care in a different way. Hospitals and health services have multiple stakeholders with differing priorities that tend to make them look at problems in different ways. Redesign has to work for the benefit of patients. It also needs to understand the needs of health workers and managers; otherwise, it cannot provide sustainable solutions.

Almost all redesign problems need to be considered in relation to three viewpoints:

1. The patient
2. The Health Care worker
3. The broader institution

The best way of getting those interests to fall in line is to go where the deck is burning: where things are so awful that something clearly needs to be done. It doesn't matter whether that is the main deck of a large service, or the quarterdeck of a small Allied Health or support service. Whatever the problem, there has to be a consensus that "things cannot go on like this"; that "something needs to be done." When that something is not clear, that is the opportunity for Process Redesign to make a difference.

A common problem statement by managers is "If this goes on, I will lose my job." That probably will not engage the people, on the ground, who are the people who have to make an improvement program work. There is always a potential problem when the "end-customer" of a program of Process Redesign is the career of a manager or a minister in a government.

Evidence

The evidence does not have to be a complex piece of statistical analysis. If the problem is big enough, common sense will do. Evidence that Emergency Department overcrowding is interfering with the primary purpose might include:

- A large number of complaints about the Emergency Department.
- A series of adverse events where we lost sight of patients and their condition deteriorated as a result.
- The staff in the Emergency Department hate it so much they are leaving in droves, and replacing permanent staff with temporary staff is costing us a fortune, so that we are having to cut back elsewhere.
- The number of people spending more than 24 hours in the Emergency Department is getting out of hand.

Some examples of problem statements and supporting evidence.

Not: "The drug cupboards are not standardised."
But: "Staff spend lots of time looking for things and going to other wards to borrow drugs or consumables. Their time would be better spent in looking after patients."
Evidence: Anecdotes, photographs of cupboards, and tracking nurses on day and night shifts.

Not: "We need another CAT scanner."
But: "It is hard to get a CAT scan when one is needed."
Evidence: Patients are being admitted to hospital for CAT scans as in-patients because they cannot get appointment as out-patients. Our monthly overtime bills for calling staff back after hours to do routine scans is cutting into our capacity to provide other services.

Keep It Simple, Be Prepared to Be Surprised

My own practice is that, once it is clear that there is good evidence of a problem that interferes with the primary purpose, I tend to say to all involved: "OK, it is clear that you have a problem. Don't tell me about how it started, who did what to whom, and what you think needs to be done. We will get to all that in good time. What we have to agree on is how to go about a program of redesign."

Sometimes, a problem can start out by seeming a bit esoteric but then become clearer on examination. I was involved in a course on Lean Thinking and Process Redesign. A laboratory manager presented a problem: a substantial number of stool specimen containers (made of plastic) were reaching the laboratory functionally empty: there was no stool sample in the specimen bottle, or there was less than the minimum amount of stool required to perform the lab tests. Recalling patients for another specimen was distressing for them, and time-consuming for the laboratory, and could cause considerable delays in the diagnosis of serious problems.

None of us could understand what all this was about, until we were shown the opaque containers into which patients were required to place their stool samples. For obvious reasons, the reception staff did not open and inspect the containers after they had been handed in, and no one looked into them until they reached an off-site laboratory. The more we thought about it, the more challenging the problem appeared.

Chapter 10

Defining the Scope

There is a problem. The problem interferes with the primary purpose. The temptation is to do what we as health workers have been trained to do: take a history. How did this happen, how long has it been going on, how did it start, who was involved?

Taking a history implies that understanding who did what to whom will help find a new way to solve the problem. It also assumes that it is important that the history taker understands the original problem. What has been done cannot be undone. As a Process Redesigner, there is little value in spending time trying to work out who was to blame. Whether the Redesigner understands the problem is not what counts. It is the people directly involved in a patient journey who need to develop a deep understanding of the work from end to end and use that understanding to develop their own solutions.

Once a problem has been articulated, it is good practice for the Process Redesigner to say to an authorizer, "Yes, the problem is clearly a problem. If we are going to use the Process Redesign methodology to try and find a workable solution, we don't need to spend time at this point trying to work out what the underlying causes are, or what needs to be done. We will find all that out. At this stage, what is most important is to define the scope of the work."

Scope is defined formally as the span between the first and last steps in the process to be redesigned. Defining the scope means defining the start and end points of the Process Redesign program. The start point is the agreed step where the work of redesign will begin. The end point is the step or point in the transformative process where the program of redesign will end. The difference between scope and all the other components of the Process Redesign method is that scope has to be specified in advance. Everything that follows is a process of discovery.

The Benefits of Starting with Scope

Starting with scope has a number of advantages. Most of all, it avoids starting with the solution.

A solution developed without creating a shared understanding of the current situation may be the right thing to do. That is beside the point. Starting with a solution that has not been developed at the coal face sends the message that "someone else knows best." Making people feel that their skills and experience count for little will not lead to sustainable change.

I had a series of discussions with a mental health services manager who had been asked to develop an implementation plan for a mental health short-stay unit. Talking him through the issues, it became clear that the problem (for which the short-stay unit was the intended solution) was that patients with mental health problems were spending too long in the hospital's Emergency Department. That was good neither for the patients nor the staff of the mental health unit, and the issue had received extensive coverage in the media. The minister had visited a service in another state that had dealt with a problem of overcrowding in the Emergency Department by opening a short-stay mental health unit next to the Emergency Department. Opening a short-stay unit is more problematic than it appears. What is the first step in the scope of work for developing a short-stay unit? Is it at the point of arrival in the Emergency Department? Is it when a patient, whom the Emergency Department staff have identified as having a mental health problem spends longer time in the Emergency Department than some external criterion requires, even if it was clear that the patient was likely to be able to go home from the department? Is it at the point that an admission to hospital was deemed necessary? What happens after the patient is admitted to the unit? Is the expectation that short-stay unit patients will go home, or is the unit going to be just a holding station for longer-term care. None of those issues had been thought about, yet they each had major implications for the scope of work involved.

A short-stay unit may, or may not, be the right solution for the service involved, but starting with it as a solution, rather than starting with a problem and defining the scope of the program of work, is just another example of ignoring the skills and expertise of the staff involved, denying them the opportunity to use their own creativity.

Defining the scope of work is very much part and parcel of authorization and permission; defining scope falls clearly within the remit of those with the relevant authority. Conversations about defining scope must begin with the people whose managerial authority covers the span of work to be tackled and must also include the extent to which the work is appropriate for a Process Redesign approach. Does a potential scope make functional sense and managerial sense? Does it allow for a viable program of redesign? Those are the issues to be covered in conversation with the authorizers.

Some of those questions also need to be taken to the key stakeholders whose work falls within the scope of work. Authorizers can say, "This is what should be done." But the people on the ground can also say, "No, I will not do it." They may not say that out loud. They do not need to. As knowledge workers, they have the negative power to ensure that imposed solutions do not last. Passive resistance is still resistance. Talking about scope clarifies a problem to be worked on in a practical, nonconfrontational, and nonblaming manner. Compromises may be necessary, but the outcome is a sustainable change.

Here is an example of the processes involved in defining scope and obtaining authorization and permission. A Department of Health made the percentage of in-patients discharged by 11 a.m. a key performance indicator for a group of hospitals. The chief executive of one of those hospitals contacted a redesign group and said, "We are well short of the target. We need to do something about it—can you help us?"

The chief executive had started with a solution dressed up as a problem: poor 11 a.m. discharge rates. But to what problem was 11 a.m. discharge a solution? After discussion, the problem was readily identified. The hospital was always full, and patients who needed to be admitted were overstaying in the Emergency Department, causing overcrowding. The Health Department had given the chief executive a solution: increase the number of patients being discharged before 11 a.m. The chief executive had no choice about trying to implement the Health Department solution, but not all the clinicians who would actually have to discharge the patients agreed that discharging by 11 a.m. was necessarily the best answer to the basic problem.

After confirming that the hospital did indeed fall well short of the target, the redesign group started discussing the scope with the chief executive. The redesign group observed that discharge was the end of a long sequence of actions and activities. Where should the redesign program begin? At the point when a final discharge decision has been confirmed, with a focus on the steps between confirmation and actual exit or at an earlier stage in the patient journey? The chief executive responded that those were reasonable questions, and she was not quite sure of the answer. She suggested that the group discuss the scope with some key stakeholders on the medical and surgical wards.

Ward-level nursing managers on some busy wards in the hospital identified two issues—(1) the frequency and timing of doctor-led ward rounds where decisions were made and (2) the more immediate problems that emerged at the point that a discharge decision was made, including waiting for discharge medication.

Should the scope reach back to the early steps that well-preceded deciding when it might be safe to send that patient home? Or should the program of work just concentrate on the mechanics of discharge itself?

There is no right or wrong answer to this kind of dilemma. Starting with the mechanics of discharge may only be a partial solution to a complicated problem, but it might nevertheless satisfy the Department of Health. Starting at a much earlier point in the overall delivery of care would probably provide a much more long-term answer. It would eventually lead to an engagement with the mechanics of discharge, but the range of stakeholders, and the complexity of the program, would be considerably increased. The final decision as to the scope has to lie with the authorizers, now better informed about the problem and who needed to be involved, in consultation with the stakeholders. In this case, they decided to confine the work to the mechanics of discharge. Another chief executive and another group of stakeholders might have come up with a different decision. It is a truism of military strategy that no plan survives the first contact with the enemy. In Process Redesign, it is the act of planning, the discussion and negotiation that is involved, which is important. The solution that emerges will be stronger and more sustainable than any that is imposed.

Sphere of Influence

Another way of looking at these kinds of issues is to consider them in relation to spheres of influence. Redesign programs begin with problems. When an area of work is proposed, it is important to be clear as to whether the potential scope of that proposal falls into the proposer's sphere of influence, or span of control. An Emergency Department is grossly overcrowded. In this case, the director of the department wants things to improve but says there is no point improving the Emergency Department if the in-patient services do not change as well. That may be right, but is the work of the in-patient services within the span of control of the head of the Emergency Department?

Hospitals and health services are complicated places. If I want to reorganize the shelves in my office, that is within my sphere of influence or span of control. A sphere of influence or span of control is the area where, provided it does not interfere with anyone else, I am free to organize things to suit me and my needs (and to influence my long-suffering administrative assistant to help me). My office shelves are within my sphere of influence. Reorganizing my shelves can make my working life easier and more enjoyable. It is very unlikely to have any noticeable impact on the work of the institution as a whole. The head of an Emergency Department wants to reorganize the work of the department from the arrival of a patient until that patient is either discharged home or referred to an in-patient unit. That falls within the sphere of influence of the Director.

Provided the Director can get the permission of the many different groups who work in the Department, and no extra resources are involved, the program of work can usually go ahead without the need for further authorization. Redesigning the work of a specific department is very important for the staff and patients involved, but its overall impact on the total system of care may again be limited.

By contrast, a physician, a unit head, or a nursing manager may want to redesign the way medical patients are managed, from the front door of the hospital until their discharge from the care of the team managing the transformative processes. That is a redesign that spans a number of different units and services. The changes involved are likely to be substantial, but the impact may benefit care across the whole institution; while permissions will have to be sought from many different provider groups, authorization will have to come from the most senior managers. The more widespread the impact, the more senior the authorizer needs to be. Commonly, in hospitals, the only person with the required span of control to authorize major system changes is the chief executive, in concert with his or her board or its equivalent.

If a proposed scope of work falls outside the proper authority of the person suggesting the work, there are two options. Confine the process improvement to a scope that falls within the proposer's sphere of influence or find a way of bringing in all the potential services as participants. There are no right or wrong answers as to which approach to take. It is a judgment call: making it should involve the participants.

Starting by defining the scope of a program of redesign also helps avoid the "scope shuffle": getting to the end of a program of work and having someone say, "That is jolly good. It's great that you have improved the rehabilitation journey of the stroke patients. It's just a shame that you didn't start in the acute stroke unit. That is where the real problems are." Or, "Halving the time taken to deliver discharge medication is great, but the decisions still get made too late in the day. Why didn't you work on the decision-making process?" Or, worse still, "It's fantastic that you have devised a great system for moving elderly patients out of the Emergency Department into an acute assessment unit, and from there into the specialized geriatric service the next day. But why didn't you work on making sure they never went to the Emergency Department in the first place?" To which, all too often, the reply is a version of, "Because primary care in the community was out of our scope. As important as it is, it is managed by a completely different group of organisations."

Defining the scope of a program of work and having that scope authorized reinforces the fact that the redesign process works in an institutional context. Redesigners are not free agents. Defining scope and getting it accepted make it clear that defining the institutional architecture of a program is very much part of the work of senior hospital managers.

Defining the scope also deals with the "everyone has a problem except me" strategy. I was part of a group asked to do some training with a small redesign unit being set up within a hospital. The head of the hospital was aware of the impact of redesign work in other hospitals and was keen to see if redesign could improve their major pressure point, an overburdened Emergency Department. The head of the hospital had called for volunteers for the redesign work. In the early part of the training, it became clear that an Emergency Department doctor had volunteered specifically because, in her view, the Emergency Department had no problems in itself. All the issues were related to the failure of other departments to remove their patients promptly, and she really wanted them to sort things out. She had volunteered for the program to make this point loud and clear.

It may well be that she was correct. But, whatever else, when a doctor in one department goes to discuss a mutual problem with colleagues in another, asks them to change their work practices, but resists accepting that he or she needs to look at some issues on his or her side of the equation, not much is going to change.

Scope and Scoping: An Evolving Task

Scoping is a verb—to scope (or scope out) a program of work. It describes an activity that can be undertaken at any point in the redesign program. It is also a noun—the scope, the span between the first and last steps to be included in the redesign program.

Commonly, the one thing that is clear at the start of a program of Process Redesign is that it is not yet clear: it is not yet clear what is really going on, or where the work is going to go. When that is the case (and it often is), the best strategy is to seek authorization and permission only to undertake the diagnostic phase of the proposed redesign program. At the end of that period, the real problem should become clear. The scope of work can then be revisited, with better information.

Even if the scope had been clearly defined at the beginning of a program, the diagnostic stage and the analysis of the real problem may have identified new areas of work. A redefined scope may evolve as part and parcel of the permission building process.

Whenever a decision has been reached as to the scope of the redesign program, write it down. That is especially important where there is conflict about what to do, and how to go about doing it. Writing down the decision makes it available to both authorizers and permission providers. Clarity about scope is the key to managing expectations about what a program of Process Redesign can, and cannot, achieve.

Writing it down also clarifies the role of the Process Redesigner. In many cases, the work of Process Redesign is undertaken by staff with existing clinical and managerial roles. However, Process Redesign works best when the Process Redesigner facilitates Redesign. The role of Process Redesigner does not easily fit into conventional hierarchical relationships, as the Process Redesigner has to act as a facilitator, not a decision maker. As a clinician or manager, I am entitled to identify areas where Process Redesign *may* be applicable. As a Process Redesigner, I can say that the relevant body of work appears to be well suited to a program of Process Redesign. But only if I am the ultimate authorizer can that work proceed without going through a further process of authorization.

To illustrate, a theater nurse opens a surgical instrument pack and finds it contaminated with dried blood and tissue from earlier operations. The theater nurse goes to the theater manager to discuss what should be done. The theater manager can say that the institution must have a zero-tolerance policy toward failures of sterilization. As a redesigner, I can say that the Central Sterile Supply Departments are well suited to improvement by Process Redesign. But redesigning the work of the Central Sterile Supply Department will involve many different groups within the hospital and may also involve the relationships with external suppliers of a range of goods and instruments. Deciding that the scope of work is an end-to-end redesign of work flows in a sensitive area such as Sterile Supply is a decision that has to be taken at the highest levels of the institution.

Chapter 11

Diagnosis (1): Mapping

Yes, a problem has been identified and confirmed as a problem, and the scope of work settled on. Now the task is to understand how the work is done. Not how it ought to be done, not how it should be done, but how it is done at present, because the only way to get to the future is from the present.

The diagnostic phase of Process Redesign is an attempt to understand how the day-to-day theory of care translates into the practice of care in a particular health service: a health service with a problem. Process Redesign for Health Care assumes that competent practitioners will be well versed in the advances in their field. The intent of Process Redesign for Health Care is not to challenge that competency but to provide a method by which those practitioners will be enabled to practice their skills in the most efficient and effective way possible.

The Big Picture and the Big Picture Map

Much of the knowledge work of Health Care is invisible to an external observer. Because an observer cannot generally see what is changing in a patient's physical or mental state, the intent of transformative work at each step cannot simply be inferred by observing people who are looking at computers, talking into phones, reading records, and talking to each other and to patients. What those people are actually doing, and how they are doing it, has to be made clear by the people doing the work. When they do that, the real problems in delivering the right care to the right patient at the right time, right the first time, will emerge.

From the very beginning of our experimentation with Process Redesign using Lean Thinking, we began the diagnostic phase with a participatory exercise that came to be called Big Picture Mapping. Some years before beginning work on Process Redesign, I had attended a session at a Safety and Quality conference where an engineer described how he did "brown paper mapping" by tracking a process through from the arrival of the raw material to the delivery of the end-product, drawing out the path of the transformation, mapping out the steps along the way, and trying to develop a detailed understanding of processes of production.

From our first attempt at Process Mapping in the Flinders Emergency Department, we have tried to do something slightly different. Big Picture Mapping is not simply about the engineer/ redesigner understanding the process. It is a collective activity in which a map is created by direct and public interaction with the participants, who describe to each other the roles that they play in the transformative process; the Redesigner facilitates and records, but it is the participants, not the Redesigner, who are the important people. It is they that need to see the process from end to end, not the redesigner. Big Picture Mapping has a number of functions, but above all, Big Picture Mapping grounds the participants in the reality of how care is currently delivered. It gives everyone involved an insight into the differences between what they profess to do and what they actually do. The various roles played by Big Picture Mapping are best illustrated by an example.

Australia is a large place. It has a limited number of major cities, each of which is surrounded by a vast and sparsely populated hinterland. Many Australians drive big, powerful cars, and drive them fast, on narrow roads. When those cars hit each other, or come off the road, serious injuries are common. So all Australian states have well-developed major trauma services that assess and manage seriously injured people at the scene of an accident, then keep them safe while they are transported (or "retrieved" as it is usually described) to hospital-based trauma services.

Thankfully, across Australia, the assessment and retrieval services available to the public at large are very effective, with well-trained staff and modern equipment. But things can always be better. In preparation for an improvement program, the senior staff of a state-wide trauma assessment and retrieval service asked me to facilitate creating a Big Picture Map of how they operated.

The scope of the mapping session was from the moment at which the emergency services were contacted by someone involved in an accident (either by a participant or a bystander) through to admission to the designated trauma service of a major hospital (if required), or alternate care.

Figure 11.1 A Big Picture Map was created during a mapping session that spread over a whole morning. The session involved about 30 participants, ranging from first-contact phone operators and ambulance staff (both state-wide and local), through to specialized retrieval teams and hospital staff. Each participant described the actions he or she undertook to respond to the report of an accident, to act at the scene, and to care for, and move, accident victims, as required. A large whiteboard quickly filled up with the post-it notes used to represent a task, a communication, or an act of documentation. Problematic issues and difficulties that emerged were written on their own post-it notes that occupied the "bottom levels" of the map.

What surprised all of us at the mapping session was the sheer complexity of the work. Because of the size of Australia, and the frequency with which accidents occur in remote locations, even before an ambulance and/or a specialized retrieval team is dispatched to the scene, the services have to resolve challenging cross-jurisdictional and cross-disciplinary issues.

But all power to the Ambos. The local knowledge and experience of the ambulance officers, who were almost always the first Health Care workers on the scene, was clearly invaluable. It became

Figure 11.1   A Big Picture Map.

clear that different hospitals and health services had different skills and capacities, and the major hospitals had evolved different ways to greet and take responsibility for patients with various levels of traumatic injury, with each hospital assuming their interpretation of the existing guide lines as correct. Experienced ambulance officers would work their way through the options and decide what was going to be best for their patients (e.g. "it's Wednesday, better bypass the Stealers Head hospital, they are always short-staffed on a Wednesday, best to go straight to St. Elsewhere"), while also managing serious injuries and aiding distressed bystanders and passengers. They would do their best to support patients until a specialized retrieval service arrived, if that was required.

Strikingly, when an injury was potentially life-threatening, its gravity seemed to provide a "forcing function" that aligned systems and cut through jurisdictional and disciplinary differences. It was in the management of serious, but not obviously life-threatening, injuries that cross-jurisdictional issues and institutional variability in policy and practice came into play.

As the session went on, a frequent comment was "I did not know you did that" followed by embarrassed laughter as a further complication emerged in undertaking something that should have been relatively straightforward. At the end of the session, a prominent trauma specialist remarked that, while each person in the room was an expert in his or her own discipline, none of them was an expert in system change, and that expertise was clearly what was needed.

The Process of Big Picture Mapping: A Social Intervention

Big Picture Mapping is not simply a method for obtaining an overview of a process; it is an intervention in the social system of a hospital or health service. Ideally, a Big Picture Map brings together, in one room, at one time, a representative group of the people who touch a process from the beginning to the end. That may be five people or one hundred, or any number between, but the task is always the same. Everyone who touches a process has to describe what it is that they do when they accept work, and what they then do to move the work along.

Health Care has many legitimized, or accepted, ways of thinking about problems. Biomedical science has developed a variety of processes and practices that have been validated and legitimized by experience. Each clinical discipline within a Health Care institution has its own body of experience and expertise. Managers can fall back on established bureaucratic processes, policy formulations, accounting practices, and health economic formulations.

Process Redesign does not yet have its own legitimized way of talking and thinking. Big Picture Mapping in an important step in providing Process Redesign with institutional legitimacy and a Process Redesign methodology.

The mapping process is democratic. In Big Picture Mapping, no one owns the authority to state what practice should be. Big Picture Mapping is not about knowledge of recent publications, scientific theories, or formal hierarchies. It focuses on what people do toward the transformation of a disordered or at-risk physical or mental state into a valued health outcome. Big Picture Mapping is specific to the hospital or service involved. Every voice is given equal weight. Every step is important.

In the 1950s, a group of researchers associated with the Tavistock Institute of Human Relations in London articulated what became known as a sociotechnical theory of institutional organization. The paper on changes in the social organization of work (Trist & Bamforth 1963), associated with the introduction of longwall coal mining, still makes fascinating reading. Also from the Tavistock Institute, Menzies (1959) produced a classic sociotechnical analysis of hospital organization that remains compelling.

Sociotechnical theories integrate the human, or social, aspects of an organization with the technical procedures and processes required to complete organizational tasks. In Big Picture Mapping, individuals with high levels of technical skills describe their contribution to the transformational purpose of the institution and make public their tacit knowledge of how to get things done. By only allowing people to describe what is done, not what should be done, all voices have legitimacy.

Mapping does not deny the importance of hierarchies. Mapping sessions cannot be undertaken without the explicit support of the authorizers of a program of redesign. But the mapping provides a link between authorization and permission.

Early on in the Redesigning Care Program, we were mapping an interventional service where multiple groups of specialists made use of a rather small intervention suite. The head of the service, who in institutional terms was the "owner" of the interventional suite, was a world leader in her field, besides being a fine and principled human being.

At a point in the mapping session, Shirley (not her real name) stood up and said, "I am glad we have got to this point, because this is what we do next." A savvy senior nurse said, "Shirley, let us hear it from the floor nurses on that one." One of the nurses responded, "Shirley, we love you, but that is not what we do next, we do it this way." To which Shirley replied, "But the literature is very clear. That is not what we should do." The nurse said, "Yes, but as you know, this gets the same result, and is a much better way of doing it in our small interventional suite. This is how we have been doing it for some time."

As the mapping wore on, Shirley regularly got up. "This is what we do here," she would say. "Let us hear it from the nurses," others would respond. And the nurses who were involved would say, "Shirley, no, that is not what we do. We do it this way." Shirley would say, "Oh, I thought what I said was the right way...." And the nurses: "Yes, but it is not the right way here, for this and that reason!"

After a while, everyone, including Shirley, started to laugh in a good-humored way. We all admired Shirley and valued her knowledge and expertise, but she clearly had got a bit out of touch with what was happening on the ground.

By the end of the morning, it was clear to all that there was work to be done. Once a clinical intervention actually got started, the technical quality of the work was excellent. What needed to be done had nothing to do with evidence-based protocols, and everything to do with queuing and scheduling. With Shirley's blessing, a long program of redesign began. We needed her authorization, and permission from her as well as the staff on the ground, to redesign the current circumstances to improve the processes of care.

When we started Big Picture Mapping, we thought the primary product of the mapping session was what was on the post-it notes. We spent long hours drawing up diagrams that reproduced the content of the map in easier-to-follow ways. Gradually, it became clear that it is the experience itself that is most important, and that photographs generally suffice as an aide-mémoire. In fact, the often chaotic nature of the map as it is generated is both the best representation of the processes involved and the best indicator of the work that needs to be done.

Setting Up and Undertaking a Big Picture Mapping

A Big Picture Mapping is a logistically challenging, human-resource-intense activity. It involves getting a lot of busy people to give up a morning or an afternoon of their time to do something that they are not familiar with and may be wary about. But the logistics and the session itself are not hindrances. They are essential aids in seeking authorization and obtaining permission.

The work starts well before the session itself. A Big Picture map is the first step in a diagnostic phase of a program in which the major authorizers and potential on-the-ground stakeholders have agreed on the problem and the scope of Redesign work. That scope forms the first and last step on the map. The Redesign expertise comes in handy in ensuring that the diagnostic process starts with a Mapping session, then working on how to get the right people in the room and identifying the major functions that will structure the map.

For a Big Picture Mapping session to be successful, the right people need to be in the room. There is no point trying to map out a process if the senior clinical stakeholders, be they doctors, nurses, or allied health practitioners, are not present. They are key members of the social system involved. There is also no point holding a mapping session if the clerical and administrative staff that do the greeting and appointing functions are not there.

How can the right people be persuaded to come together at one point in time? The key strategy is to get the authorizer whose sphere of influence includes all the parties involved, to issue the invitation to attend a Big Picture Mapping session, to be held at a time and place that has been chosen so as to maximize the likelihood of participation.

For an authorizer to issue an invitation, the authorizer has to know about the work, and support it. Helping the authorizer understand what Big Picture Mapping involves, and why he or she needs to use up some of his or her authority capital on issuing the invitation, is very much part of the work of Process Redesign. It tests the extent to which a senior manager is willing to go beyond lip service in supporting a Process Redesign program, and confirms that the chosen authorizer has enough authority to at least get a diagnostic phase working. The issuing of the invitation by the authorizer also demonstrates to everyone involved that authorization is in place.

If the process spans several different groups or disciplines, getting authorization will almost always involve going high up in the organization. Many times, invitations will need to come from the chief executive or a general manager. Before the invitation is issued, some thought needs to be given to a good time and place to hold the mapping, so as to make it hard for people to decline because it clashes with important direct care activities.

Once the appropriate authority has been obtained, and the invitations issued, attention can turn to the identification of major functions. Experience is that Big Picture Mapping sessions work best when the overall process being mapped is broken down into a series of major functions, each of which may involve a number of components. Major functions are groupings of tasks that relate to each other. Their completion is marked by a change in the state of the raw material of the abnormal or at-risk physical or mental states or conditions.

As a general rule, almost all end-to-end processes in Health Care are made up from a set of basic functions:

- A "work comes in" function (referral)
- An "initial sorting" function (what kind of work/patient is it?)
- An "allocation" function (to an individual, a team, etc.)
- A "doing the work" function or functions
- A "work completion and transfer of care" function

So for mapping an out-patient service, there would be "how does a patient get referred to the clinic" function, a "how does the referral get dealt with" function, a "what happens on the day" function, and a "communication with referrer and follow-up" function. For mapping an Emergency Department, there would be an "Arrival, greet, and triage" function, an "initial assessment and allocation" function, a "definitive treatment" function, a "referral or discharge" function, and, if necessary, a "boarding in" function, and so on. The identification of major functions is best done by the mapping session facilitator talking things over with knowledgeable stakeholders— those conversations help build permission and increase the likelihood of participation.

Come the day, attention needs to be given to an environment that will maximize participation. Our practice is to sit people in a semicircle facing a wall or whiteboard, then use post-it notes to record the acts and actions as they are described by the participant. Having people sit in a semicircle facing the facilitator whose questions move the process along, rather than sitting in interest groups at tables, is a further sociotechnical intervention. It embodies a democratic, cross-functional approach in which every voice has equal value and can be spoken out without fear of interruption or retribution. This requires both the authorizer and the major stakeholders to acknowledge that the Big Picture Mapping is a safe-zone where truth can be told to power without fear of repercussion, a further demonstration of the nature of Process Redesign.

Mapping is not therapy. Mapping is about what people do, not what they feel about doing it. It is about what is done, not what should be done. If people interrupt someone describing how the work is done, to say "that is not we should do," they need to be reminded of the task and the importance of listening to each other and accepting that the starting point of a Process Redesign program is deeply understanding the present, warts and all.

In a Health Care transformation process, every step is important. It is easy to overlook the key role played by clerical and administrative staff who deal with referrals, set up appointments, and greet and manage anxious patients. Paying particular attention to the clerical and administrative work pays great redesign dividends, both practically and in demonstrating that every voice counts in redesign.

Is it helpful to have active end-customer participation? Yes, but the more acute the clinical problem and brief the process, the harder it is for patients to provide a representative point of view. But having patients participate keeps a mapping grounded and is always worth doing.

Closing the Session

Big Picture Mapping is done because there is a problem with the service involved. By the end of the session, the real complexities and difficulties in the way the services are currently provided should have become obvious to all involved. If everything is already working pretty well, the problem probably does not warrant redesign. My practice is to say at the beginning of a Big Picture Mapping session. "We should not assume there is a problem with the processes we are going to map. If everything is working well, that will become clear, and we can just move on. If not, we will all have to think about what to do next." Of course, by the time a Big Picture Mapping has been authorized, it is unlikely that things are working okay, but it will surely happen one day.

The Big Picture Mapping that reveals a whole set of process difficulties is a key step in creating permission to proceed. The opportunity must not be missed, and the way the session is closed is the key to using the experience in a creative way. At the end of the mapping session, I ask the participants to sit back and look at the map as a whole and ask themselves "Is this a good way to do things?" If the general answer is "No" (and very often it is), "Can it be done better; is it worth trying to improve the processes involved, and; are you willing to be involved in improving it?"

If there is general agreement to participate, and permission has been obtained, a work group can be formed to work on the next steps in the diagnostic element of the Process Redesign methodology.

Chapter 12

Diagnosis (2): Direct Observation

Sustainable redesign needs to be based on what people actually do. My practice is to call the direct observation phase of Process Redesign "Learning to See", a phrase that acknowledges the insights of Lean teachers such as John Shook, gathered both in person and from his text with Mike Rother (Rother and Shook 2003). It also allows me to refer to the work of one of my intellectual heroes, the late David Marr (1976), a pioneering cognitive neuroscientist who was interested in human vision, in how we humans learn to see. For David Marr, bringing something into vision is not a passive process. The brain and the mind do not simply function as a kind of video camera attached to the retina. Neural code is transformed into a picture of the external world by reference to a detailed model of that world based on learning, experience, and innate processing capacity. Bringing an object into vision requires seeing and looking. Seeing is the process of the external world impinging on the vision faculties. Looking involves choosing where to direct attention. Seeing a scene, the brain starts by developing a simplified model of what is looked at, which is then further processed into a detailed representation of the external world that allows the looker to make sense of what he or she is looking at.

In an analogous way, Scoping defines where to look and the Big Picture Map creates a simplified model of the Health Care processes involved. That model provides clues as to what to look at more closely and what to then look for. The detailed work of bringing the processes truly into vision involves both direct observations of process steps as they are undertaken and the analysis of available data sources related to the processes in question.

The aim is to use tracking and data analysis to generate a model of the current state that is detailed enough to provide a platform for improvement.

External or Internal Redesign Capacity?

Redesign involves skills that are not part and parcel of the discipline-based trainings currently available to Health Care workers and their managers. If a health service manager becomes convinced that an institutional problem might benefit from a Lean Thinking approach but the institution lacks the internal capacity to introduce that approach, one strategy is to "buy in" redesign expertise from external consultants. The consultants will generally take information obtained from direct observation and existing data sources, and turn it into a model of the current state, feeding this back to the client and other key stakeholders. While consultants are often highly skilled at that task, it is clearly in their interests to hold on to the analytic and design skills involved. It is those skills that are at the heart of the product the consultant is selling.

Much of the rest of this book is based on the assumption that a Process Redesign for Health Care using Lean Thinking program involves one, or more, staff member(s) from within a health organization developing sufficient Process Redesign skills to facilitate a Process Redesign program in their organization. Going down the internal route takes time and is less predictable than buying in expertise from consultants. As the saying goes, no senior manager ever got the sack for employing one of the big consulting companies. But developing the capacity for the staff of an institution, or service, to build their own solutions is time well spent. Sustainable change is much more likely when people learn to see their own processes clearly enough to develop the changes that are necessary.

The Structure of the Learning to See Phase

Structuring the Learning to See phase revolves around answering the following questions:

- Who should learn to see?
- What do the visionaries need to look for to learn to see the work in a new way?
- Where and how should they look?
- How can they use data to guide and confirm their vision?
- How can they present their vision, and to whom?
- How can they use the new vision to generate metrics for monitoring and evaluation?

What Do the Visionaries Need to Look for?

The basic proposition of this book is the process view. That the transformation of the raw material of a patient's abnormal (or at-risk) underlying physical or mental state(s) or condition(s) into a valued health outcome is undertaken by a sequence of task and knowledge steps. The challenge is how to identify and then separate out the relevant steps from the overwhelming busyness of everyday Health Care.

Taiichi Ohno is reputed to have drawn chalk circles next to production lines and then required newly employed production engineers to stand in them for long periods before reporting back what they had seen. Ohno would dismiss their first reports out of hand. Ohno knew that really understanding the sequence of work involved took hours, not minutes, and he required his engineers to stay in the circle until he was satisfied that they were really seeing what was in front of them.

A similar, but not quite as confronting, process can be helpful in a busy Health Care environment.

Find a slightly out-of-the-way spot, and just stand and watch. Patience is important. At first, it may be hard to make much sense of what you are looking at. Gradually, the pattern of the work will start to come into vision.

These are the kinds of questions to ask yourself as you are watching. What are the major sequences? How much time seemed to be spent on value-adding activities, and how much on looking for things and asking the same questions over and again? How do people relate to each other?

Are they working as a team? Are they helping each other, or are people focused on their own work, ignoring everything else that is going on?

I did this in an Emergency Department, pairing myself with various members of the senior staff from that department. As is common in all institutions, it is unusual for people to have the opportunity to just stand and look at the way their group, department, division, or institution works.

In this case, there was a lot of friction between the Emergency Department and various clinical units in the body of the hospital. It was striking how, when doctors and nurses from those units came into the Emergency Department, they would look lost, not clear as to who to ask for further information about the patients that had been referred to them. Eventually, they would find their patient, do what they had come to do, try again, often unsuccessfully, to find someone to talk the assessment over with, not find anyone, just write something in the notes, and leave.

It was hardly surprising that all parties complained that communication was difficult. As the observers from the Emergency Department staff began to look at their own colleagues, they learned to see how the behavior of their colleagues, and (by extension, themselves), was contributing to the difficulties.

Follow the Raw Material as It Is Transformed

The raw material of a patient's abnormal (or at-risk) physical or mental state is transformed into a valued health outcome by a series of task and knowledge steps:

- A paper prescription is transformed into a drug that is administered, hopefully to a patient's benefit.
- A note on a request form is transformed into an image on a screen or X-ray plate.
- Blood in a tube is transformed into information about levels of substances in the body.
- A beating heart is transformed into a line on an electrocardiogram.
- An awake, conscious person is transformed into the work site of a surgeon.
- A phone call or an electronic request is transformed into a meeting with a doctor or nurse that can change the course of a person's life.

The best way to understand the transformative sequence is to follow the transformation as it takes place. In this context, the redesign process takes on the qualities of an engineering design task, that of following the raw material as it is being transformed into an end-product. Where does each step begin and end, how long does each step take, how long is the wait between steps, who or what is involved, and what is the state of the raw material at the end of each step?

Tracking individual patient journeys, end to end from admission right through to discharge, can be time-consuming. Patients may stay in hospital for many days, and capturing whole journeys as they happen may not be practical. One strategy is to divide the journey up into the major stages, track each stage in a number of patients, and put the results together using the structure of the major functions discussed in Big Picture Mapping. Figure 12.1 depicts a section of the chest pain journey in a hospital. It is an adapted extract taken from a larger end-to-end map of a chest pain journey. The map was put together by local staff who observed over 20 patients at various stages of the journey in question.

Tracking is a skill particularly developed by the Redesigning Care Team members, and the expertise and dedication shown by Denise Bennett, Jane Bassham, Margaret Martin, and Melissa Lewis in extending and developing tracking methodologies need to be specifically acknowledged.

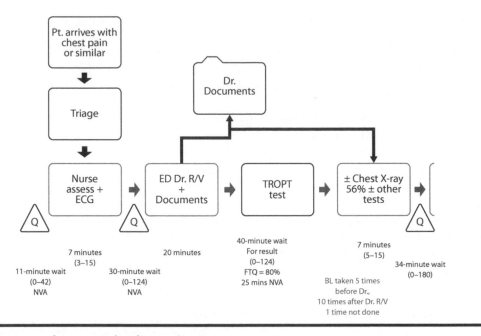

Figure 12.1 A fragment of a chest pain map.

A number of the examples provided here began life in the work they did, although the examples have been modified and figures redrawn so as to ensure that anonymity is preserved.

Following specific elements of care can also be extremely revealing, but it requires perseverance.

As part of the redesign of ordering and dispensing discharge medication at Flinders, Melissa Lewis tracked a number of scripts from the moment of writing through to a dispensed script arriving back on the ward.

She tells the story of attempting to track a script written by a junior doctor during a ward round. Later in the morning, as the doctor emerged from a toilet, she saw Mel waiting nearby. "Why are you following me around?" she asked. Mel replied, "I am not following you, I am tracking the discharge script you put in your bag rather than in the tray where it was meant to go."

The observations made during a tracking sequence can be written as a process flow map in different ways. Figure 12.2 portrays a cardiac-related journey. The figure is again an extract from a more detailed cardiac journey map. What is important in both maps is that the transformation process is laid out step by step, and the waiting time between each step is identified. In Figure 12.1, the value-adding time is 13% of the total journey time, and in Figure 12.2, the value-adding time is around 8% of the total journey time. The fact that time spent in the transformation of the underlying abnormal or at-risk state into a valued health outcome is only about one-tenth of the time spent waiting or queuing is common both to Health Care and many industrial processes. It shows the potential gains to be made by process redesign.

Tracking the Machine

Health Care is basically a human-scale, knowledge-based industry. Yes, there are many complicated and advanced technologies employed at various stages of many care journeys. But, understanding how a complex piece of technology, such as a blood auto-analyzer or an MRI scanner, fits into a process cannot be understood by simply looking at the machine as it is working. The task is

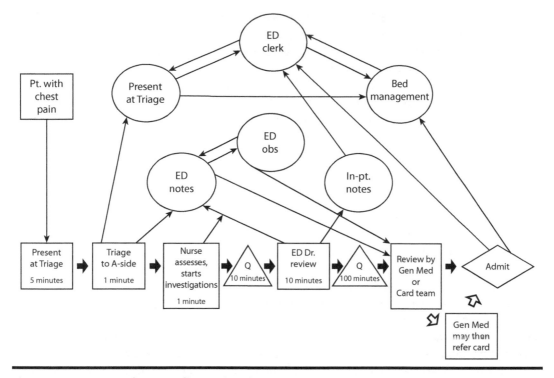

Figure 12.2 Extract from cardiac Patient journey.

to see how any one machine fits into the process as a whole, and how much of that machine's potential capacity is being utilized. How many minutes per hour is the machine actually working at transforming raw material, and how many minutes per hour is it standing idle?

The machine may be an actual machine, such as an X-ray machine or a laboratory analyzer. The machine analogy can also be used to think about a processing unit whose elements are so closely integrated that the various separate human participants link together to make up a de-facto machine. An out-patient clinic can be thought of as a machine with a material receiving area (the reception desk), a raw material holding area (the waiting room), and a processing unit (the clinic room) whose products exit or return to the receiving area for repackaging (next appointments).

Understanding how a single machine works, whether it is an actual machine or a clinic service, is relatively straightforward. It is when a second machine is added that things start to get more complicated, and mapping and tracking comes into its own.

A large general practice worked out of a substantial building, with a number of doctors on duty at any one time, plus two nurses running treatment rooms. Most patients who needed to see a nurse for a service started with a brief encounter with a doctor. The practice prided itself on not keeping patients waiting to see the doctor, but while the doctors ran to time, there was often a queue outside the nurses' work area, much to the annoyance of the patients and the distress of the nurses. What was going on?

A period of observation made it clear that the receptionists who booked the practice appointments were highly skilled and tried to minimize the time patients had to wait. But they booked the patients in relation to the doctor's available time slots even if it was clear in advance that the nursing encounter would be more time-consuming than the doctor element. But the availability of the nurse and the treatment room was not part of the booking process; each booking was entirely structured around the doctor's slots, without any regard to the availability of a nurse. It would have made more sense to book to the nurse appointment slots, and fit the medical component in, than book to the medical slot and try to fit the nurse component in, but the booking process did not take the sequences involved into account.

Things become even more complicated where the "machine" is a person and that person goes to the raw material, the patient, rather than the raw material moving from machine to machine. The sheet metal used to make car parts is moved around the factory on production lines, hoists, and pulleys. Hospital in-patients tend to stay still.

On an in-patient ward, once the patient is in a bed, he or she generally stays there. The "machines" (doctors reviewing, examining, prescribing; nurses taking observations, giving out medications, providing care and attention; physiotherapists exercising; social workers consulting; assistants giving out food and water; and family and friends) mostly come to the patient, rather than the patient being transported to the "machines." In Ford's terms, the "man" [or woman] comes to the work, not the work to the man [or woman].

Finding out how the health workforce uses its time is a major piece of the redesign puzzle. It is common for Health Care workers to complain that they do not have enough time to do their work. They may well be overburdened, but tracking assesses whether that is with value-adding work.

I did some work with a group of Allied Health workers who felt particularly overburdened. Tracking revealed that the staff involved spent just 9% of their time on face-to-face care of patients. The rest was spent on a variety of activities. Some of these were necessary but not directly value-adding. Some, such as putting stickers in referred patients' notes that read, "Thank you for referring Mr. X for assessment and treatment, I am too busy to take the referral at present" were, in Lean terms, pure waste.

Tracking a person involves a minute-by-minute observation of what that person actually does. To make the tracking process more straightforward, it is useful to draw up a series of categories in advance, to choose a "refresh" period for each assessment note—30 seconds, 1 minute, 2 minutes—and then write down the predominant activity undertaken in each period. Using simple charting tools, such as those in Excel or similar software, it is possible to develop a picture of how people spend their time. If the tracker notes where a person is in each period, it is also possible to identify where people spend their time, as well as identify what they are doing.

There are many different ways to organize a tracking session, and many different kinds of information produced by actually following how work is done.

Figure 12.3 shows some notes made after observing the care of a group of patients with chest pain. The notes relate to delays and difficulties in progressing care. Similar observations could be made about staff relationships, staff–patient interactions, and the like.

Figure 12.4 shows a simple tracking chart used to track individual patients moving through a multidisciplinary clinic in which patients first see a doctor and then an Allied Health staff member. The tracking tool provides a row per patient, and the columns identify the scheduled appointment time for the patient, the actual arrival time, the time they completed the first component of care (the medical clinic, plus the total amount of time from arrival to leaving the clinic), the arrival time at the Allied Health component, the waiting time, the time called into the Allied Health consulting room, treatment time and time completing the service and leaving the therapy area. As can be seen, patients were booked to arrive at 5-minute intervals, but the duration of waiting (plus consultations) in the initial medical clinic meant that, predictably, patients spent a long time in the clinic.

One of the interesting questions about tracking is who should actually do the tracking. It is tempting to think that tracking should be the special province of the process redesigner.

0830 hrs	ED	CP patient has had beta blocker this morning, limiting EST results
0830 hrs	ED	CP patient × 1 has not had a second set of cardiac markers
0900 hrs	4D	No beds available for 2 × CP patients waiting in the ED
1030 hrs	CP	Nurse contacted RMO to commence ESTs for CPAU patients
1100 hrs	CCU	Late doctors round
1100 hrs	CCU	Problem accessing MI beds, registrar receiving referrals for patients requiring cardiac beds
1120 hrs	4D	CPAU patient awaiting later TropT result
1130 hrs	CP	RMO work load—still reviewing CP patients prior to ESTs

Figure 12.3   A sample of tracking data.

PT ID	Overall clinic times (hrs)			Total Clinic Time	Allied health component (hrs)				
	Sched Appt Time	Arrive	Left		Arrive AH	Wait for AH	AH call	AH Tx time	Left AH Dep
5	930	800	1000	120	1010	5	1015	107	1210
6	925	Dr. only 915	1010		1015	10	1025	31	1100
7	950	935	1020	45	1025	5	1030	25	1100
8	915	845	1030	105	1035	30	1105	41	1145
9	940	915	1030	75	1035	5	1040	22	1105
10	940	930	1035	65	1035	30	1105	95	1250
11	950	950	1045	55	1050	55	1145	68	1255

Figure 12.4   Tracking an Allied Health Clinic.

Our experience is that the most productive use of tracking time is to get the people who do the work, or who manage the process, to do the tracking themselves. Managers spend much of their life in offices, and when they do "go on the floor," it is often to undertake a kind of ritualized procession where no one talks about the real issues. With tracking, managers have a legitimized way of seeing what is actually going on. There may be some concern that the people who are being tracked will modify their behavior when they are being observed. Our experience is that modification does not last long. As long as the tracker just observes, people quickly revert to their usual behavior.

Analysis

The best way to present tracking data is the simplest way that works for you, the process redesigner. If the data are transposed to an Excel spreadsheet, a variety of analyses and charts can be produced using the tools embedded in the program. The advantage of using a program such as Excel is that, once the redesigner has mastered the basics, it provides a versatile platform for analyses both by the authorizers and the frontline staff. Figures 12.5 and 12.6 show some data gathered from medical officers over a tracking program. Figure 12.5 shows the communication patterns for a surgical

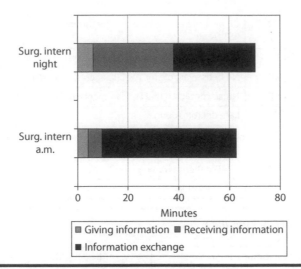

Figure 12.5   Tracking information exchanges.

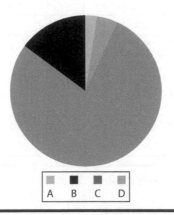

Figure 12.6   Tracking ward locations.

intern on a night or day shift. The chart shows that communication patterns differ in hours and out of hours, reflecting the differential availability of staff over a 24-hour period. Figure 12.6 is a pie chart, derived from data in an Excel spread sheet. It shows the locations a surgical intern worked in during a daytime shift, where each major location is, in this case, identified by a letter A–D. Actual location names would be used in a real-life tracking chart.

However it is analyzed, once the raw data on activity have been generated by the tracking process, it can be used to flesh out the Big Picture Map and give a more accurate representation of the current state of the process to be redesigned.

There are no hard-and-fast rules on how to work out the translation and present the results. The formats that work best are the ones that make sense to the people who do the work, and that tell the story of the present state in an easy-to-understand manner. Redesign is not a scholarly activity. The tracking material will identify where the work flows easily, and where there are major delays on the way.

Chapter 13

Identifying the Real Problem

By the end of the diagnostic phase, the current state should be clearly defined and understood. What was the real problem identified by the diagnostic phase? Was it the problem identified during the earlier Big Picture Mapping, or has the problem evolved over the course of the diagnostic work?

One way of thinking about the diagnostic phase is to see it as a kind of funnel. Into the top of the funnel go all the different kinds of problems that set the Process Redesign program in motion, mixed in with the information generated by the diagnostic phase. As the diagnostic process proceeds, the funnel narrows and the real problem pushes its way through, ready to be tackled.

I was involved in a large program of work whose starting problem was that, after usual business hours, the hospital was not an acceptable place to work or be a patient. Only a skeleton crew of junior medical staff were left to manage the many areas of the hospital after hours. They were struggling, and they showed their unhappiness, among other things, by leaving just before they were rostered to be on night shifts.

All sorts of issues emerged as the diagnostic phase proceeded, but eventually it became clear that there were a small number of real problems (see Chapter 21). As we attacked the real problems, the hospital became a more acceptable place to work at night and a more acceptable place to be a patient.

Root Cause Analysis, the Five Whys, and Effect-and-Cause Analysis

Sometimes, a clear description of the current state will be sufficient to identify the real problem, but often it is necessary to go deeper to seek out the root cause.

A meeting room attached to a small hotel in Las Vegas is an unlikely setting in which to be introduced to process thinking. But that was where a group of us from South Australia attended a training session in root cause analysis, run by Dr. Jim Bagian and colleagues from the American Veterans Health Administration in the United States. Jim Bagian is a doctor-astronaut who was heavily involved in improving the safety and quality of Health Care in the American Veteran Health Administration system (Bagian et al. 2001). He is a passionate advocate for methods such as root cause analysis, a general investigative strategy that is used to work out what went wrong after a tragedy such as a plane crash or a nuclear power plant accident. Root cause analysis has been widely taken up in relation to the analysis of serious adverse event occurrences in Health Care.

Root cause analysis is an extended version of what many Lean thinkers call "the five whys." When you don't understand what is happening, ask why at least five times, until you get to the bottom of the problem. For example:

- Why did the patient die in the Emergency Department?
  Because the doctor did not recognize the seriousness of the problem.

- Why did the doctor fail to recognize the seriousness of the problem?
  Because he was a surgical intern, with little relevant experience.

- Why was the surgical intern seeing the patient, not the Emergency Department staff?
  Because the patient was a transfer from another hospital, so the Emergency Department staff were by-passed and responsibility was handed over to the surgical team as soon as the patient arrived, and it was 4 a.m. and the intern's superior, the Surgical registrar, was busy.

- Why weren't other surgical doctors available?
  Because doctors had had their working hours reduced as a result of a wage negotiation but nothing else had been changed.

- Why had nothing been done about reducing the risks posed by reduced numbers of doctors?
  Because after hours is out of sight as well as out of mind.

In root cause analysis, an effort is made to track the sequence of events that led up to something going wrong, develop an effect-and-cause diagram that starts with the effect (a patient death, a wrongly delivered drug, or the like), and then trace that event back to its cause. It is a process analysis that starts with an outcome and works back to causes.

Process Redesign for Health Care does not start with an adverse event. It starts with a problem in the delivery of care and tracks the operational steps forward that make up the processes involved. Root cause analysis looks back from an event. Process Redesign looks forward from the initiation of a process through to its conclusion. The initiation is generally the arrival of a raw material, the abnormal or at-risk physical or mental state that underlies a patient's presenting concerns. But, it could be the arrival of a drug, a form, or even a batch of laundry. Root cause analysis and Process Redesign are both about learning to see the process steps and their outcome, but they take different vantage points.

During the diagnostic phase of process redesign, identifying a delay, a queue, or a variation that increases the risk but has limited or no benefit, or identifying a step whose first-time quality is low is not enough on its own. The question has to be "Why?," "Why do patients have to wait?," "Why do nurses spend 70% of their time away from the bedside?," "Why do we roster staff so that they are not available when they are needed?," "Why do people get interrupted while they are seeing patients?" Very often, the answer is simply because that is how it is always done, and change is hard, and improvement uncertain.

Asking why, looking at problems as effects, and seeking the causes from the mapping and the tracking, all help identify the root cause. Working on the root cause is working to solve the real problem and develop a sustainable solution.

Chapter 14

Measurement

At this point in the redesign sequence, it is necessary to think about issues of measurement. Numbers are a powerful tool. They challenge myths and help in countering resistance to redesign that is based on self-interest rather than genuine concerns about the process of change and the quality of outcomes. While numbers are not everything, there is no way of getting away from the power of numbers to demonstrate that a problem is a problem, and to effectively monitor and evaluate the impact of whatever is put forward as a way of improving the real problem.

Measurement for Redesign—Types of Measurement

It is commonly said that we manage what we measure. Ensuring that a Process Redesign program meets the goals of the various stakeholders requires a well thought through, and appropriately implemented, program of evaluation. Evaluation is not only asking participants how they feel about the changes. It also involves measuring things to see if they change. To be a redesigner is to be a scientist, experimenting and evaluating the outcomes of the redesign experiments. Effective scientists know how to create and use simple measurement tools that suit their purposes, and redesigners need the same skills.

Redesign involves three viewpoints:

1. The patients
2. The staff that deliver care
3. The institutional view

To cover such a wide and diverse range of stakeholders, measurement for redesign requires access to the whole range of measurement techniques available to Health Care practitioners: qualitative and quantitative measures that are either parametric or nonparametric.

Qualitative and Quantitative Measures

The distinction between qualitative and quantitative measures is fundamental to measurement processes for any area of Health Care, let alone Process Redesign.

Qualitative measures concentrate on using words and images to represent the essential characteristics of the subject at hand. Qualitative methods are a good way of getting at what the users of Health Care services feel is really important to them. The classic example of a qualitative method in Process Redesign is patient stories captured in words or short videos. Patient stories provide powerful insights into the experience of care. They are great motivators.

Early on in the redesign program at Flinders, we organized a series of roundtable discussions with groups of patients. The wards at Flinders are built on the "race track" principle. There is a large central nursing station where notes are kept, computers are located, ward clerks sit, nurses have handover, and much else besides. The patients' beds are arranged around the nurses' station in a large oval (the race track).

One of the focus group participants described how he felt about the way nursing care was delivered during his numerous hospital visits for a chronic health problem. He said the nurses reminded him of bungee jumpers. The bungee was anchored at the nursing station. Nurses "jumped out" to the bay that he was in, did something, then were "snapped back" toward the nursing station on the bungee. This evocative and instantly recognizable simile laid the foundation for a whole program of work (O'Neill et al. 2011) to help nurses spend more time at the bedside and less time being jerked back and forward to the nursing station, the store room, the drug cupboard, and the like.

A useful concept for integrating patient experience into redesign is the patient touchpoint (or "moment of truth," as it is sometimes known in various business Process Redesign approaches). A touchpoint is a point of contact between a customer and an organization that gives the customer an opportunity to form (or change) an impression about the organization.

The mapping and tracking of the diagnostic phase will have identified the major patient touchpoints along the journey. They are commonly the points where patients and staff interact at a moment when a new segment of the transformative process begins or ends; the most useful moments to engage with patients is at the end of a care segment, such as leaving an Emergency Department, at the point of completing an admission process, leaving the out-patient clinic, and so on.

How do patients experience those touchpoints? The only way to find out is to ask the patients themselves, at the time, or soon afterward. Fully describing how best to ask would fill another book. But the most important tool for putting anyone at ease is to make it clear that you are going to listen carefully, and that you have the time to listen. The best way to make it clear that it is the patient's story that you are interested in is to use open-ended questions, such as "Tell me about your visit to the department," "What led up to it?," "How did you find it?," "What did you feel went well?," "What could we do to improve the experience?," and so on.

Once the interviews have been concluded, they need to be carefully reviewed, and any common themes identified. For instance, a number of patients who had been interviewed immediately after their treatment in an Emergency Department all said that waiting was not the problem. It was waiting without anyone telling them what was going on. And interestingly, alarms on monitors going off and no one seeming to respond to them were particularly concerning "that could have been me that was being ignored."

Quantitative measures are those that can be expressed in terms of definite numbers or amounts. A crucial issue in quantitative measurement is the distinction between parametric and nonparametric measures. In the absence of a statistical background, the distinction may seem technical and not of much interest. The distinction is important because it influences almost every element of quantitative measurement.

Parametric and Nonparametric Measures

Parametric measures are exact measures. They are measures of entities with exact values measured by reference to some external standard. Length of stay is an exact measure which is "parametric" because a day is defined externally by reference to clocks whose capacity to measure time refers back to standardization with other clocks, which in turn refer back through a chain of clocks to end up with an atomic clock that is used as an absolute standard of a length of time. So, a length of stay of 2 days is exactly double the length of stay of 1 day. Two 24-hour periods are not "a bit longer" or "quite a lot longer" than one 24-hour period. They are exactly double. You can add, divide, and otherwise manipulate parametric numbers and know exactly what the results of the manipulations will be. Powerful analytic techniques are available for parametric measures.

Nonparametric measures can be put into ranks (more than, less than) but, unlike parametric measures, cannot be added or subtracted, multiplied or divided. While statistical techniques are available for analyzing nonparametric measures, they are not as powerful as those for parametric measures. Nevertheless, nonparametric measures can be very useful in Process Redesign.

The most common nonparametric measures used in measurement for improvement are measures of staff or patient attitudes. Surveys may be undertaken before a program begins, and then repeated afterward. The responses will fall into groups that can be ranked in order. Because the differences are not exact, the measure is nonparametric. "Strongly approve," "approve," "neither approve nor disapprove," "disapprove," and "strongly disapprove" are genuinely different categories, but units of approval cannot be added or subtracted. The sum of four units of approval minus two units of approval is not two units of approval. It is '50% 'more people approve than disapprove'.

In measurement for Process Redesign, it is often useful to put things in rank order, accepting that differences between ranks may be somewhat approximate. Very simple mathematical approaches work best with such measures, for example, 10% of people think nothing has changed, 20% think things have got worse, but 70% think things have improved or improved greatly.

Turning to parametric measures, the simplest illustrations of the difference between parametric and nonparametric measures are sports results. In the 100-meter final of the 2012 Olympic Games, Usain Bolt came first, Yohan Blake second, and Justin Gatlin third. As Blake and Gatlin would know, adding second and third place together does not make a value that outranks first. Ranks are nonparametric. They do not simply add or subtract. But the time taken by each runner to complete the course is parametric. A hundredth of a second is the same in the London Olympics as it was in the Beijing Olympics.

Bolt took 9.63 seconds to complete the course, Blake 9.75 seconds, and Gatlin 9.79 seconds. The time difference between first and second (9.75−9.63 = 0.12 seconds) is three times the gap between second and third (9.79−9.75 = 0.04 seconds; 0.12 ÷ 0.04 = 3). Bolt was not just the fastest. The use of exact numbers shows just how big the gap was between Bolt and his rivals. But on average, the top three athletes were not only the three fastest runners in the world on that day. They took, on average, just 9.72 seconds (9.63 + 9.75 + 9.79 ÷ 3 = 9.72 seconds) to run 100 meters, the fastest average winning time in Olympic history at that point.

Computers or Paper and Pencil

There is a large gap between simple parametric or nonparametric analyses using paper and pencil and parametric analyses that require a computer. Hospitals are filled with data, gathered for all sorts of uses. They appear to invite further analyses for redesign purposes. But this kind of data are filled with traps for the unwary. Unless the Process Redesign Team has good access to informatics advice to tell them exactly what is being measured, and a biostatistician or equivalent to make sure that analyses are statistically sound, most of what is really useful in measuring for improvement can be worked out by hand or with a calculator. Process Redesign is not about subtle differences. It is making things work better on the ground. Meaningful improvements are usually easy to detect.

Advanced statistical techniques are most valuable when trying to pick out a relatively weak improvement "signal" in a context where there is lots of statistical "noise." Such techniques are useful when trying to identify a 10% improvement in a system where there are lots of day-by-day variations, and where many different kinds of patients may be involved. But the analyses involved are not simple. There are important issues to do with the distribution of Health Care variables, which are often skewed in one way or another, and problems when mixing up yes/no (admitted/discharged) with variables such as length of stay that are continuous (could be any number of days and portions of days), and so on. Simple is almost always best in Process Redesign. However, even simple techniques can be improved by taking basic issues into account when designing an analysis.

The Basic Triad of Analysis Design

The basic task of measurement in Process Redesign is to answer the question, "Has the program made things better?" No matter what is measured, and no matter from whose point of view improvement is considered, analyses that are designed to answer the has-it-made-things-better-question will fit into one of three basic kinds of design:

1. Comparisons against an external standard
2. Between-group comparison
3. Change over time

Alfred Sloan would feel comfortable managing a modern health service. "Making your numbers" seems to be the lot of modern Health Care managers, whose expertise is often judged in relation to large numbers of institutional key performance indicators, or KPIs. KPIs are external standards against which current performance is judged. "What percentage of patients was discharged before 11 a.m.?," "Did ninety-five percent of patients spend less than 4 hours in an Emergency Department?," "What percent of surgical patients were operated upon within their priority?," and so on. As various people promote their favorite KPI, new ones get added to the list, but existing ones are rarely removed. As a result, it is not unusual for hospital managers to be given more than 100 KPIs against which to report.

The usual statistical test for when a difference is a real difference, rather than just the ups and downs of chance, is if the odds on getting a result as extreme as the one that was seen was at least 20 to 1 against. If 100 indicators are measured each month, then every month, there will be a 20 to 1 chance that at least 5 will be different from the average by chance alone. Should those five poor outcomes be ignored and put down to chance, or should each one be examined more closely? There is no good answer to that, other than waiting for a trend to emerge. It makes much more sense to take one or two well-chosen standards that directly relate to the problem being redesigned and concentrate on those as the standard against which to judge outcomes. The challenge remains though as to specificity.

A key question for any Process Redesign program is what has been the specific impact of that program. Were things changing anyway, so that the program made little or no contribution to changes already in place? Were things changing, but only slowly, and the program speeded things up? Were things static, or getting worse, and the program turned things around? The best way to identify the specific impact of a program of Process Redesign would be a controlled comparison.

The specific impact of an intervention is best seen when a comparison can be made between a study group exposed to the intervention and a control group that is similar in every way except that it has not been exposed to the intervention. If the study group changes much more than the control group, it is reasonable to assume that the intervention has had a decisive impact.

The double-blind, placebo-controlled random allocation clinical trial is the gold standard of evidence-based medicine. It requires that subjects be allocated to either a treatment or a comparison or control group using some kind of random number allocation process, and that neither the experimenter nor the participants are able to guess whether they are in the treatment group or the control group. The experiment then runs for a defined period of time using a protocol that is fixed in advance. There is no cross-over between the study and control groups, and outcomes are only looked at the end of the experiment.

Process change does not work in this way. Process improvements have to involve the people who provide care. They will know if they are doing what they usually do, or something that is very different, so that the basic criteria for randomization and blinding cannot be met. Also, the double-blind, placebo-controlled randomized clinical trial assumes that there is no diffusion of the thing being tested from the study group to the comparison group. That is hardly possible in hospitals, where people talk to each other and are keen to introduce changes that improve care or work practices. Indeed, diffusion of techniques is a mainstay of improvement processes.

So robust (in statistical terms at least) between-group comparisons are hard to perform in process improvement programs. In many ways, the most realistic approach to measuring the introduction and outcomes of programs of Process Redesign is to introduce time as the basic measurement strategy. In which case, having defined the key measures of improvement, baseline measurements are made before the introduction of the improvement program. Recording continues as the Process Redesign program is introduced and undertaken, and extended until well after the formal improvement program has been completed. The timing of any interventions are noted and the measurements charted to see if a measured change coincides with the period when changes in processes were introduced.

If an external standard has to be reached, this can be incorporated into the measurement program. The most important aspect of measurement over time is to use the current state of a service, or institution's own performance, as the baseline against which to identify improvement.

Technically, statistical testing of progress over time to separate the ups and downs of chance from statistically significant improvements is the province of what are called "time series analyses." For a variety of reasons, the mathematics of time series is among some of the most complex in Health Care outcome analysis. Simpler methods are required.

The Run Chart

The most common way to monitor and track the progress of improvement programs is to use a run chart, a measurement method in common use in manufacturing and service industries of many kinds. A run chart takes whatever measure is being recorded, charts its value at predetermined time intervals (every hour, every day, every week, whatever is relevant for the program of interest), and then joins the values up together to provide an easy to visualize measure of change over time.

Figure 14.1 depicts the general format of a run chart. Values of the item to be measured (number of patients, percentage occupancy, or whatever) are on the vertical axis, and time periods (days, weeks, months, etc.) on the horizontal axis. Each individual point on the run chart is a specific value at a specific point in time.

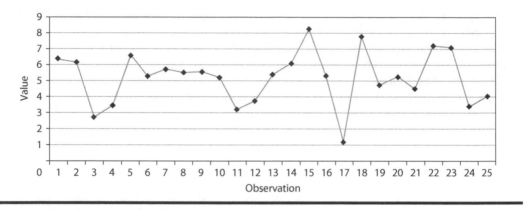

Figure 14.1   A simple run chart.

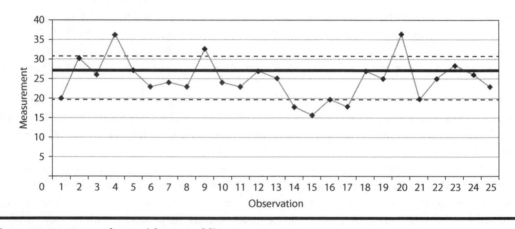

Figure 14.2   A run chart with control lines.

Just looking at the chart makes it clear that values vary over time. In Figure 14.2, statistical techniques have been used to locate the mean, or average, and to identify those values that are so different from the mean (i.e. beyond 2 or 3 Standard Deviation values, expressed as 2SD or 3SD) that they are really different from differences due to the rise and fall of chance.

The dilemma for Health Care is that simple methods for calculating the mean and standard deviation lines make assumptions about the distributional characteristics of values (the underlying way the values vary), which commonly do not actually apply to the kinds of things that a Process Redesign program is designed to change. Statistical methods that identify and then take distributional characteristics into account are best left to professional bio-statisticians.

Also, in most programs of Process Redesign, we are not really interested in one or two moments of difference. We are dealing with systems that are often very variable, and we are looking for meaningful and sustainable change that brings both consistency and noticeable differences in outcome that will persist over time. So again, run charts where differences are very obvious, and relate closely to when interventions were introduced, are as good as charts with sophisticated mathematics. Process Redesign programs with a sustained impact generate run charts where the changes are clear to see.

Measurement Focus: Time, Money, and Outcomes

While common and important questions asked of process improvement programs, "Do they work?," "Work for who?," and "Work for what?," might be good starting points, Process Redesign programs may be focussed on further issues such as:

- Releasing time and resources
- Saving money
- Increasing adherence to standards
- Improving access
- Improving care outcomes
- Combinations of some, or all, of the above

Patients and clinicians are interested in improving the outcomes of care. A program of Process Redesign can also properly focus on reducing the time staff spend on wasteful, nonvalue-adding activities, such as looking for things or people, starting tasks over again because of interruptions, and so on. Reducing waste releases the time spent on wasteful activities. How that time is then spent may be outside the scope of the Process Redesign program itself. It will be for the staff and their managers involved to make that decision.

It may be that, translated into savings, the time released is returned to the treasury and the savings made available for other activities. In the heavily regulated environment of a public hospital, this may be more of an aspiration than reality. Most hospital staff are not paid by the minute or by the hour. Enabling a staff member to spend 40% of his or her time on value-adding activities instead of 30% may be really useful for that staff member and the patients for whom he or she is caring. But the staff member is on a full-time contract, so no direct savings are achieved. Indeed, it may enable the staff member to see more patients, who generate costs. Directly equating time released with a quantum of money saved is a common, but inappropriate, method of evaluating redesign programs. Releasing 10% of nursing hours by reducing waste will not simply lead to a 10% reduction in staffing costs.

It may be decided in advance that any time released will be used to implement pre-specified tasks and priorities. Improving the work organization of the nursing day should release nursing time. It may be decided in advance that some of that time will be spent on reducing the incidence of pressure ulcers. Standards for activities such as pressure area care may be in place, so that increased adherence to those standards is an appropriate measure for the improvement program. Hopefully, improved adherence to the standards will decrease the pressure ulcer rates (see the discussion on Process and Outcomes). Or, a program of work may focus on releasing the patients' time by minimizing their waiting times in an out-patient clinic, or by ensuring that they can leave hospital earlier in the day or after a shorter total length of stay. For the individual patient, the qualitative measure will be satisfaction; the quantitative measure will be reduction in waiting time, length of stay, and so on.

In hospitals and health services where staff have tenure and are hard to dismiss, realizing savings through Process Redesign is difficult because people are the largest component of Health Care costs. Reducing waste releases the time of the staff. But real-money savings will occur only if the staff leave and are not replaced. When cost-cutting is signaled in advance, it risks an obvious problem. Why would a large group of staff invest substantial amounts of time and energy in working themselves out of a job?

Process Redesign is not a quick-fix for a budget problem. It is worth doing because it addresses the primary purpose of Health Care: providing quality care. Over time, productivity will increase and savings can be made, but not quickly or easily. Process Redesign can certainly increase the capacity of an organization. Focusing on reducing the time spent on wasteful steps or other flow improvement strategies can increase the number of patients that can complete the required process in a given period. Resources can be better utilized. Improving the scheduling of X-rays can decrease set-up times and increase the number of patients who can be X-rayed in a day or a week. Starting clinics on time and making sure that everything needed during a consultation is on hand can decrease the time taken to see individual patients and increase the number of patients seen during a clinic.

But Health Care gets more expensive every year, and budget pressures continue. The place to begin the search for real-money savings, rather than improved productivity and quality of care, will often be in areas such as supply chains for commonly used consumables such as towels or bed linen and more expensive items such as pharmaceuticals. Not very glamorous but very practical.

Measuring Processes or Outcomes

There is much debate in measurement circles as to whether to concentrate on process measures or outcome measures. When a patient arrives at an Emergency Department, the Triage nurse will perform a very quick review and allocate that patient to a Triage category. Triage categories are the predetermined time in minutes that a patient should wait before the initiation of meaningful treatment within the body of the Emergency Department. The percentage of patients who are seen within their Triage time is a process measure. But patients come to Emergency Departments to have their abnormal (or at-risk) physical or mental states transformed into valued health outcomes. To only measure adherence to Triage times is to assume that that alone is enough to ensure a good outcome from Emergency Department care. It may be necessary, but it certainly is not sufficient.

Emergency Department outcomes are influenced by many factors other than adherence to Triage times. Improvement programs in Emergency Departments should be measured by clinical outcomes as well as adherence to process standards. Outcome measures include issues such as patient satisfaction, unplanned returns to Emergency Departments within 24 or 48 hours, and mortality in the Emergency Department (and during the remainder of a hospital stay).

When there is certainty that doing the process right will improve the outcome, process measures may be enough. But if the relationship between a process measure and the final outcome is less than certain, outcomes need to be measured as well.

Summary

The capacity to measure is at the heart of the scientific process. Measurement holds the mirror of objectivity up to the effort to redesign. If something is hard, as Process Redesign often is, it is only too easy to feel that effort alone is enough. We are all human, and none of us likes to think that our efforts are in vain. But a commitment to measurement is a commitment to being sure that process improvement is actually making a difference, and to learn from one's mistakes as well as one's successes.

Chapter 15

Goals, the Scientific Method, and the Future State

The complete transformation of an abnormal or at-risk physical or mental state into a valued health outcome requires three elements to work in harmony:

1. Doing the right thing (what)
2. Doing it at the right time and in the right place (where and when)
3. Getting it done safely, effectively, and efficiently (how)

Getting the "what" right is the province of codified biomedical knowledge. Improving the likelihood of getting both "where and when" right, and ensuring that the "how" works as well as is possible are what drives Process Redesign (Bohmer 2009).

Health Care is full of problem solvers. Every day, doctors, receptionists, lab technicians, service assistants, radiographers, and anyone else involved in the care of patients solve the problems created by Health Care systems that were not designed to cater from end to end or did not suit the present circumstances.

Every patient is different and every hospital and health service works in its own unique context. But certain kinds of problems recur, and the next three chapters describe a number of strategies that are likely to be particularly useful.

Far and away, the most important starting point for an intervention is not any one particular strategy. It is a spirit of learning and experimentation. Ignoring the skills and experience of the people doing the work is the essence of waste. The best way to make use of those skills is to work with them to devise experiments that they will then implement, using the Plan–Do–Study–Act (PDSA) cycle of improvement.

Experiments and the Plan–Do–Study–Act Cycle

PDSA is the quality improvement method championed by Walter Shewart and Edward Deming, the fathers of contemporary approaches to quality improvement. The basic concept is that an improvement intervention follows four phases:

1. Planning what to do
2. Doing the improvement
3. Studying its impact
4. Acting on the results of that study to revise and improve on what was done

The PDSA cycle is modeled on the scientific method. Start with a hypothesis or hunch about something. Plan an experiment to test your hunch. Conduct the experiment. Review the outcome of the experiment. Revise your hypothesis in response to what you have found. Use what you have learned to plan a new experiment to test the revised hypothesis.

The PDSA approach is a learning approach. Giving out medications requires precision and care. A nurse doing a medication round is visible to everybody and is frequently interrupted by people looking for information and delivering things. Interruptions spoil concentration and are a fertile breeding ground for medication errors. How to reduce interruptions during medication rounds?

In a series of PDSA cycles, the first experiment involved putting a do not interrupt sign on the medication trolley. It was ineffective.

The next experiment involved the nurses putting on a high-visibility orange slip-on vest during medication rounds. The study phase demonstrated that although the vests were quite effective, they made the nurses who wore them feel silly, and so the orange vests were not a sustainable solution.

In the next experiment, blue vests with "medication round in progress, do not interrupt" were made up. They worked well and were adopted as a standard practice.

A ward decided that the noninterruption policy was so well established that the vests were not needed. They experimented with stopping them. The study phase demonstrated that while the nurses were constant, the patients and other staff changed all the time. The interruptions recurred. The ward returned to using the vests. The interruptions decreased.

People resist change when they have not been consulted about the new way. They fear that the change will make things worse and that they will be left spending time and energy finding a way to work around it. A commitment to PDSA builds authorization and permission because:

■ Involving the people who do the work in planning the experiment ensures permission for the experiment and the new processes that emerge
■ The requirement that the experiment needs to be described in sufficient detail for authorizers to sign off ensures that the "do" of PDSA will be thought through
■ Reporting back on the outcomes of the experiment makes study mandatory

In the early years of Process Redesign, I was uncomfortable with words like "experiment," I associated it with the kinds of experiments I did during an earlier period in my practice when I was working on my Ph.D, and I was worried that it would alienate staff without a strong scientific background. But I have come to value the term, as it expresses the fact that every Health Care practitioner is capable of finding new solutions to their problems if they are provided with the right opportunities. Saying "What will our first experiment be?" is to say "Let us try something, and learn from what we try. It does not matter if we do not get it quite right first time, provided we evaluate and learn from what we try."

Good scientists know what their experiments are trying to achieve. Defining the goal of a Process Redesign experiment ensures that its impact will be properly evaluated.

Goals

What is the goal of the redesign program you are working on? Is it to make a process quicker, easier to accomplish, with fewer errors, more cost-efficient, or all of the above?

It is often said that the best goals are SMART goals:

S: specific
M: measureable
A: attainable
R: relevant
T: time-bound

SMART goals drive changes. In the UK Labor government's 10-year plan for the National Health Service, promulgated in 2000, the government set a SMART goal for English hospital Emergency Departments: that 98% of all patients should complete their Emergency Department journey in 4 hours or less. There has been plenty of argument about that, but the goal itself was specific, measureable, attainable (the vast majority of English hospitals achieved it), relevant to reducing congestion and delay, and time-bound because hospitals were told by what time they had to achieve it.

In 2002, when the Emergency Department at Flinders was in difficulties, a group of us visited a number of Emergency Departments in Central London that had achieved the 4-hour target. They were all busy places, and, uniformly, they described how the 4-hour target had transformed their Emergency Departments from war zones into good places to work and safer places to be a patient.

What was particularly SMART about the 4-hour target was that it was a flow and redesign target. To achieve patient movement in 4 hours or less, the work had to flow from beginning to end in a smooth and effective manner. The target did not tell people how to do it. It defined a future state, and left it up to the people who knew the work as to how to get from the present to the future.

Trying to imagine what the future looks like is the essence of moving from the diagnostic phase of redesign to the intervention phase. The diagnostic phase describes the present state. It allows the redesigners and the people to do the work to share a common understanding of what is happening now. It helps them identify their SMART goals for the future and get those goals approved by the authorizers of the work. Permission to work toward those goals comes from a redesign program that has involved the people who will need to make the changes in the scoping and diagnostic program and the analysis and articulation of the real problem. All that is left is to work out how to get from the present to the future.

Chapter 16

Strategies (1): Value Stream, Batching, and Flow Improvement

Redesign endlessly confronts the problem of managers and leaders being in a hurry. In most health systems, the higher you climb up the ladder, the greater the likelihood of being in your office. People make appointments to see you. They come to you with problems. At the end of your visitors' appointed time, your assistant hovers at your door, waiting to interrupt you to make sure you are on time for your next meeting. The people who do get to see you expect to go away with instructions as to what to do. The more severe the problem appears to be, the more urgent the need is to find a quick answer before the next appointment.

To use an analogy, managers in a hurry like a recipe. They like a recipe that says: to make the perfect clinic, take a kilogram of waiting list strategy, mix in two spoons of triaging into three categories, add one manager and a good serve of performance management, and bake for 2 hours.

There is nothing wrong with management by recipe, provided it works. It assumes that all ingredients are the same, that all Health Care ovens are the same, and most importantly, that all Health Care cooks are equally skilled.

In our experience, those conditions are true only for the minority of the organizational problems managers are presented with. The larger the number of people the problem involves, the less effective the recipe is likely to be. Complicating things further is the fact that the customers of public-sector managers include the careers of the government officials to whom they answer, and the advancement of the ministers to whom those officials answer. That particular group of customers is not generally interested in why things are complicated or difficult; they just want results.

Reconciling the kinds of results senior government officials want with the needs of current and future patients and the needs and ambitions of the staff who work in an organization can be very difficult. That is why across Australia the average tenure of a health service chief executive is about 2 years! No wonder they are usually in a hurry.

Sustainable redesign is not about applying recipes. It is the much more difficult process of learning to cook, and using those cooking skills to match the ingredients at hand to the needs of the diners who need the nourishment.

Think of the redesign strategies that follow as basic cookery skills for Process Redesign for Healthcare using Lean Thinking: "How to use a frying pan?," "How to bake a cake?," and "How to prepare a joint of meat for roasting?". Examples are provided here as to how those cooking skills have been applied in practice. But the examples are not intended to be recipes to be followed step by step in a hospital or health service. They are simply illustrations of how cooking skills can be used. What is important about the examples is the strategies followed, not the specifics. The strategies are the cooking skills needed to turn your own ingredients into Process Redesigned Health Care dishes!

Making the Process Visible

The outcome of a diagnostic phase should be an understanding of the steps involved in the process as it is currently undertaken. Seeing the work as a series of process steps designed to provide value for patients is itself an intervention. People get used to things. No matter how chaotic everyday reality is, it can come to be seen as normal. You get used to how you live. It is only when your partner's parents are coming to visit for the first time that you look around and realize how much tidying up there is to do.

I was doing a Big Picture Mapping of an Emergency Department. The hospital involved was in a regional center. Its radiology service was provided by an external contractor whose radiographers went off duty at 8 p.m. They were on-call after that, but calling them back to the hospital after 8 p.m. was expensive.

The Big Picture Mapping made it clear that getting patients without life-threatening injuries through the Emergency Department's triage and initial reviews processing steps usually took more than an hour. It also became clear that standard practice was that if a patient with a possible fracture arrived in the Emergency Department after 7 p.m. and the injury did not look too bad (i.e. was probably a sprain) no X-ray was taken. The limb was stabilized with a plaster slab, and the patient was asked to come back the next morning for an X-ray and further treatment. This avoided the expense of having to call the radiographer back after hours. Whatever the clinical and economic virtues of the system, the staff said that it had apparently led to a number of angry scenes in the department unrelated to the immediate practice itself.

I assumed that the angry scenes occurred when patients were sent home. The staff said, "No, this is a country town. People are pretty accepting round here, and we make sure they have good pain relief." Then, I asked, "So when do people get angry?," to which the staff replied, "When they come back next day," and I asked, "How come?"

It emerged that the hospital had a strict policy that patients in the Emergency Department were to be seen in triage category order from Category 1 (life and death) to Category 5 (a problem that could safely wait 2 hours for a review), and patients in a lower category were only seen when there was no higher category patient waiting, no matter how long the lower category patients had already waited.

The patients who were told to come back the next morning were clinically safe because the limb was stable in a backslab, and they were not in severe pain. Technically, they were Category 5 patients and could legitimately wait up to 2 hours to be seen. In practice, if the Emergency Department was busy in the morning, they could spend even longer to get to X-ray and complete their treatment. They spent those hours watching newly arrived patients come in after them but get seen before them. Those patients did not have life-and-death problems. They could have had relatively minor conditions but could have been designated as a Category 4 or Category 3, rather than a Category 5, patient, and no Category 5 patient was seen if there was a Category 3 or Category 4 patient in the waiting room, no matter how long the Category 5 patient had been waiting.

Not surprisingly, the backslab patients got angry. "I waited last night. I was asked to come back, and now you are keeping me waiting again. Patients come in after me, and they get seen before me. And frankly, they don't look like they are dying. Don't you think I have better things to do? What is going on around here?"

Just mapping out the steps end to end and seeing them as part of a single process made the absurdity of the situation clear. With just a little flexibility, it was easy to ensure that the returning patients from the night before could be seen promptly.

Mind you, this is not as bad as the hospital where the drop-off spot for patients being admitted had a high kerb that a wheelchair could not get over, and no ramp. When I asked what had been done about the problem of the patients who needed a wheelchair, the staff pointed to a large sign above head height on the side of the building. The sign read "Beware of the kerb."

Splitting into Value Streams

Making the process visible is a key step, but commonly it is not enough on its own. Over and again, we have found it useful to think about splitting the existing process into specific value streams. A particularly useful method of allocating processes to value streams is to use a two-axis format: short and long, planned and unplanned, as shown in Figure 16.1.

Short and Long

Process Redesign starts with a raw material (a patient's concern, the delivery of pharmaceuticals to a hospital store, an operating theater schedule) and transforms it step by step into a valued health outcome. A short value stream is a process in which the step-by-step transformation is accomplished by a short and relatively clear-cut sequence of actions. A long value stream is a transformation that requires a long and complicated sequence, with many possible variations, and much uncertainty.

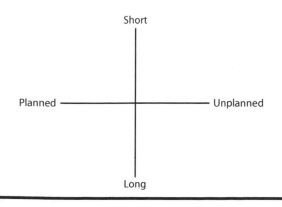

Figure 16.1   Value stream axes.

Long and short are not absolute terms. They have to be seen in context of the transformation required and the setting involved. It is hard to define short and long with absolute precision. Process Redesign is a practical business; most participants in a redesign program know a short when they see it!

Short and long are more appropriate than terms such as simple and complex. There is very little that is genuinely simple in Health Care. Things have become short because they involve highly skilled and relatively standard actions that replace activities that previously took multiple, but often less highly skilled, steps.

An excellent example is removing an appendix by a laparoscope, rather than by an open operation. Appendicitis used to involve major abdominal surgery and a multiday stay in hospital. Some years ago, the Redesigning Care Group at Flinders, in conjunction with the Australasian Lean Healthcare Network and Lean Enterprise Australia, organized a national conference on redesign and Lean Thinking. A senior colleague from a hospital group in another state was due to attend. Unfortunately, she developed severe stomach pain on the plane as she was travelling to the conference. She was brought straight from the airport to the Flinders Medical Centre. She was admitted to the short-stay Medical–Surgical Emergency Ward. She was admitted in the morning, had a laparoscopic removal of her appendix that evening, and was discharged 24 hours later. She took a few days off work and wrote to us to say how smoothly her care had gone! Short: but not at all simple.

Removing an ingrowing toenail is a short procedure, usually done under local anesthetic, and necessary if the toenail is causing some infection in the patient's body. When I was an intern, this was a job allocated to the newly arrived surgical interns. I think I did a reasonable job, but compare the cosmetic outcome of toenail removal by an intern with that by an experienced Plastic Surgeon. Short is about the sequence, not the specific way a practitioner undertakes a specific step; that is a professional matter, not a redesign matter.

Planned and Unplanned

Planned work is work that can be planned in advance. In relation to patient care, the conventional view is that a care process that can be planned at least 24 hours in advance is described as planned because it is the Health Care system that makes the decision as to the exact point in time the "processing" component of transformation is initiated.

Unplanned work is work in which the patient (the end-customer) decides the specific moment when the actual transformation of a particular abnormal or at-risk physical or mental state gets started. I will return to this issue at greater length in Chapter 19.

A more conventional way to describe planned and unplanned work is to talk about elective and emergency work. The word "elective" has the flavor of something discretionary or optional. Many planned courses of treatment are in no way discretionary. Surgery for cancer can be planned but is not discretionary, which is why I prefer to stay with the terms "planned" and "unplanned."

Splitting, Segmenting

The strategy of splitting an existing process into value streams that are then redesigned is sometimes known as segmentation. It can be useful to think of splitting, or segmentation, in general terms. Figure 16.2 shows a generic value stream. The raw material (patient, blood sample, imprest system order, etc.) arrives and is greeted or received, depending on whether the raw material is a person or an inanimate object of some kind. The format of the raw material is then checked to see if it is

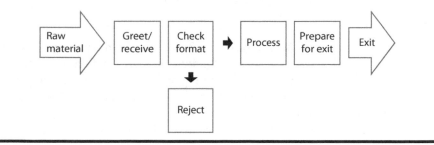

Figure 16.2   A generic value stream.

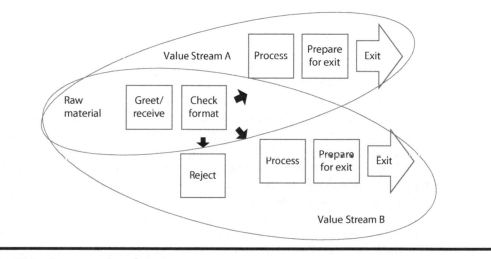

Figure 16.3   Two generic value streams.

compatible with the likely processing steps involved. It is either rejected and referred elsewhere or accepted and processed. At the end of processing, the material is prepared for exit (home or to the next step), and the material moves on.

In value stream segmentation, the raw material is first sorted and then allocated to a specific value stream using some kind of rule system, or standard work. Value stream segmentation is portrayed in Figure 16.3.

Health Care has long made use of these concepts in areas such as Day Surgery Suites. Patients are assessed in clinics or other settings. The patients are then sorted into those with conditions suitable for management in a Day Surgery Unit, and those whose condition requires an overnight or multiday stay. Suitable patients are allocated to Day Surgery Units where their care is well understood and the processes are largely standardized.

Day Surgery Units that are used for orthopedic procedures such as knee arthroscopy can turn over two or three groups of patients per day, and multipurpose suites can be used for orthopedic procedures one day and hepatobiliary or plastic procedures the next. The case studies later in the book will show how this concept can be extended into other unplanned work areas.

In planned work, the initial greeting, checking, translating, and allocating are commonly done in a different location from the treatment areas and at a separate time from the actual processing. Unplanned work can be segmented in similar ways, but the sorting and allocation are immediately followed by the care itself.

High Volume

Health Care practitioners tend to be smart, self-motivated, and hard-working. They love a challenge. So they are attracted to the unusual and the difficult, and may find more straightforward work mundane and lacking in excitement. But focusing on high-volume work and getting it done really efficiently not only means that large numbers of patients are provided with a good service. It also liberates time for the out-of-the-ordinary.

In most Emergency Departments, only a very small number of patients need immediate resuscitation by large teams of medical and nursing staff. Around 60–70% of patients have a restricted range of problems that can be dealt with completely within the department. The remaining 30% percent of patients will be admitted to the body of the hospital. But it is not always easy to get Emergency Department staff to concentrate on providing an excellent service to the large number of dischargeable patients, Emergency Department care only, patients. They are not as excited by that work as the drama of life and death.

Redesigners need to be on the lookout for a high-volume, short work stream. Find it and concentrate on getting that stream of work to run smoothly, without interruption, and with little or no waste, and there will be more than enough time for the complicated work. Chapter 20 describes the dramatic outcome of such a redesign in an Emergency Department.

Looking for, and improving, high-volume value streams apply to every area of work, not only the clinical. A group of staff from a nonhealth care building and environmental services group came to talk to me. They said that they had a number of difficult projects on the go and were getting bogged down. During the discussion, I asked if all the projects were equally complicated. "Oh no, we get asked to do quite a lot of really quick pieces of work, but we find it hard to get round to them because we are so tied up with the complicated projects."

One obvious approach that emerged during that conversation was to form a short work team to look after the quick pieces of work. Drawing on my experience, I suggested that, counterintuitively, the short work team should be made up of very experienced staff. They would get the work done really efficiently, with little or no supervision. There are lots of opportunities for less experienced staff to get experience by working with more experienced colleagues on long projects. But short work is best done by people who are experienced in the work. Short is not simple.

Flow

Once a process has been defined, and the series of steps involved are clear, the workgroup involved can turn its attention to improving the flow of work through the process. Improving flow lies at the heart of Lean Thinking and is central to Process Redesign work.

First, whatever is being worked on has to leave each step fit for processing at the next step. Otherwise, the overall process is hopelessly inefficient.

Second, the pace of production at each step needs to take into account capacity at the following step. Otherwise, delays occur as the excess product of one step has to be stored before it can be used by a slower step. Uneven flow can also lead to unused capacity, as machines and people wait excessive periods of time for material to be produced by earlier steps.

In manufacturing, storage occurs in warehouses and storage areas, and delays in production mean that orders can be lost. In hospitals, patients can get lost also. But they are not stored in warehouses. "Storage" of patients occurs in waiting rooms, hospital wards and clinics, and on waiting lists, which are especially common places for patients to get lost in.

One clinic that we worked with had a large group of patients on a waiting list with "next available" against their names. When asked what was the average delay for the next available appointments, the booking officer said, "next available" actually meant "never." Patients in this group were never offered an appointment, but the Health Department involved would not let anyone say that a clinic was rationing its services. How could a patient get off the next available list? By getting their Minister of Parliament to write a letter of complaint!

Taiichi Ohno made improving the scheduling and coordination of the processes of production central to improving Toyota's competitiveness. A process that flows evenly from step to step is one where the steps are well balanced, and where the pace of production is matched to the requirements of the market. And it is likely to be safer than a process whose flow is chaotic and poorly organized.

Takt Time

Many texts on Lean Thinking emphasize the importance of takt time. Takt is derived from the German word *taktzeit*, which translates to "cycle time." The takt time is a fixed time within which each step in a process needs to be completed. The time is the same for every step, and if every step is completed within that time, there will be no delays or holdups. The question is how to set the takt time? As used in flow production, the cycle time is set by the marketplace. Here is a simplified example that illustrates the basic concepts.

- A company sells 100 cars per day.
- The production line is working for 8 hours a day (8 × 60 minutes = 480 minutes).
- Taking away 80 minutes for breaks gives 400 minutes of available processing time.
- 100 cars are to be produced. So a car needs to roll off the line every 4 minutes to produce 100 per day.
- Setting the takt time at 3 minutes 30 seconds allows leeway for natural variation.
- The company sets a processing time of 3 minutes 30 seconds for each step.

If producing one car involves 10 steps, and each step takes 3 minutes 30 seconds, it will take 33 minutes to produce any one car. So the first car rolls of the line 33 minutes after work begins. And 330 minutes later, 10 cars have been produced.

If a step takes more than 3 minutes 30 seconds, it has to be balanced by a step that takes less time. If a step takes 7 minutes, or 10 minutes, then the work has to be duplicated or triplicated, so that a finished part is still available every 3 minutes 30 seconds. And so on, step by step.

Producing to a takt time immediately shows up any problems. Inefficiencies are obvious because they cause blockages. Because there is no allowance for repairing components that are sub-standard, quality rapidly improves because the line stops while a new part is substituted for a sub-standard part.

If demand varies, takt time has to vary as well. If demand increases, overtime may need to be worked. If demand falls, work has to stop early, or more cars are produced than can be sold. Eventually, if production continues to exceed demand, the price of the finished goods has to be reduced to get rid of the surplus.

It is hard to reproduce the exactness required to work to a precise takt time in a Health Care context. Patients with the same primary condition vary in age, have other things wrong with them, and have varying responses to treatment. And for hospitals that have large numbers of unplanned arrivals, caseloads vary day by day. Producing to takt can be done, but it is difficult, and it requires separating out planned and unplanned (usually emergency) work. But the concept of balancing production along a production line, to produce an even flow, remains relevant.

A natural consequence of flow production to a specified cycle time is that individuals cannot be overburdened. A person cannot be asked to do more than he or she is capable of within a specified takt time. To do so would cause a delay at that point. In a sequential "making" process, overburden at one point will involve delays as work banks up in front of the worker who is struggling with the workload. In turn, this leads to under-utilization as people twiddle their thumbs waiting for the overburdened worker to complete his or her tasks and hand the work on. Line-balancing involves structuring the work so that the tasks are evenly distributed, either by redistributing work between processing steps or by adding extra capacity for longer tasks.

Take

All hospitals with large emergency loads struggle with the problem of how to provide care 24 hours a day. A common practice is to allocate a large proportion of admissions to a "take team," with medical (or surgical teams) taking turns to be on take. The inevitable result is day-by-day variation in workloads. As one medical team explained it to us, for the 24 hours the team is on take, they rush about trying to keep up with the work. The day after a take day is taken up with a whole-day ward round, the team sprints all over the hospital reviewing their patients. They have to speed around the hospital because there is almost never enough room on their home ward for all the patients that need to be admitted. The second day after take is taken up with trying to move patients back to the home wards (both to improve their care and because the beds are needed for the next take team's patients). Day 4 is for reviewing progress and generally sorting things out, and by day 5, things quieten down and it is possible to get home early. Then round again.

Take systems mean that workloads are unbalanced across days and across teams, because the make-up of the patients admitted on take will vary, and workloads will then vary unpredictably.

After a great deal of debate, the various general medical units involved in a take system at Flinders decided to test out a line-balancing strategy. At 8 o'clock every morning, all admissions from the previous 24 hours were reviewed at a unit meeting and allocated to consultant-based teams, with the allocations based on the current workloads of each team. The aim was to balance workloads so that each team had roughly the same number of in-patients. In this system, teams took new patients every day rather than one in four or one in five. But, as one of the senior consultants put it at the end of a winter using the new system: "We are busier than we used to be, but it does not feel busier. The work is more even, and it feels fairer. We are all managing similar workloads, with fewer outliers and less running around." Of course, peer pressure is needed so that all teams play by the same rules and none holds on to patients so as to avoid taking new cases. However, no matter how logical load-leveling is, many consultants have an emotional attachment to take because that is how they were trained, and they are always looking for an opportunity to bring it back. Human nature: it keeps popping up!

Batching

In Process Redesign, the general principle is to organize work processes around predictable patterns of demand, rather than to suit the preferences of the staff in an institution. This strategy influences many aspects of redesign, especially the need to reduce batching.

Human beings have a natural tendency to see the world from their own point of view, and to value their time and convenience ahead of the time and convenience of others. Health Care, with its relative imbalance of power and knowledge between patient and care provider, is particularly prone to this tendency. It is only too easy to place a high value on the time and convenience of medical and nursing staff, and to put a low-to-zero value on patients' time and convenience.

Fracture clinics are busy places. Patients with limb fractures that were set in places such as Emergency Departments may need to be followed up a day or so later to check the plaster and have a further X-ray to make sure everything is going to plan. These reviews are commonly done in an orthopedic surgery fracture clinic.

The traditional way to organize a fracture clinic is to give every patient the same appointment time of 9 a.m. That way, with all the patients arriving in a batch, the doctors do not waste a second of their time because there is always a patient waiting to be seen. But no matter what time you, as a patient, arrived for your appointment, you can wait hours to be seen.

Asking patients to arrive in a batch and then keeping them waiting for long periods of time reflects the assumption that the doctor's time is valuable, and the patients' time (and convenience) is of no value and no importance. Not an acceptable position, unless you see public patients as undeserving of respect, even if it is the public purse that is paying your salary.

The general structure of batching is that when a process has several steps that follow on after each other, processing at a particular step is done in a batch, and nothing moves until the whole batch is complete. Referrals for a surgical clinic come in every day and are triaged in a batch by a surgeon once a week. They are then passed on to an appointments officer, who works through the batch two days later and sends out all the appointments the day after that. An appointment that misses the surgeons review day can wait a whole extra week to be processed, let alone the other delays. In batching, every element that is processed in a batch has to wait until all the elements in a batch have been processed, before being moved on to the next step.

Figure 16.4 provides a simplified comparison of batching versus a continuous flow process. The figure shows a process with three steps, with a processing time of 1 minute per item at all steps.

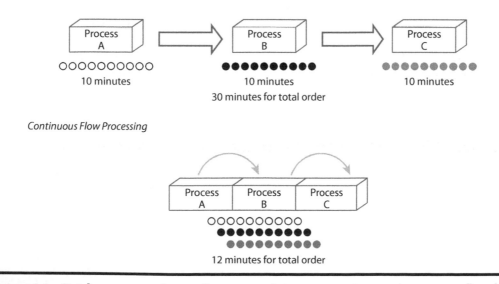

Figure 16.4   Batch versus continuous flow processing.

When 10 widgets are processed in a batch, it takes the first widget 21 minutes to get through the system (two sequences in a batch, then first off the line in the third sequence). The whole order is complete in 30 minutes. If each widget completes the three steps without batching, the first widget is processed in 3 minutes, and the complete order is finished in 12 minutes.

Health Care is full of batching of this kind, done for the convenience of the batcher, rather than with the total process in mind. I visited one hospital where the physicians were all part-time and ran private practices alongside their public hospital duties. It was their custom to come into the hospital in the morning, see new patients as a batch, go back to their private practice, then come back to the hospital at the end of their working day to briefly review their existing patients in a ward-round type batch, and declare them fit for discharge or not. This would regularly delay the discharge of patients by a whole working day, greatly to the frustration of the nurses and the patients involved.

Batching not only relates to decision-making. In most hospitals, "imprest" supplies are stock items that are ordered from an imprest list, or menu of stock items. The list reflects the commonly used items in any particular ward.

It is usual to restock wards once a week. If the imprest items are high-volume items, such as towels, pads, tissues, and swabs, large volumes of stocks have to be held on the wards. The wards then need large stock rooms, which get out of order very easily, contributing to the common problem of running out of stock items, especially during busy periods in winter, a season that always seems to come as a surprise, despite the fact that it happens each year. When wards run out of supplies, staffs either spend time "borrowing" from other wards or re-ordering to get stock delivered between runs. This takes time away from patient care and, if nurses have to be sent off the ward to get the re-ordered stock, reduces the staff available to provide care just at the busy time when they are needed most.

A visit to a large regional hospital provided another nonclinical example of the problems of batching. Out-patients were seen in a clinic some distance away from the main hospital building. But the patient records were kept in the main building. It was the usual practice to take the notes for the day over to the clinic on the day of the clinic itself, as lists were often only finalized late on the day before. The distance was too great for the notes to be transported by hand, so they were driven over in a small van. The driver did not like to waste time or petrol, so waited until he had enough notes to justify a trip. As a result, the notes were almost never available for morning clinics until close to midday and if a patient turned up unexpectedly at a clinic, there was no chance of getting access to his or her notes.

It may not be easy to do away with batching altogether. But once people become aware of the issue, batches can be reduced in size, and run more frequently so as to minimize delays. Imprest can be delivered twice a week, and the smaller volumes can make the deliverables quicker. It can be done.

Improving Flow: Eliminate, Combine, Reduce, and Simplify

Reducing or eliminating batching is one step in a more general strategy to improve flow:

- Look end to end at all the process steps
- Eliminate waste by improving or eliminating a step
- Combine steps where there are overlaps
- Eliminate batches where possible
- Reduce the size of the batches if they cannot be eliminated
- Try to make the flow as simple as possible

Removing waste is an excellent starting point. Early on in a redesign program, we were working through the paperwork involved in registering and then admitting patients from an Emergency Department. Just as it appeared that we had worked through the whole process, one of the clerical staff said, "And of course, there is the paediatric admissions form if the patient is under 16." We asked, "Why a paediatric admission form as well as a generic one: what additional information is on the paediatric form?" The clerks replied, "Nothing actually, it is just some of the questions on the generic form, laid out differently and labelled paediatric." "So what happens to the form?" None of the clerical staff were sure. As far as they knew, the forms were collected once a month and taken to the Records Department. We asked the Records Department what was done with the forms. They replied that they were taken to the off-site archives at the end of the year, stored for 3 years, then as far as they knew, they were destroyed. No one had ever actually asked to see them.

It seemed likely that a few years ago there was some problem with pediatric admissions. A new form was created. The problem was sorted out. The new forms were not necessary any more, but no one had told the clerks to stop completing them, and the clerks did not have the authority to stop filling them in, even though it was clear that the forms had no function.

It took the support of the supervisor, and further lengthy discussion before the clerical staff would agree to a trial of not completing the pediatric form. Just scrapping the forms would have meant that years of time and energy had been wasted, and it was hard for the clerks to accept that. But by the end of a month's trial, it was clear that nothing terrible had happened, and everyone agreed to scrap the pediatric admission form.

This kind of story is familiar to Health Care Process Redesigners. A problem occurs; an error is made. A checking step is added, which is in fact unnecessary once the problem has been rectified, but it is much harder to stop an extra process than to add one, even if the problem that prompted it has been sorted out.

Health Care is filled with add-on, just-in-case processes. But add-on steps are self-defeating. If every step has an error rate of only 5%, and a process has 10 steps, by the time the process has been completed, the likelihood of an error somewhere in the process has risen to at least 50%. A vicious circle sets in. Because the process is complicated, it is prone to error. Because it is prone to error, extra checking and just-in-case steps are added. Because each step has its own error rate, the likelihood of error does not decrease. Extra steps are added with their own error rate, so mistakes still get made. And so on, round and round.

Redundancy

But extra steps are not always waste. Redundancy in safety systems is the concept of duplicating critical components of a system so as to increase the reliability of that system. For instance, many hospitals have "mirror servers" that duplicate information stored in the mission-critical computer systems. The mirror servers are located in sites well away from the hospital itself so that, in the event of disaster, patient-related information is not lost.

More commonly, some Health Care tasks, such as proper identification of patients and operation sites before procedures, have human "redundancy" built into them. Several different people will ask you to tell them your name and to point to the operation site to be operated on, and hopefully that ensures that it is the bit that gets operated on.

But a lot of waste and duplication is just that. Cutting it out generates capacity, and improves the working day of the staff involved.

Chapter 17

Strategies (2): Targeted Interventions—5S, Visual Management, and Visual Systems

5S

It is common to talk about "surgical precision." But lots of places in hospitals are seriously messy. 5S is the name given to a structured process of putting workplaces in order. Putting things in order makes things easier to find. 5S is about more than simply putting things into some kind of order. It is about how things are used, who uses them, when and where they are used, and how to organize their storage and retrieval so that commonly used things are close to hand. It is process thinking in action. Many areas in hospitals are in common use. Putting things in order means thinking about how to standardize and simplify storage and retrieval so that, for all users, access is easy.

5S (Table 17.1) is a translation of a set of Japanese words, *seiri*, *seiton*, *seiso*, *seiketsu*, and *shitsuke* (translated as sort, shine, set in order, standardize, and sustain). 5S is a program with five phases that follow an orderly sequence. 5S makes daily work easier to manage. It also educates about redesign as a sequential methodology.

5S is a practical activity. Like all redesign programs, 5S begins with a problem. The evidence that things are in a mess and need tidying up is usually pretty obvious but the need to put things in order may have been revealed by a tracking process that makes it clear how much time is spent looking for things. Is it hard to find commonly used items? Is time that could be used to add value to patient care being spent on looking for things, rather than on the transformation process itself? If so, then 5S may be a good place to start. And because most people really do not like working in a mess, 5S is a great way to generate permission for Process Redesign.

In the Care after Hours improvement program described in Chapter 21, tracking junior doctors after hours demonstrated just how much time they spent looking for the equipment they

Table 17.1 The elements of 5S

Sort	Take everything out. Sort into things to throw away, things to keep, and things to review
Shine	Take the opportunity to clean up
Set in order	Develop a structure for access and storage based on use patterns
Standardize	Formalize the structure, so that the storage and retrieval solutions become standard practice
Sustain	Define the "ownership" of the storage area and assign responsibility for its maintenance

needed to put up a drip because every ward stored its equipment in a different area, and in a different way. Time spent looking for commonly used items is pure waste.

The permission building element is enhanced by the fact that 5S needs a team. While 5S can involve just one person, such as a clerical officer, organizing his or her work area, or a doctor, organizing his or her office, 5S is most frequently applied to a shared work area.

If the area is of any size, 5S will need a team, and the most effective teams contain both people with experience in 5S and participants from the work area itself. Initially, the 5S expert might be the redesigner, but as the staff members get the hang of 5S, they need less support from redesigners, and it is increasingly common to see teams of frontline supervisors and staff members implementing 5S their own work areas.

When you start to clean out an area that has got into a mess, there are things that are broken and clearly unusable, and things in current use. There are also things whose status is not certain. Good practice is to put a tag on such objects, and leave the tag on for a defined period, to see if anyone claims the object for future use. When tidying up an Emergency Department, a 5S team came across an odd assortment of small bottles and probes. It was not clear what they were for. Tagging them lead to a senior nurse being able to identify them as part of the equipment eye surgeons used when they were called down to deal with certain eye injuries. This did not happen very often, but when it did, it was a real emergency. Rather than just leaving the bottles in a mess, the 5S team created a special labeled cupboard for eye equipment, an initiative gratefully received by the eye team.

Take the Doors Off, Support the Processes, and Standardize Where Possible

When we 5S a large complex, like an Emergency Department, or a large storage area outside an operating theater complex, we bring along a carpenter, because one of the first rules of 5S is to take cupboard doors off. A closed door is an invitation to disorder. Take the doors off, and let the sunshine in! Once the doors are off, it is time to think about the processes the storage area supports. What are the high volume processes? Are the objects required to support the high volume processes easy to find, and stored in a logical way, so that time and effort wasted in movement are minimized?

Once a good system has been developed, can the lessons learned be applied to other areas? Does every drug cupboard need to be organized in a different way? Can storage systems be made easier to follow and more predictable for users new to a particular area but already used to working in the hospital itself? The simpler it is to find things, the easier it will be to get people to "own" their storage and keep it in order.

Visual Management

Health Care practice is dominated by voice, text, and numbers. For generations, doctors, nurses, and all the other professionals involved in Health Care have talked to each other and to patients, and recorded those conversations in text-based patient records. Nowadays, text is commonly supplemented by numbers: numbers generated by diagnostic tests, and by all the other thousand and one sources of data in a modern hospital. Historically, the final repository of text and numbers has been on paper, although increasing numbers of hospitals and health services are starting to store records in the form of bits and bytes in computers.

I am a part-time member of a quasi-judicial tribunal that hears actions brought by individuals who feel aggrieved by administrative decisions of various kinds. The tribunal has the authority to subpoena documents. It is not uncommon for us to wade through volumes of handwritten medical records or computer print-outs. There is no substitute for the medical record as a record of events. But the medical record, however formatted, is a terrible way to manage the hour-by-hour, and day-by-day, communications necessary to organize process flows. The medical record was never intended for that purpose, and there is an urgent need to supplement the record with strategies to support Process Redesign and Health Care flow.

Visual Systems: Symbols, Signs, and Signals

"Visual management" is the term commonly used to describe the range of strategies that use visual systems to support process management and process control. It is appropriate at this point to acknowledge the pioneering work of Gwendolyn Galsworthy (1997) from whom my colleagues and I have learned a great deal about visual management.

Visual management does not sit alone; it is the outcome of the development of underlying visual systems made up from various combinations of visual signs and symbols. It is usual to separate form from content in visual systems. The form developed to represent the area of interest is usually described as the signifier, whereas the content that is actually being represented is the signified. Traffic lights are universal visual systems that organize the flow of traffic along and across streets and highways. The form is a light box containing different colored lights that work in pre-specified sequences. The content is stop (red), caution (amber), and go (green). The combination of signifier and the signified creates a symbolic system, such as traffic lights.

In general, visual symbols can be divided into signals that point to something and signs that contain a specific content. I am marooned on a desert island. A plane passes overhead, and I light a fire, hoping that the smoke will be a signal that points to my presence. But the smoke is ambiguous; it could be a signal of human habitation or a natural phenomenon. If I have a flare gun and flares, I can send up a red flare as a sign that unambiguously indicates both my presence and my distress. While the distinction between signals and signs is of considerable interest in many areas of clinical medicine (is an elevated blood pressure a signal of a potential problem or a sign of a specific disease?), visual systems in Process Redesign usually involve the construction of symbols that combine signals and signs.

Simple written signs, and more complex visual symbols, can indicate a thing's status, direct, and locate the viewer in relation to the signified content of the sign or symbol, identify actions that need to be taken in relation to the signified content, and, sometimes, can take the form of a command.

Status

A symbolic system can indicate the status of an object or a process. Because of its association with heat and fire, red is often a symbol of danger or caution. When the sign, the brake lights of a car come on, this is a sign that the status of the brakes is "on," and the car is likely to slow down. Induction stove-tops do not change color when they are active. They need a sign, usually a red light, to indicate their status as "on."

A much more abstract visual system is an ECG tracing. The heart is an extraordinary natural pump whose muscles are activated by electrical pulses from the sinoatrial node. After activation, these muscles depolarize, and the overall rhythmic changes in the electrical potential of the heart are picked up by electrodes placed on the skin of the chest wall and reproduced as a trace on paper or a screen. The form of the representation (the signifier) of the underlying functioning of the heart is a visual trace; it can also be an auditory representation as a series of beeps. The content (the signified) is the status of the heart (beating or still) and the functioning of the cardiac musculature and its electronic controls. ECGs can be recorded for short periods of time or continuously in heart monitors. A common problem with heart monitors is that the electrodes become detached, an event that is signaled by a loud alarm. The dilemma is that that the auditory signal does not necessarily differentiate between an electrode displacement and an alert signaling a cardiac arrest. While staff can become tolerant of the sound of false alarms, those alarms may, as discussed earlier, be a source of distress for patients and visitors.

At a less technical level, any period of observation in a busy ward or department will reveal endless conversations that start with, "Where are we up to with Mr. Smith?" or "Have you got the referral for Mrs. Jones?" The visual management case study in Chapter 22 describes the extensive use of a signaling system, originating in industry, to indicate the status of inter-disciplinary referrals (begun, in progress, complete, etc.).

Direct

Visual systems not only inform, they also direct. Road signs combine information and direction (as in "Exit for Manchester 15 km") while also locating (Durham Road is identified as Durham Road by text-based name boards at the ends of the street and at major crossroads). Hospitals and health services are filled with signs that try to direct people to specific locations and signs that then locate those destinations, such as Ward 6G. "Way-finding" is the term given to the attempts to make it simple to get where you want to go in hospitals. The older the hospital, the more it will have been modified over the years, and the harder it will be to find your way around. Many hospitals use visual systems such as colored lines painted on the floor to direct visitors from entrances to locations such as "Admissions," "Emergency Department," "Ward block C," etc. No doubt, in time, large institutions will provide electronic mapping software that will allow visitors to navigate their way through the institution following the institutional equivalent of Google Maps.

Affordance

The basic principles behind many of the visual management strategies that work go back to the insights of an important figure in perceptual psychology, J.J. Gibson (1979). Gibson talked about environmental affordances, which he defined as "all actions latent in the environment," but more easily understood as those features of the environment that instruct you. The designer Donald Norman (2013) developed the concept further by discussing how objects can be well designed so that they clearly suggest how a person has to interact with them. Some designed objects have "good" (i.e. easily identifiable) affordances, telling you how to hold them and how to use them, while others need further work on their affordances. When we see a door with a handle, we instinctively assume that we pull to open it. When we see a door with a flat plate, we instinctively assume we push to open it. Health Care is full of instruments that tell you how to hold, open, and use them (scalpels, syringes, pill boxes, folders of patient notes, and the like), and things that do not instruct you and have to be learned. At one time, I did a weekly clinic in a particular health service. As clinicians, in fulfillment of a national documentation program, we were suddenly required to collect a suite of standardized clinical information from patients. The suite had to be collected using particular software program that, when implemented on the hospital's computer system, required the opening of six different screens in a hard to remember sequence. Completing the forms took almost as long as seeing the patients.

The concept of environmental affordances can be expanded to the broader features of an environment. When the environment incorporates a well-organized visual management system, the environment "tells" you where to find things, "tells" you where things are up to, and "tells" you what to do next. To make sure that they are used to maximize effect, car parks have lines painted on their surfaces to indicate where a car should be parked. The signal "the white lines" signifies the right orientation and location to park a car. Crossing the lines signifies a car parked in the wrong way. The environment is telling the driver how to use it.

But Health Care processes are rarely designed. They usually evolve in a haphazard manner. It is uncommon to find a Health Care environment that tells you what to do next. But imagine a waiting area for a machine (an X-ray) or a person, a triage nurse. You as a patient have no idea how long you have to wait, and it is not clear to the staff who is next, or who has been waiting for a long time to be seen. Now imagine a series of squares painted on the floor next to the Triage Desk or the X-ray department. Each square is large enough for a barouche (a moveable patient trolley). Each square is numbered. Provided the squares and the barouches are kept up to date as people are moved on, the squares can tell the staff the order of arrival of patients. They also give you, as a patient, an idea of how long you will have to wait and inform you when a later arrival is being seen before you!

Affordances do not only apply to fixed symbols. When patients leave the hospital, a variety of forms and documents have to be completed, as well as medication gathered. A hospital developed a green bin system for managing the documentation related to discharge. Wards throughout the hospital had a series of small green bins that could be put on the counter of the nursing stations, each with the capacity to have a patient's name clipped to the front. The bins are "discharge" bins that tell people where to put all the documents related to that particular patient's discharge. The environment says, "Put the notes and the discharge forms in the bin. Do not keep them in an office or on a shelf somewhere where having to look for them wastes time and energy, and delays discharge."

Commands

Sometimes, signs or symbols go from instructions to commands. Signs that say, "Stop, gown-up before entering" are prominently displayed on doors and curtains of patients suffering from an infection that could be transferred to others. Gown-up signs instruct staff to take precautions to avoid becoming carriers of those infections and protect patients against infections carried by staff members.

The Ideal Visual Management System

The ideal visual management system is simple, easy to understand, and democratic. It is a signaling system that all users, from senior consultants to junior clerical officers, should be able to understand and act on appropriately. Visual management systems that work are systems that have been designed and developed by the people who use them. Given the opportunity, the ingenuity of the health workforce is boundless, provided they are in control, as is seen in Chapter 22, which is devoted to a description of the development of a particular visual management program.

It is inevitable that visual management systems will be increasingly implemented in digital media of various types. Such systems are very appealing. They look innovative and exciting. The danger is that digital systems take control away from the users. They are most useful when they truly reflect the needs of the user rather than the enthusiasm of the software developers. As redesigners, my colleagues and I love whiteboards, bits of cardboard, cheap-colored plastic bins, fishing-tackle boxes, and all sorts of affordable and available storage solutions. In a series of PDSAs devised and managed by the people who will use the signs and symbols, they can, as needed, be experimented with, tested out, modified, retained, or scrapped. At the point when the processes are deeply understood, and provided users stay in charge of the development, digital systems can be of great value. Process Redesign needs to harness their power. But when a software writer asks you for the "specs" for a system, so that he or she can go away and develop a system for you: beware. Control is moving from the user to the software engineer, and anything may happen.

Chapter 18

Strategies (3): Queues, Prioritizing, Capacity, and Demand

This chapter is all about queues, queuing, and waiting. Queues are not things of beauty. There is nothing to admire about patients waiting for things to happen. The 1971 film *The Hospital* is a bitter black comedy about problems with adverse events and delays in hospitals—the sort of problems that Process Redesign is still grappling with today. It starred the late George C. Scott and had screenplay by the playwright and screen writer, Paddy Chayefsky. During the course of the film, a nurse is rendered unconscious and her assailant has to find somewhere to keep her. He leaves her on a stretcher in the X-ray waiting area. Why the X-ray area? Because, according to the film, a sedated body lying around for 5 hours would not seem unusual.

An exaggeration? Certainly, but earlier on in the film, another character died because of being lost sight of in a busy Emergency Department. One of the precipitants for the whole program of Process Redesign was an investigation into the death of a patient who had been lost sight of in an Emergency Department for several hours.

Some hospitals become super-specialized "factories," restricting their work to a narrow range of surgical procedures, such as hernias or hip and knee replacements. These treatment "factories" screen potential patients very carefully, so that they admit only the kind of patients they can manage in a standardized way. By such means, the specialized treatment factories can function much as other manufacturing or service industries that have stable and predictable demands for a narrow range of products.

For the rest of us, especially if we work in public-sector hospitals with large emergency loads, the variability of the caseloads and the obligation to treat what comes through the door mean that queues cannot easily be prevented. But they can be brought under control, if the behavior of queues, and the dynamics of queue formation, are better understood.

The scientific study of queues and queuing is the province of the mathematical discipline of queuing theory, a discipline with a 100-year history. Queuing theory and, its practical counterpart, Operational Research are heavy-duty mathematical disciplines, and contemporary Operational research in Health Care has become the province of computer modelers, trying to develop mathematical algorithms that mirror the true complexity of Health Care. It is easy to be put off by the difficulty of the mathematics and the ranges of simplifying assumptions that are required to get anywhere near a mathematically robust set of expressions. But the underlying Operational Research are important and readily understood, as are some of the more accessible strategies for managing both queues and queuing. This chapter uses a variety of unfamiliar terms. This is not to dehumanize the provision of care but to provide some distance between queuing theory and Health Care, so that the principles come better into view, unimpeded by prior assumptions and prejudices.

Acknowledging Erlang—The Calling Population

Queuing theory emerged in the early part of the twentieth century with the work of Agnar Erlang (Brockmeyer et al. 1948), a Danish engineer, who was engaged to design economically viable telephone exchanges that had enough capacity to respond to calls made by subscribers.

In Erlang's day, telephone exchanges had a number of subscribers attached to exchanges where operators connected incoming calls to the relevant subscriber's line. A subscriber might realize that it was some time since he last called his mother, and decide to phone her. If he phoned at 11 p.m., he was likely to find an operator free but his mother asleep. If he phoned at a popular time, say 6 p.m. on a Sunday, many subscribers in the calling population were likely to be having the same thought, and the operators would be busy, so the caller might not be able to get through. While mechanical, and more recently digital, switches have made congestion at the exchange largely a thing of the past, it can still be difficult to make an overseas phone call on Christmas Day. You may need to make several attempts.

Erlang developed a number of mathematical formulae that explored the relationship between jobs and the places, like exchanges, where services were provided (service stations) in an effort to predict the likelihood of a caller finding an operator free when trying to make a call. In honor of Erlang, a population whose members might want to access a service will continue to be identified here as a "calling" population. A calling population will generate a number of "jobs" (calls to an exchange or, in the case of hospitals, patients presenting for care) and present them to a service station (a telephone operator, a Triage nurse). Jobs are then processed at a relevant service station, so that a telephone connection is made, a patient is assessed, or a basket of shopping is processes at a supermarket till.

Erlang developed two formulae: one that assumed that if the service station was busy when the job arrived, the job would be lost (the caller would ring off, the patient would leave the Emergency Department, or the shopper would abandon the basket of goods). The other formula assumed that the job joined a queue of jobs waiting to access the process station. We will come back to the formulae in due course.

At this point, there are two possibilities:

1. If the service station is available to process a job at the moment it is presented, the job is serviced and leaves the system.
2. If the service station is not available, the job either joins a queue or is lost.

Thinking in terms of patients and hospitals, an individual within the catchment population of a hospital presents for care. If the processing station, be that a doctor, a nurse or another kind of Health Care worker is free at the moment the patient presents, the patient is attended to.

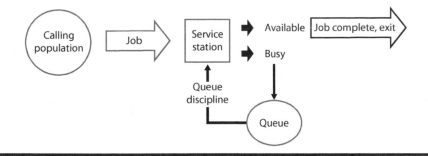

Figure 18.1   Basic queuing and queue discipline.

The patient is immediately treated and, from a queuing theory point of view, exits the system or presents to the next service station along the invisible production line that is the complete treatment process. If the Health Care provider/service station is not available at the moment the patient presents, the patient either gives up and goes away or joins a queue to access the service station. If there is a very long delay between the first step and the next step in a process—whether the first step is a Triage nurse in the Emergency Department or an initial review of a referral by a clerical officer—patients can and do give up and leave the system. However, from here on, to make things easier to follow, it will be assumed that if a service station is busy, patients join a queue to be serviced at that station.

The order in which a job (or patient) leaves a queue to access a service station is called the "queue discipline." Figure 18.1 shows the basic system in graphical form.

A great deal of Queuing Theory and Operational Research concerns how different kinds of queue disciplines will affect the length of time individuals, or groups of individuals, will spend in queues. Not all queues are equal. Health Care commonly involves short-term queues and long-term queues. Short-term queues are the queues that form within hospitals, in Emergency Departments, X-ray services, out-patient clinics, and hospital wards. While they may not seem to be short term to the patients waiting in them, we can describe them as short term because they are queues formed within hospitals when patients, already in the hospital, have to wait for a hospital service station to be free to provide a service.

Long-term queues are made up from patients waiting, in their own homes or other facilities, to be called into the hospital to begin to receive the definitive care they need. Long-term queues are usually known as waiting lists.

Short-term queues are common in unplanned work. In unplanned work, the patient presents directly to the service station. Even when the service station is very busy, the patients cannot be sent home unassessed, so a queue forms that has to be worked through. The paradigmatic location for unplanned work in a hospital is the Emergency Department, where all patients have to be assessed and a definitive plan of management put in place before the patient can leave. The doors cannot just be shut and the full sign put out.

In planned work, the hospital or health service can receive a referral or other request for treatment, and after a desk-top assessment, put that patient's treatment request into a long-term queue (i.e. add the patient to some kind of waiting list). It is then up to the hospital to choose in what order to take treatment requests out of the long-term queue and move them into the hospital.

I prefer the term "planned" to the more usual "elective." Elective has a discretionary feel about it, implying that the patient can choose to have it or not. But many treatments for cancer are planned, in that while the day of treatment is under the control of the health service, the treatment itself is hardly discretionary.

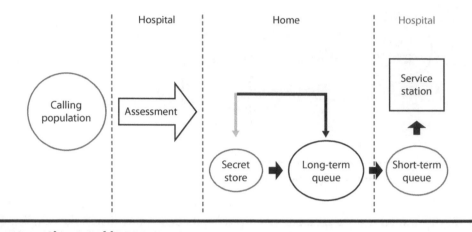

Figure 18.2 Short- and long-term queues.

If planned work is under the control of the hospital, it would be easy to assume that it would be slotted in around the unplanned work, timed so that it minimizes overburden of staff and resources. That is often not the case. Numbers of elective admissions usually fall dramatically during holiday periods when unplanned work also falls, and elective work is concentrated in the working week, rather than being spread evenly over seven days. In Australia at least, numbers of elective surgical procedures fall during the conference season of May and June, when many professional societies have their annual meetings. Unplanned work does not show any such movement. It goes on at similar levels day by day, although with predictable seasonal variations.

What this demonstrates is that unplanned work is the outcome of independent decision-making by individuals within a population and, at a population level, is very consistent. By contrast, the availability of a small number of key individuals can affect large volumes of planned work.

As a rule of thumb, large movements in utilization of health services are almost never due to changes within the population. They are generally a consequence of decisions within the health system. Populations change slowly, so the number of "jobs" generated does not alter rapidly. It is the availability of Health Care service stations that can be changed rapidly by key individuals with administrative or clinical decision-making authority.

The queues that patients experience can be a combination of long-term and short-term queues or just short-term queues depending on the nature of the care required. Figure 18.2 shows both types of queues.

Queue Discipline

Unplanned Work and FIFO

There are various kinds of queue discipline, some of which will be more familiar than others.

FIFO stands for "first in, first out." You arrive at a busy supermarket delicatessen counter; you take a ticket with a number on it from a ticket machine; you get served when your number comes up. You are seen in order of arrival. You wait for a bus. As people arrive, a queue forms, and you get on the bus in order of arrival in the queue.

FIFO is a classic queue discipline, one that everyone understands. My father was a single-handed family doctor in West London. He used FIFO for all his work. The surgery opened at 9 a.m.

From about 8.30 a.m., patients started queuing outside the front door. They knew the order that they arrived in, so once the door was opened, the patients went into the waiting room and the surgery began. The patients knew the order in which they had arrived. My father buzzed a buzzer for the next patient, and each patient saw him in FIFO order.

FIFO is simple and equitable. It minimizes the overall amount of time that individuals wait in a queue, provided that no one gets moved out of order to the head of the queue. If they do, everyone in the queue has that patient's treatment time added to their wait. Without doubt, FIFO is what works best for unplanned work. Chapter 21 shows the impact that moving to a FIFO system can have in a setting such as an Emergency Department.

Long-Term Queues

Figure 18.2 includes a reference to what I have called a secret store, or shadow queue. Patients seek out, or are referred, to a service center such as an out-patient clinic or a specialist's practice. They are assessed as needing a service at some point in the future. There are two common routes that can then be followed. In the first route, the job (the patient) is placed in a shadow queue that can only be accessed by the specialist. This shadow queue is not visible to any governance entity over and above the specialist (and the patient). Shadow queues are almost entirely maintained so as to avoid institutions or individual practices being seen to be noncompliant with externally imposed indicators such as designated periods in a long-term queue (e.g. no patient will wait more than 12 months for a planned procedure). Shadow queues certainly exist, but they are best seen as a design failure for the basic system. If detected, they should be taken as an opportunity for Process Redesign.

The second, more transparent, route is for the job to be placed directly in a long-term queue (a waiting list). The patient waits at home until called into the hospital. The way jobs are ordered, or stored, within the long-term queue, and then called into the hospital or other service station is discussed in the section on priorities later on in this chapter. But once in hospital, it is common for planned work patients to be put into short-term queues to access a specific service, and at this point, I look at a variety of issues around the relationship between a service station and the short-term queue for planned work. The issues are relevant for any kind of service station but are most obvious in relation to settings such as operating theaters and out-patient clinics.

Shortest Service Time Queue Discipline

A set of patients are taken out of the store (admitted from a waiting list) and assembled into a group waiting for the service station to begin treating them (in the operating theater, radiology suite, etc.). With no new arrivals to be added, a Shortest Service Time queue discipline can be used to minimize waiting times in the short-term queue for the service.

The Shortest Service Time queue discipline is of greatest value when the jobs in the queue take variable amounts of time, while the total time available is fixed or limited. Common examples are theater lists of operations, and out-patient clinics. Patients on an operating list may take different amounts of time, but all the operations need to be got through within an available theater session. Out-patient clinics are commonly a mixture of new and old patients, each of whom require a varying amount of time for their consultation, but all of whom have to be seen within a single clinic session that is fixed in length (3 hours, 4 hours, etc.)

Shortest Service Time is the queue discipline in which the short-term queue is arranged so that people with the shorter jobs are treated before the people with the longer jobs. Get the short jobs

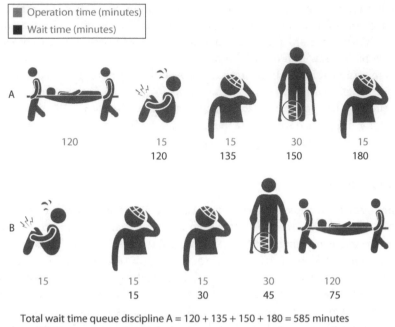

Total wait time queue discipline A = 120 + 135 + 150 + 180 = 585 minutes

Total wait shortest service time discipline B = 15 + 30 + 45 + 75 = 165 minutes

Figure 18.3 Shortest service time queue discipline.

over and done with before starting on the long jobs. The advantages of this for hospitals can be seen by thinking about theater lists.

Figure 18.3 illustrates two basic scenarios. In the first scenario (A), the long cases are done first. Taking the queue as a whole, the total waiting time for the patients going to theater is 585 minutes. The longest wait to be operated on is 180 minutes. In scenario (B), the shortest that uses the Shortest Service Time queue discipline the short cases are done first. The total time in the queue is 165 minutes. The longest wait is 75 minutes. Doing short cases first minimizes the time patients have to spend nil by mouth, and decreases the likelihood that short cases will be bumped off at the end of the list.

Shortest Service Time is a general queue discipline that can be used for work with any group of planned work jobs in a queue that is self-contained. That is, the jobs are being worked through with no new jobs being added and the task is how best to manage the jobs in the queue. A hospital ward round is another setting in which patients are in a short-term queue waiting for the round to get to them. The round has to review a fixed number of cases and will try to do so in a reasonably fixed period of time. Seeing the quick cases (usually discharge decisions) before the new cases will certainly shorten total waiting times both for the patients who are actually waiting to go home, and for soon to be in-patients who are in a short-term queue in the Emergency Department, waiting to be admitted.

Mixing Planned and Unplanned Work: Minimizing Impact on the Short-Term Queue—Intrusions and Buffer Slots

A number of strategies can be used to minimize short-term queues. These include getting clinics to start on time and fitting slot times to job requirements. But a major and common source of short-term queue chaos is the problem of mixing planned and unplanned work in a planned work setting. Large contemporary family medicine practices are very familiar with this problem. My father only saw patients in an unplanned way. Telephones were not common in our part of London when I was growing up, and an appointment system would not have suited my father's kind of practice. Nowadays, most family medicine practitioners use an appointment system of some kind to give a structure to their practice. But patients who need to be seen urgently still walk in. A common strategy is to use buffer slots to ensure that intrusions into planned work schedules do not interfere with the smooth running of the clinic.

A buffer slot is a designated clinic appointment or slot that is kept free. Receptionists are not allowed to book a patient into a buffer slot. A busy clinic may have more than one buffer slot spread over a clinic session. Patients are not necessarily seen in the buffer slot appointment. That is not what the buffer is for. The unplanned arrival is slotted in whenever it is convenient. The buffer slot is there to contain the disruption caused by having to fit in an emergency patient. The appointments affected by slotting in the unplanned arrival can run up to and fill the buffer. The buffer is there to absorb the extra time taken up by the emergency, so that the remainder of the clinic runs to time.

If only one buffer slot is provided, it is usual to slot that in around the middle of the clinic. If more than one is provided, they can be spread out about one-third and two-thirds of the way through the clinic. Too early and they will not be useful; too late and the purpose of containing disruptions will not be fulfilled.

Buffer slots require discipline. It is only too tempting to override them when the appointment times build up. But that is a self-defeating strategy, as the disrupted clinic keeps everyone waiting. As a rule of thumb, if the intrusions represent more than 10% of the workload of the clinic, then mixing unplanned and planned work will not work. In such cases, it is better to create a separate work stream for the unplanned work. That separate work stream can be in a different area of the hospital or be provided by a different team. When that is not possible, a common strategy is to "bundle up" the unplanned jobs and put them at the end of the designated clinic time and then see the patients on a FIFO basis. This is a widely used strategy in settings where patients are used to just turning up. A Health Care system may be trying to move to an appointment-based program, but nevertheless, considerable numbers of patients stay with the familiar process of just turning up. Eventually, the community will get used to an appointment system, but there needs to be some kind of transitional process in place.

Slot Time Adjustment

Slot times are the specific times allocated by the service station for particular kinds of job. Most service stations have a limited palette of slot times of varying and predetermined lengths, and then force jobs into those slot times. For instance, a morning clinic in a health service of 3 hours duration may provide 20-minute slots for new patients and 15-minute slots for follow-ups. The slots are embedded in the clinic templates provided in computerized (or paper and pencil) booking sheets. The template for this exemplar clinic is two slots for new patients, and eight slots for follow-up; 10 patients in total, with one break for coffee.

Patients do not always fit neatly into the predetermined slot times. Experienced receptionists are aware of this and will attempt to manipulate the booking system to fit the clinic requirements by doing things like booking two quick patients into one follow-up slot. Many booking systems are so rigid that they do not easily allow this, and short-term queues build up as early patients overrun.

An alternative strategy is to:

- Determine the shortest usual time for a consultation
- Divide the whole clinic period up into equal time slots using the shortest time as the slot time
- Say the following to the clinician running the clinic

"You can have as many, or as few, slots as you need for each patient. Look at your clinic list, and nominate the number of slots you need for each patient. And after a consultation, when you send the patient back for a follow-up appointment, please nominate the number of slots you need for that patient".

To make this clear, using the morning clinic as an example, let us assume that in practice, the shortest actual time to see an uncomplicated follow-up is 5 minutes. Then, using 5 minutes as the universal slot duration, divide the 3 hours into 5-minute slots, so that a 3-hour clinic has 36 5-minute slots. Allow clinicians as many (or as few) 5-minute slots as they need for each patient, based either on their experience with the patients who require follow-up, or on their assessment of new referrals. As clinicians get used to the system, they start to build up clinics that efficiently use the available time.

In the example, the existing clinic template for the exemplar clinic had 10 slots in all. Building the clinic using short slot times, a clinician may nominate three 5-minute slots for one new patient, and four for another (15 + 20 = 35 minutes), a single 5-minute slot for each of four follow-up patients (= 5 × 4 = 20 minutes); two 5-minute slots for each of four follow-ups (= 5 × 2 × 4 = 40 minutes), and three 5-minute slots for each of three follow-ups (= 5 × 3 × 3 = 45 minutes). Thus, the clinician plans to see 13 patients instead of the 10 on the existing template, and still have 40 minutes left in the clinic for overruns, paperwork, coffee, or a crisis.

Many computerized clinic templates are unwieldy and difficult to change. In our experience, a good start point is for receptionists to get bits of A3 paper, rule the slots up for each clinic on the paper, and then keep a paper and pencil record of slot times allocated by the new system for as long as it takes to see what the clinic structure really should be.

All this might sound simplistic, but it has been described in some detail because it is striking how confined people are by what are actually arbitrary rule systems in computerized booking systems. In our experience, once clinicians start thinking about the actual time they need for each patient, they start structuring the clinic to make the best and most efficient use of the time available (see Chapter 23).

Partial Booking and the Infinite Queue

It is part of human nature to enjoy being busy. When specialists get together, after they have discussed important things like holiday plans and investment strategies, they ask each other how things are going. Status comes with being able to say, "I am just so busy. I hate having to ask patients to wait for an appointment, but I just can't keep up." As a result, many practitioners get into the infinite queue situation.

They have a group of patients they need to see regularly. Once they see a patient, he or she is sent back to the receptionist with a note saying he or she is to be seen again in 3 months, 6 months, or 1 year. The receptionist duly makes an appointment for that time ahead. The patient leaves with a fixed appointment time, and the practitioner has the satisfaction of a full order book stretching months or years ahead. But the capacity of the clinic is determined by the clinician's time, which is limited. Gradually, all the available slots get taken up months or even years in advance. But, over the period covered by the ever-lengthening queue, capacity is lost but the demand moves forward.

When a shopkeeper closes a shop for a day, the customers wanting a service will look elsewhere. If a clinician with a full clinic order book misses a clinic because of ill-health, a domestic crisis, an unplanned emergency, or simply fails to tell the receptionist about a planned holiday until the week before going on leave, the booked patients do not go away. The clinic capacity for that day is lost forever but the demand moves forward. Now a group of patients have to be slotted into a system that has no spare slots, because every slot is taken up months or years in advance. Hours of time are taken up trying to squeeze patients into fully booked clinics. And woe betide a patient who needs to change an appointment. Even if that patient gives several months' notice, there are no available slots for the patient to give the patient, so the patient is at risk of being moved to the back of the appointment queue. Yet, when the day of the clinic comes, there are empty slots, because, for all sorts of good reasons, some of the booked patients do not turn up for an appointment they made a year earlier. As a result, some clinics overbook on the assumption that there will be no-shows. But overbooking is problematic as the overbooked patients do not necessarily arrive at the exact time of a no-show (and sometimes, all the booked patients turn up!). The clinic becomes chaotic, leading to short-term queues that are unpredictable and hard to manage, resulting in the patients being unhappy and the clinic staff being harassed.

The root cause of the chaos is failure to apply Lean Thinking principle number one, "Specify value from the viewpoint of the end-customer." What a customer needs is timely, prompt, and predictable care. It is the provider, not the patient, who needs the full appointment book. How can the provider with a busy practice provide a good service that also values the patient's time? Partial or patient-centered booking is a process whereby clinics are only booked for a limited time in advance. A month is a good period. Patients are told that they will be seen in a month, 3 months, 6 months, 1 year, or whatever time ahead is appropriate. But they are not given a fixed date. They are told that they will be offered a specific appointment closer (2–3 weeks works well) to the time. They can then take up that appointment or an alternative can be arranged.

A partial booking system that works relies on:

■ Getting patients' contact details right (a requirement that relies on and that, in turn, will improve the accuracy of patients records)
■ A notification system that tells the booking clerk when patients are due to be seen (a variant of the closest due date system)
■ The ability to get in touch with people to give them an appointment when the appointment is due

Partial booking is more demanding than just giving a patient an appointment for a fixed period— weeks or months in advance. But it minimizes very complicated shuffling of appointments, because the clinic slots are not taken up months in advance. And it minimizes no-shows, so clinics can run smoothly on the day. Time not taken up with shuffling hundreds of appointments to manage a clinic cancelled at short notice, can be used to contact patients who are due to be seen in the next week or two to confirm that they are taking up the offered appointment, or to arrange a suitable alternative.

Managing Long-Term Queues

Now we move back into the long-term queue, and consider how to exit the long-term queue when there is a date for a job to be exited from the queue after which a job is considered to be "overdue." Many different kinds of clinical services have defined periods of time within which patients should be seen. If they have to wait longer than is acceptable, they become overdue. The closest due date queue discipline applies whether there is one list (one acceptable time), or if there are multiple lists of patients in different priorities, each with his or her own acceptable period and consequent "due date"; the vexed issue of allocation to priorities will be dealt with in due course.

The issues when taking patients off waiting lists are analogous to the decisions a supermarket manager has to make when attempting to keep refrigerators stocked. Supermarkets have limited amounts of refrigerator space that their customers can access. To keep the refrigerators stocked, the supermarket may have a large cold store at the back of the shop. Each packet in the cold store has its own use-by date. The order in which the packets are taken out of the cold store and placed in the refrigerators to be sold will be very important for the supermarket manager who is trying to balance having enough in store to make sure the refrigerators are well stocked, while minimizing goods that have already been paid for going past their use-by date.

The exact health analogy of the cold store is the long-term waiting list. A clinic gets a referral. Patients are seen, put on a waiting list, and allocated a surgical priority, but not an actual operation date. Effectively, the surgical priority is a use-by date:

■ *Category 1*: use-by/operate within 30 days
■ *Category 2*: use-by/operate within 90 days
■ *Category 3*: use-by/operate within 365 days.

A common practice is to take people off the waiting list from each category, in that category's FIFO orders. That is, treat each category as an independent store, and minimize waiting within each store, ignoring the impact on patients in other stores. This risks some patients being treated too early, and others too late. There may be a limited number of Category 1 patients, so that any Category 1 patient can be treated within seven days. This might be very good for those patients, but they are being seen earlier than their care mandates.

An alternative, that decreases the likelihood of patients going past the use-by date, is to remove patients from the waiting list not in the order in which they were put on their list, but in the closest due date order. Look at all the jobs in relation to their due or use-by dates and identify the jobs that are closest to expiry. Complete those before jobs with a less immediate expiry date.

Look at all the patients on the waiting list and admit those who are closest to becoming overdue, irrespective of when they were put on the list or what category they are in. If a Category 1 patient has only been on the list for a week (but whose due date is in 4 weeks), do not admit that patient in preference to a Category 2 patient who has been waiting for 88 days. There is still time to treat the Category 1 patient within the due date, but the Category 2 patient is about to become time-expired. The closest due date system takes advantage of the natural variations in the timing of patients being put "into store" (on a list) to even out overall waiting times.

The closest due date approach requires an information system that provides a complete view of all the patients' use-by or due dates. But it minimizes overdue patients.

Queues and Priorities—Little's Law in Action

When writing this chapter, I had to decide what order to write in—should I start with patients leaving queues or with the internal organization of queues themselves? Changing the processes that lead to some groups of planned patients spending very long periods within queues before they are even considered for care is very challenging. Some of the practices that lead to queuing problems seem hard-wired into Health Care. They are not there to make things difficult for patients.

They are often a consequence of trying to do the right thing by patients, but in so doing, creating problems as well as solving them.

The simplest way to order the people in a queue is FIFO. That is the most equitable internal queue structure, and it minimizes average waiting times. But it does not differentiate between patients, and there are many situations where service providers feel swamped by the number of potential jobs that are presented to them and worried that seriously ill patients will be missed.

A common response is to prioritize, to define various categories of urgency, and then allocate each referral to an urgency category, ranging from "see very soon" to "none of the above." As numbers in each category increase, there is a tendency to further subdivide, with clinicians becoming more and more idiosyncratic in their interpretation of categories. It is not uncommon to find clinics with five or six urgency categories within their overall "patient store" or waiting list, and less and less clarity as to category boundaries.

Process Redesigners dislike prioritization. Process Redesigners can count to two: (1) life or death (2) everyone else. Or maybe to three: (1) life and death, (2) see very soon, and (3) everyone else. But, not more than three. The reasons why Process Redesigners dislike prioritization go back to a combination of common sense and Little's Law.

Common sense tells us that our capacity to predict the future in relation to the unfolding of illness is limited. More than three categories represent an overoptimistic view about our own predictive skills. What is the real difference between fairly urgent (Category 3), quite urgent (Category 4), and hardly urgent at all (Category 5) The differences are often impossible to operationalize. In the analysis of these issues, common sense can be supplemented by Little's Law. It is one of the basic mathematical laws in queuing theory, and while real life is not usually as tidy as mathematical theorems, Little's Law is very informative.

Little's Law and the Impact of Prioritization

John Little (1961) first described the relationship that has since been known as Little's Law, in the late 1950s. Little's Law states that in the long term, the average number of customers in a stable system is equal to the long-term average effective arrival rate, multiplied by the average time a customer spends in the system. Despite their apparent unpredictability, Emergency Departments' short-term queues can be considered to be stable systems, because the underlying characteristics of times and numbers of patient arrivals vary little from day to day. And long-term queues, or waiting lists, are by their nature stable systems with planned exits and defined internal structures. Moreover, Little's Law has been found to be a robust law that operates under a wide variety of conditions.

In comparison to a simple queue discipline like FIFO, prioritization increases the average time spent in a system. It has to; otherwise, it is not worth doing. Prioritization is only relevant if there appear to be more patients arriving in the long-term queue than there are service station slots to see them in.

The best way of understanding all this is to work through a hypothetical example. To make it more accessible, the following example does not try to provide a nuanced mathematical analysis. It takes a somewhat simplified approach. The hypothetical example centers on a surgical clinic that receives 24 referrals each week, and has four slots available for new cases.

The clinic is held on a Friday, and each Friday, the appointment clerk looks at the referrals that have arrived during the week and appoints them. The clinic starts life using a FIFO approach. Once it is up and running, under FIFO, every patient referred during a week will wait six weeks before being seen, as previous weekly batches are worked through. Then, with four new patients being reviewed per week, the average waiting time for a batch of 24 patients to be seen is 9.5 weeks. Applying Little's Law, the total number of patients waiting per week is 24 (the arrival rate per week) × 9.5 = 228.

A waiting time of 9.5 weeks is a long time, and the surgeon in charge gets worried about patients whose condition is very urgent. She says she will have a quick look at the referrals on Fridays, identify anyone who must be seen very soon (a very urgent group), and squeeze them in somehow outside the new patient slots.

This now leaves 23 patients to be appointed to the four new slots per week, which slightly reduces the total number of patients in the system (to 218) without, after rounding, having much impact on the average waiting time.

Encouraged, the surgeon says "9.5 weeks is still a long time to wait. I will look through the referrals on Fridays, identify some pretty urgent cases, and see them early." It turns out that there are around four such cases per referral batch, and it is decided to allocate two slots each week to see them in.

The average wait for the semi-urgent patients is 3.5 weeks (each has to wait at least 2 weeks for the previous batch to be worked through). But the remaining 19 cases now have only two slots per week allocated to them. Once the system gets going, each of those patients has to wait 9.5 weeks for each patient in the previous batch to clear plus clearing their own batch = 19 weeks. This gives a total of 391 patients in the system.

Now the surgeon becomes concerned. Nineteen weeks is a very long time to wait, so she adds another category—fairly urgent. It turns out that there are four such patients per week, and one slot per week is allocated to them.

So now, of the 23 noncritical patients, 4 are urgent, 4 fairly urgent, and 15 "other" urgent. The fairly urgent patients on average wait 6.5 weeks (each has to wait four weeks for the previous fairly urgent batch to clear, and then there is their own batch to work through). With one slot available for other patients, each of the "other urgent" patients has to wait 22.5 weeks (15 weeks for the previous batch to completely clear plus 7.5 weeks on average for their own batch). The total number of patients in the system is now 377.

Using two categories has increased the total number of patients in the system by around 50%, and crucially, while the overall numbers may eventually stabilize, in the example, the longest wait for the nonurgent group goes from 9.5 weeks to 22.5 weeks (an increase of over 200%).

At this point, because 22.5 weeks seems a long time, the risk is that the response is to make yet another category of urgency and see the "a little bit more urgent" patients before the remaining "not urgent at all" patients. The upshot of this is the creation of a majority group (the "not urgent at all" group) who attract terms such as "see next appointment," or some such category, that actually mean "never see unless someone like a local politician makes a fuss."

The general point is that prioritization in any service enables a small number of patients to be seen relatively quickly. But one person's priority is another person's wait. What are the alternatives to prioritization? When eventually someone says, "this is not right, we must do something about the next available patient group", the first thing is to do go through and ask every next available patient on the waiting list (assuming they are still at the same address) if they still need the service they have never in practice been offered. Commonly, of those that have survived, a substantial percentage have either recovered or received the service elsewhere. After that, the best thing to do before simplifying the prioritizing process is go back to the beginning and look at the capacity of the system and the demand the arrivals make on it.

Analysis of Capacity and Demand

Faced with increasing demand, the opening gambit for both clinical and nonclinical units is to ask for more resources. When I was doing my post-graduate training, I visited a large rehabilitation hospital set in immaculately tended grounds spread over many acres. The grounds included an elaborate set of internal roads that were slightly odd because they rose unusually high above the surrounding lawns. I had the opportunity to ask the hospital Superintendent about the roads. The Superintendant said, "My ambition is always to come in 5% over budget. In that way, my budget will grow each year. If it looks like I will come in under my preferred overspend, I resurface the roads. Resurfacing has no long-term cost implications and can be done at short notice."

Those days are over. There is much more scrutiny on costs and cost-efficiency nowadays. When a unit bids for more resources, it is important that it can demonstrate that it is as cost-efficient and time-efficient as possible. Otherwise, the bid will be sent back to the drawing board. There is, however, a balance to be struck between cost-efficiency and the need for spare capacity to reduce queuing and avoid congestion.

Erlang Variables

As previously discussed, Agnar Erlang developed two formulae that form the basis of queuing theory. Erlang's formulae are quite complicated, and I will not attempt to present them in full, but they are so important that the basics need to be explained.

The first, and most important, thing is to express all variables in the same basic unit of measurement, even if on the surface, the variables themselves appear quite different. The underlying unit of measurement that is commonly adopted is a period of time.

There are two basic variables at the heart of all queuing computations. They are the arrival rate and the service rate.

The arrival rate (λ) of jobs is usually identified in terms of arrivals per unit of time. For convenience, we commonly use per hour as the unit of time, but could use per minute or per day.

To get from a number of arrivals to an arrival rate, we look at the average number of jobs currently arriving per hour. The arrival rate should be easily identified by direct observation of the service station.

$$\lambda = \text{the average number of jobs arriving per hour.}$$

Using per hour as the common denominator (it could be per minute or per day; what matters is that it is the same time interval as the arrival rate), the service rate (μ) is the average number of jobs that the existing resources are able to service per hour if every available second was used for processing. By observation, it is possible to identify how long a job takes, and use that to calculate the number that is **possible** to complete per hour.

$$\mu = \text{the average number of jobs that can be completed per hour.}$$

The key to a practical analysis of capacity and demand is the service rate. Note that the service rate is number of jobs that can be completed in an hour, not the number that is currently being completed. What is currently being done has to be separated from what is possible to do.

Work as it is currently done is made up from three elements: value-adding work, necessary but not intrinsically value-adding ("necessary" in the following sections), and waste.

An ultrasound machine is used for a variety of purposes. A radiographer does ultrasounds each morning, and each morning, a short-term queue builds up outside the room where the machine is kept. As the queue lengthens, patients start to get angry, and the radiographer feels the pressure. The ultrasound machine is switched on at 8.30 a.m. and is switched off at the end of the morning session at 1 p.m. So in principle, the machine is staffed and available for 270 minutes. The questions are, "What is the service rate?," "What proportion of that time is taken up with value-adding and necessary work?," and "How much of the available time is used up by waste?" Direct observation will allow an observer to identify pure waste, because it is time taken up looking for things like notes and extra equipment and dealing with interruptions. Staff may feel and be busy, not because they are doing value-added work but because the system of care is not well designed and waste is inescapable.

The importance of waste is that the potential service rate for a service station excluding waste should be compared against the existing service time, because the aim of redesign is to drive out the waste. By discounting the time taken up by waste, the underlying service rate of the service station can be calculated, and the potential operational capacity identified.

Let us say that after a period of observation of a service station, it is possible to say that 20% of time is wasted (the machine is idle while the operator is looking for things or people, and not able to perform the value-added or necessary actions).

In our radiographer example, each job appears to take 12 minutes, five patients arrive per hour, and the service rate is 100%, yet a queue builds up. If, by observation, it seems that 20% of the service time is waste, then the service rate without waste is six jobs per hour (5 + 20% of 5 (5 + 1 = 6)). At six jobs per hour, the queue will disappear.

Another way of looking at this is to divide the number of jobs currently done, by the service rate without waste. In this example, five jobs are done per hour, while the number of jobs that could be done if there was no waste is six—so the machine is working at 83.3% of its full capacity. This is usually called the utilization rate (5/6 expressed as a percentage).

In the above example, waste is identified by direct observation. An alternative is to record value-adding time and necessary time, and assume that everything else is waste. For example, in an operating theater, for each operation, knife-to-skin time and the time at which operations end may be recorded. If the total time taken for actually performing operations each day is added up, and a nominal time is allowed for the induction of anesthesia and writing of an operation note, then the rest of the time the theater is staffed and available, but not being used for performing operations is waste. It should be possible to work out how many extra operations could be done in the waste period, and thus the current utilization rate.

Another approach is to use external benchmarks for how long a job should take. A service station performs five jobs per hour, each taking 12 minutes. The benchmark time for that kind of job is 10 minutes. So using the benchmark rate as the standard, utilization rate per hour is 5/6 = 83.3%.

If utilization rates are well below 85%, there is every likelihood that driving out the waste will ensure that short-term, and long-term, queues can be reduced or eliminated, allowing the claim for additional resources to be reassessed.

Here is an example from direct experience. During a mapping session for the flow of medical in-patients through a general hospital, a number of staff members identified access to CAT scans as a common problem. The Radiology Department did both emergency and planned CAT scans. It was clear that access to the CAT scanner was a problem because:

■ There were delays in getting CAT scans done for emergency patients coming through the Emergency Department.
■ Radiographers were paid overtime to come in after 8 p.m., and overtime was regularly being used to complete routine work.
■ In-patients were prioritized, so out-patients waited days or weeks for a CAT scan. If patients needed a follow-up scan shortly after discharge, they were being kept in hospital to have them as in-patients, rather than being discharged and risk delays for an out-patient scan.

The department was developing a business case for a second scanner. Observation of the Radiology Suite revealed that a patient was only actively being scanned 60% of the time. For 40% of the remaining fully staffed hours, the X-ray beam was not being used fruitfully.

The wastes included:

- The CAT scanner did not scan while a patient got undressed before a scan and dressed again afterward.
- Radiographers all took their meal breaks at the same time.
- Many scans required injections of contrast: the time spent doing the infusion was necessary, but time spent looking for a radiologist who was willing to do the infusion was a waste.

The scanner was doing three scans per hour (one every 20 minutes). Without the 40% waste, it could do five scans (one every 12 minutes). The utilization rate for the CAT scanner was 3/5 = 60%.

A number of simple strategies quickly increased utilization rates on average, a little over 4 per hour, or 85%. Radiologists agreed to develop a roster for giving contrast injections. This reduced delays in the CAT suite, and it also improved reporting times, because radiologists had protected time for reporting, free of haphazard interruptions. An extra changing room was developed to reduce delays due to patients not being ready, and scanning sequences were altered to enable radiographers to set up for scans in a time-efficient manner. Work was done in working hours, overtime rates decreased, and waiting times for out-patient scans were also reduced. The required work could now be done within the existing capacity, and there was no objective case for a new scanner.

Utilization at 85% and Above; Exponential Delay

If the amount of obvious waste is low and utilization is already around 85% or over, improvement will not be easy. It becomes necessary to look in greater detail at exactly how the steps are done, particularly the necessary but not intrinsically value-adding work. Are there small improvements that can save minutes? Can some steps be eliminated, or merged, or simplified? This is challenging work, and it will call on the flexibility and ingenuity of all the staff involved.

It is also very important to acknowledge that at utilization rates of 85% and over, queues start to become inevitable with even small increases in the number of arrivals. In the above example, the implication is that having machines stand idle is a bad thing, and expensive machines should be worked as hard as possible. The dilemma is that working at close to full capacity for much of the time takes all the buffers out of the system and makes the build-up of queues very likely if the numbers of jobs increase by even a small amount. In a system with lots of capacity, there will be staff members and machines standing ready for use, so patients have a good chance of being seen as soon as, or shortly after, they arrive, and extra arrivals can be easily accommodated.

Adding a small number of extra cases to already stretched systems, results in congestion. The underlying relationship between queue length and extra arrivals in a system working at close to capacity was demonstrated more than 100 years ago by Erlang, but it still remains out of sight in Health Care. It is basically common sense. The exact arrival time of a job is unpredictable from moment to moment. The busier the station, the less likely that it will be free at the moment a job arrives, so that job will join a queue. And that queue will grow as the arrivals continue. The proof of this is best demonstrated by using a simple numerical example based on a very simplified form of Erlang's formulae. If, like many of us, you do not like formulae, Figure 18.4 tells the story.

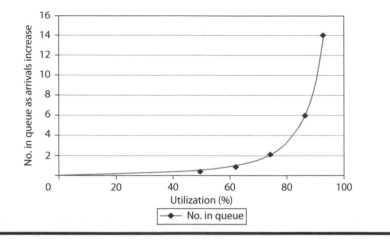

Figure 18.4   Queue length impact of new arrivals at increasing levels of utilization.

I have already defined arrival rate as λ and service rate as μ. I will start with a system that is not at all under strain. As previously identified:

$$P \text{ (the utilization rate)} = \lambda/\mu.$$

- If on average four patients arrive per hour at a service that can handle up to eight patients per hour, P (the utilization rate of the service) will be 4/8 =0.5, which is 50% utilization.
- L (the average number of jobs in the system at any one point in time) = μ/μ – λ.
- That is, with four jobs per hour and a service rate of eight, L = 4/8 – 4 = 1. So on average there will be one patient, who is getting serviced, in the system at any one moment in time.
- Lq (the number of jobs that are likely to be in a queue at any point in time) = the utilization rate × the number of jobs in a system = P × L.
- That is, with four jobs per hour and a service rate of eight, Lq = 0.5 × 1 = 0.5.
- W (the average time a job spends in a system) = 1/μ – λ.
- That is, with four jobs per hour and a service rate of eight, each job/patient will spend W = 1/8 – 4 = 1/4 = 0.25 of an hour in the system. The average amount of time likely to be spent waiting, rather than actually receiving care, is Wq = P × W.
- That is, with four jobs per hour and a service rate of eight, then Wq, the time that a patient can expect to wait = 0.5 × 0.25 = 0.125 of an hour, which is 7.5 minutes.

Exponential Growth in Queue Length with Small Changes in the Number of Arrivals

Having created the variables already described, we are now in a position to understand the effect that extra arrivals have on waiting time and the number of people in a system. What is particularly important to understand is what happens in a service functioning at high level of utilization when even a small number of extra patients arrive for a service. Table 18.1 assumes that the service rate (the number of jobs that can be served, the basic measure of capacity in the system) remains unchanged, but the arrival rate, the number of jobs that do arrive per hour, steadily increases.

Table 18.1   The Impact of Increasing Numbers of Arrivals at High Level of Utilization

If μ (service rate) = 8 per hour					
λ (arrival rate)	ρ (utilization %)	L (av. no. pts in system)	Lq (av. no. pts in queue)	W (av. time in system)	Wq (av. time in queue)
4	0.5 (50)	1	0.5	0.25 (15 mins)	0.125 (7.5 mins)
5	0.625 (62.5)	1.6	1	0.33 (20 mins)	0.2 (12 mins)
6	0.75 (75)	3	2.25	0.5 (30 mins)	0.325 (22.5 mins)
7	0.875 (87.5)	7	6.12	1 (1 hour)	0.875 (52 mins)
7.5	0.937 (94)	15	14	2 (2 hours)	1.97 (1 hour, 52 mins)

At high rates of utilization, small numbers of extra arrivals per hour have a disproportionate impact. At 7 patients per hour, the average time in the queue is 52 minutes. Adding half a patient per hour (or one every two hours) takes the system to over 90% utilization. An extra half-a-patient increases the number of patients in the system from 7 to 15, and the average waiting time in the queue from 52 minutes to 1 hour and 52 minutes.

The impact of working at a high level of utilization is most easily visualized by means of the graph shown in Figure 18.4.

Hospitals and health services are expensive resources. Common practice is to run them at very high levels of occupancy, as this is seen to be more cost-efficient. But at high levels of occupancy, queues are inevitable. So the apparent cost-efficiency of working at 98% occupancy is only real if it is assumed that the time patients spend waiting in places such as Emergency Departments has no value for those patients and can be ignored in the calculation of value for money.

The task of Process Redesign is not to get rid of queues, which is often very hard to do, but rather to limit their exponential growth as much as possible. At high levels of occupancy, one more patient really can tip a service past the point of viability.

Pre-emption and Impossible Jobs

So far, the analysis of queues, capacity, and demand has made the assumption of an ordered system with definable arrival rates and service times, and orderly queues whose disciplines can be understood and reproduced. If only real-life hospitals and health services were like that.

In the earlier description of Little's Law and prioritization, it was assumed that slots were allocated to specific priorities. But there are many situations in Health Care where slot disciplines are not maintained. Instead, classes of patients pre-empt the places in a short-term or long-term queue of other, "lower" classes of patients.

In simple pre-emption systems, there are two classes of patients—high priority and low priority. When high-priority patients arrive, the care of low-priority patients is suspended, and it is not resumed until the high-priority patients have been cleared. The dilemma is that in settings such as Emergency Departments, the time of arrival of both high-priority and low-priority patients is random in relation to each other.

In many Australian Emergency Departments, patients are allocated to one of five priorities, with any higher priority patient pre-empting any lower priority patient. This kind of system is very hard on low-priority patients. They are just starting to move up the queue to be seen when they are pre-empted by a higher priority patient, but who arrived more recently. In fact, they are pre-empted by any higher priority patient, no matter how long they have been waiting compared with the higher priority arrival.

What makes this particularly problematic from lower priority patients' point of view is that the lower priority patients do not receive any partial credit for the time they have already waited; they are stuck in a queue that does not make any progress while everyone in the queue has to wait for all higher priority queues to be cleared.

In practice, in a busy Emergency Department, this can mean that lower priority patients can wait 8–9 hours to be seen for a condition that probably can be resolved in a few minutes. During that time, they become increasingly distressed, and there is always a risk that their condition will deteriorate. Systems such as this are only made to work by a constant effort from floor managers and unit schedulers, who try to juggle patients.

If a mathematician is asked to provide a fully functioning model of the interactions between five priorities, each with a varying and unpredictable arrival time, and pre-emption at every level, they would turn to mathematical strategies such as negative exponentials, Laplace transforms, complex service time distributions, and the like, and even then, they would struggle. It is a tough call to ask an Emergency Department shift manager to do that kind of model building for five classes of priority, in his or her head, while also looking after the patients and the staff. But that is not the full extent of the problem.

Most queuing analyses make the assumptions of predictable service times and rates. It is assumed that the actual process of looking after patients is reasonably predictable and uniform across patient types. In other words, once a service station gets to actually do a job, things are reasonably predictable. But that is clearly not the case in many general hospital environments, where their size means that they rely on complex staff rosters made up from staff of varying skills, competencies, and length of experience. Also, the more senior the staff member, the more idiosyncratic his or her behavior can become. On one occasion, during the mapping of the workings of a large teaching hospital's Emergency Department, the senior medical staff said, "we do not like seeing skin rashes." "Why not?" "We just do not like them, and we encourage the Triage team to divert them to a local general practice." Which the Triage nurses tried to do. But not when the hospital was busy, because it took so much longer diverting patients than having them seen and treated in the Emergency Department.

All in all, very many large hospital units with complex scheduling requirements present what are called nondeterministic polynomial time hard problems (NP Hard problems). NP Hard problems do not have complete and elegant mathematical solutions. They can only be approached on a trial-and-error basis, where all potential solutions to any one scheduling decision have to be computed and sorted through to see what might work best for that problem at that time. That might be acceptable if you are a large digital computer whose electrons move at the speed of light. For the floor managers, shift managers, or theater schedulers who actually have to get the work done, and whose mental processes work at human speed, it all comes back to experience and feel ("I think that will work"). Human ingenuity is such that mostly it does work. But, because each trial-and-error solution is the best that can be done under settings of incomputable complexity, there is always a danger that someone, somewhere, will feel that they have missed out and complain bitterly, unaware of the true complexity of the scheduling task.

When pre-emption and high levels of staff and patient variability go together, hospitals and health services are routinely asking nurses, clerical officers, and other shop-floor staff to do impossible scheduling jobs that the world's largest and most sophisticated supercomputers struggle to.

They generally get paid a pittance in comparison with more senior doctors and nurses, and, only too often, do not get thanked for their efforts.

What can we do to make things easier for them, their customers, their fellow staff, and the patients they serve? Keep it simple; separate value streams; challenge prioritizing wherever you see it. We can count to three. Immediate threats to life and limb, and then other very urgent problems, have to be prioritized, but try to leave it at that and see the rest of the patients in order of registration or arrival. Acknowledge the extraordinary skill and ingenuity shop-floor staff display as they keep the work going. Try not to take them for granted. And when you really do not know what to do, try FIFO. It is simple, easy to explain, and easy to manage. FIFO definitely saves lives.

Chapter 19

Embedding and Sustaining

The real test of a program of Process Redesign is not simply getting people to behave in a different way. It is turning the new way of working into "the way we do things around here."

When we began working in the Emergency Department at Flinders, patients were first put into one of five Triage categories, then seen in the Triage category order, with pre-emption and no credit for time spent waiting. Some years later, we had an occasion to ask some recently graduated nurses, "How do patients get seen in the Flinders Emergency Department? What determines which patient is seen next?" The nurses replied, "They are first streamed into A-side (likely to be admitted stream) or B-side (likely to be discharged stream). But whatever stream they are in, unless they have to go to *resus*, they are seen in order of arrival." And there was an unspoken question "How else is there to do it?" What had seemed revolutionary had become "the way it's done around here."

There is no specific route to that point, no single correct way to ensure that the changes Process Redesign for Health Care programs bring will become embedded in the everyday life of a service. A well-planned program of Process Redesign—one that starts with a problem, defines the scope of work clearly, has a governance structure that brings together the authorizers and the key stakeholders, builds permission through a diagnostic process, engages with the people who do the work, and allows and supports them to create their own experiments that are designed to solve the real problem—is a program likely to generate changes that have a chance of enduring. Experience indicates that what is important is not to miss a step.

However, there are some strategies that will make the improvements the Process Redesign program brings more likely to endure.

Measure, Monitor, and Evaluate

Sustainable changes are much more likely when the consequences of a problem have been measured at the start of the work, and the impact of the program monitored by simple measures that will reflect to the problem the program was designed to alleviate. Monitoring demonstrates that the program of work is actually working; it is only too easy to assume that all that hard work must be doing something useful, when it is not.

Good practice is to start the intervention phase with a public commitment to formally evaluate the outcome at a fixed point. Around three months time after the last experiment has run its course is a good time for an major evaluation. It is time enough for a new way to start becoming everyday practice but not long enough for people to have forgotten what was in place before.

The evaluation should be quantitative, measuring the impact of the program on the problem to be solved. It should also be qualitative. Health Care is hierarchical. It is common to introduce a change and then not ask the people on the shop-floor what they really think about it. That is asking for passive resistance and outright sabotage. Simple surveys of what staff members feel about the new way are really important. It is important to ask as many as possible of the people who do the work, what they think about the redesigned processes. The people who do not like it will make their views known anyway. But it may turn out that they are a small minority, and their views should not be allowed to derail the changes. Questions such as, "Are things different from how they used to be?," "Is the work easier or harder to do?," "Are patients getting a better service?," and "Should we go on with the new way of working?" are simple questions, but the answers provide very important information.

There is no point asking the people what they think if you are not prepared to listen to their views. If a group is unhappy about what is happening, the members of that group need to be heard and their concerns responded to, not glossed over. This can be uncomfortable, but it is necessary. We were involved in a major program of reorganizing the flow of work in some medical units. The nurses and consultants liked the new way, but the junior doctors were unhappy. They said it made it harder for them to get the experience they felt they needed. We had to respond to that, otherwise the program was not going to be sustained.

Should there be a formal decision to adopt the new way as a hospital policy or a new procedure? When we started the Redesigning Care Unit, we were keen on getting formal endorsement for the new way at the end of an evaluation. Over time, we have found that less important because if we have been measuring and monitoring, there should be no surprises in the evaluation. If it is not obvious that things are better, the new way is unlikely to be sustained, no matter what.

The Frontline Managers

Early on, we learned to our cost that nursing and other line managers had to be key participants in the programs of redesign. It is only too easy for an overeager redesigner to try and work around the experienced line manager (noting that doctors do not usually 'do' line management in the way that nurses and other disciplines do), assuming that the line manager is the reason why change is so difficult. A couple of times, as redesigners, we worked with the direct-care nursing or other staff groups, and let line managers watch from the sidelines. When the experiments were concluded, and we thought the Process Redesign work was done, the line managers were still there, only too often saying to their staff, "That was fun, I hope you enjoyed it, but I am still here and I am in charge, and I didn't agree to any of that, so I don't think we will go on with it." Why? Not because the new way was not a good way but because the program of work excluded and undermined them, and they were reasserting their authority.

We came to realize that, in relation to redesign, the work of the line manager or immediate supervisor is not to impede change. It is to take the results of the redesign experiments and turn them into an everyday practice that can be supervised, managed, quality controlled, and, if necessary, delivered to new recruits to the unit, by training. That work will not be done unless the line manager is part of the team that devises the new way, and thus comes to own the new way of working. That can take time, and may need a lot of diplomacy, but line managers must be part of any workgroup or development process. There is no alternative if the new way is to be sustained.

Constancy of Purpose

So far, I have focused on how a specific program of work goes from being an experiment to everyday practice. How can a culture of continuous improvement be developed in which the people involved in a process continue to try and improve that process? We have no easy answer to that. Some people get the hang of Process Redesign very quickly and make it their own. Others are happy to go back to their usual way of professional life as soon as the piece of work they are involved in reaches stability. Education in Process Redesign; networks of support throughout an institution: and a deep commitment to making Process Redesign an institutional way of life, will all help. Above all, as Edward Deming (1986) wrote in the first of his 14 points for management: "Create constancy of purpose for the improvement of product and service…."

CASE STUDIES: MAKING IT WORK

Chapter 20

Redesigning Emergency Department Flows: Case Study

Redesigning patient flows in the Flinders Medical Centre Emergency Department was where our Process Redesign journey started. Many of the most important things we learned about Process Redesign had their roots in the work in the Emergency Department. The Emergency Department Redesign also demonstrated that striking improvements can be made simply by changing the design of patient flows. While the redesigned flows described here represented a major break from Australian Emergency Department practices at that time, the models we developed (King et al. 2006) have subsequently been widely adopted by Emergency Departments across Australia and elsewhere. What is important in this, as in the other case reports, is not the specifics of what we did. The case reports are included to give a feel of how Process Redesign for Healthcare using Lean Thinking works in practice. What is important are the principles involved and the methods by which they were implemented.

I am a psychiatrist by background, but I am also trained in Clinical Epidemiology. After 25 years as a full-time psychiatrist seeing patients and managing a psychiatric unit, plus a variety of other tasks, I took on the development of a Clinical Epidemiology Unit which focused on the analysis of patterns of service delivery across a health service, linking service delivery with population structures. From there, I became the inaugural Director of Clinical Governance for the Flinders Medical Centre. My role was essentially that of the chief safety and quality officer for the hospital, and our activities included the introduction of Root Cause Analysis for serious adverse events into South Australia Health Care practice, among others.

The Problem

In my role as Director of Clinical Governance, I made a written declaration to the Hospital Board, and the hospital's senior managers, that I was not confident that the hospital's Emergency Department was capable of providing safe care to its patients. The document included a systematic analysis of why that was the case. It was because of that declaration that I first became involved in a large-scale, systemic redesign intervention.

The Flinders Medical Centre Emergency Department is the major provider for Emergency Care for a population of more than 300,000 people. It is a busy department. Its patients span the age range from the very young to the very old. It provides the whole range of care that a modern teaching hospital undertakes, including major trauma patients who arrive via the hospital's integrated helipad. My concerns about the Department's capacity to provide safe care were confirmed by an external review.

While I had come to my own conclusions about the Emergency Department, the clinical managers of the Department were well aware that they had a problem. They were just not clear what to do about it.

Evidence

My views did not come as a surprise because the problems had been mounting for some time. The evidence that there was a problem was everywhere to see. The Department had become dangerously overcrowded. Unrelated areas such as the Recovery area of the main Operating Theater suite had been conscripted into use as supplementary Emergency Department cubicles. A Recovery suite is designed to manage patients for a brief period after an operation. There are a limited number of patient bathrooms, no facilities for visitors, and not even a modicum of privacy. Yet, emergency medical and surgical patients were spending days in the Recovery suite. This disrupted the operating theater schedules, because patients had to recover from anesthetics in the operating theater, rather than in Recovery, and dangerously overstretched the Emergency Department staff. Furthermore, since becoming Director of Clinical Governance, there had been a number of serious Emergency Department adverse events with poor outcomes that we had been required to investigate. There was also some indication that the overall Emergency Department mortality outcomes were beginning to deteriorate, although the statistics were hard to interpret. What was clear was that the Department was doing badly against many other performance indicators. Morale was low and staffing levels were hard to sustain. Relations between the Emergency Department staff and the staff from within the body of the hospital had deteriorated. Blame was endemic.

The Emergency Department was staffed by highly skilled individuals whose clinical expertise was not in doubt. They had not been sitting on their hands while the situation deteriorated. Unfortunately, none of the many attempts they had made to improve the situation had made a lasting impact.

The problems could not be blamed on excess demand. Our Clinical Epidemiology Unit had demonstrated that the Emergency Department was only being asked to manage the expected demand generated by the community it served. The Hospital Board, and the Chief Executive, accepted my concerns and began the process of trying to improve the situation. But again, none of the initial attempts at improving the situation proved fruitful, and I was then fully authorized to try and sort things out. While the senior Emergency Department staff accepted that something needed to be done, gaining the permission of the larger Emergency Department staff group—wary, weary, and embattled as they were—was another thing.

Scoping

Emergency Departments are a major gateway between the community at large and the body of the hospital. Friction is common between Emergency Departments and the "downstream" units that admit patients after an initial review in Emergency. It is not unusual for the people who staff Emergency Departments to feel that the in-patient units do not pull their weight when it comes to admitting patients in a prompt and timely manner. Emergency Department staff tend to seek solace in the assumption that all would be well if, by the wave of a magic wand, a large number of extra hospital beds could be found for in-patient units to admit patients into. Contrawise, in-patient teams often come to feel that Emergency Department staffs are unhelpful, do not understand the pressures the in-patient units are under, and have a tendency toward an unhealthy regard for their own clinical expertise.

Flinders had its fair share of this kind of inter-group blame and general name-calling. However, after we had got through that, the senior staff in the Flinders Emergency Department accepted that there was little to be gained by expecting everyone else to behave better while the Emergency Department just stayed as it was. As a first step, a decision was made to start the scope of any Emergency Department redesign work from the point of arrival of a patient at the Emergency Department, and to conclude it at the point where a patient physically left the Department, either to go home or to be admitted to an in-patient unit. Focusing on improving the situation within the Emergency Department meant that the improvement work would not be held hostage to a requirement for downstream units to change their behavior.

Diagnosis

Big Picture Mapping

It was not immediately clear where to start trying to understand what was going wrong in the Emergency Department, and I co-opted Melissa Lewis, who worked in the Clinical Epidemiology Unit that I directed, to help me. She and I, and a group of enthusiastic medical students, followed a group of Emergency Department staff around as they went about their business. We learned that everyone was very busy. What it was they were doing was not so obvious, and it was clear that another approach was necessary.

Melissa read about Process Mapping online. I had previously been to a workshop where a production engineer had described creating a "brown paper" process map by personally following all the steps involved in making a product, interviewing the people involved, and writing the results up on large sheets of brown paper tacked to a wall. The brief attempt at following staff around the department made it clear that simply following staff or patients would not shed light on the basic issues. We instinctively felt that the existing "brown paper" approach would not work without modification.

The description of Process Mapping that Melissa came across involved bringing people together to describe what it was that they did. That appealed to us. The senior staff of the Emergency Department were fairly skeptical that anything much would be learned that way, but Australians are a "can do," egalitarian, kind of people. The senior Emergency Department medical and nursing managers agreed to bring together a representative group of all staff members to map out how the department functioned. In time, we came to call this Big Picture Mapping, but at that moment, it was a leap in the dark.

So, a group gathered in the Emergency Department seminar room and we began. Joining Melissa and I were senior Emergency Physicians, nurse managers (including Jane Bassham, who later became a key member of the Redesigning Care Team), senior and junior registered and enrolled nurses, junior medical staff, clerical and administrative staff, and Patient Service Assistants (PSAs). Whilst we were not very clear on how to proceed, but both Melissa and I had had enough experience of meetings where it was not clear what was going to happen next, to make a start.

We decided to follow a basic "brown paper"—type method of tracing the steps involved in tracking a production process from the arrival of the raw material through to the finished product, but in this case, doing it collectively. The main difference between the process at Flinders and what is usually understood in industry as Process Mapping was that people were asked what they did and how they did it, rather than creating the map by following the product as it was transformed. The mapping process worked by inquiry, not observation. This made the mapping a public process, rather than being the product of a series of tracking and one-on-one private interviews.

We opened by being honest. We said this was an exercise in understanding. "Because we don't work in the Emergency Departments, the only way we will get a sense of how the department functions is to trace the journey of how patients are managed step by step as they move through the Department. So how do people get here? Where do they present? Who greets them?"

"They come by car, by ambulance, by plane, or on foot and they arrive at the glass doors at the front of the department," came the reply. And so it began.

We both asked questions, but Melissa mostly wrote down the information that emerged, using post-it notes on a whiteboard. Intuitively, we sensed that mapping with a large group of participants was likely to be a two-person job, with one person asking questions, and the other both listening closely to what was being said to make sure that everyone has a chance to have their say, and writing down a summary. Melissa was the obvious candidate to do the writing because of her excellent handwriting, and her high degree of inter-personal skills made her an excellent question asker as well. The structure of the room meant that we sat facing a single large group, rather than the Emergency Department staff being broken up at small tables. It was a happy accident, as it helped the participants work together rather than sticking in discipline groups, which they would have done if they had been grouped around separate small tables.

Good to Get to Know You

Right from the start, there were some extraordinary revelations, revelations that have however been reproduced over and again at Big Picture Mapping sessions. At the beginning of these initial sessions, we did not know who people were, so we asked everyone present to say who they were and what their job was. When it was the turn of the senior PSA to introduce himself, he said who he was and what he did, and what a good thing this meeting was. When asked why, he pointed to a senior Emergency Physician and said that he had been working in the department for a number of years, and had often seen the physician around the place but had not known his name or quite what he did. The physician acknowledged that he had seen the PSA around. He clearly did a great job, and was relied upon by all the staff, but the Emergency Department physician acknowledged that he did not know the PSA's name either. Both said it was good to get to know each other.

The PSA

Although people tried to rush through it, we got the participants to describe the patient arrival process in some detail. The Emergency Department has since been rebuilt, but at that time, its main entrance was made up by two sets of sliding glass doors with a space in between. The space between the two sets of doors was known locally as "the air-lock" (it was intended to ensure that an even temperature could be maintained in the department, although it was not very effective). A small PSA station looked out into the air-lock.

PSAs are the blue-collar workers of patient care. They have emerged from the more traditional hospital porter and hospital cleaner roles. They move patients around the hospital, and at Flinders they clean and do a variety of other fetching and carrying jobs. Cleaning is especially important for the prevention of cross-infection. The mapping revealed that they also had a crucial role directing patients, family members, and ambulances when they first arrived. In many ways, it became clear that the PSAs were key members of what has become known in other settings as a "first-responder" team.

South Australia has a bigger land mass than France and Italy combined but has a population of a little more than 1.5 million people. Most, but not all, South Australians live in Adelaide, the state capital. People, who travel between Adelaide and outlying small towns and communities, drive fast, in powerful cars, along long, narrow roads through a vast, empty hinterland. When those vehicles hit each other, or run off the road, serious injuries are common.

Because accidents often occur on rural roads surrounded by open spaces, critically injured accident victims are often transported to an Emergency Department by helicopter. At Flinders, the helicopters land on a helipad on the roof of the car park next to the Emergency Department. It is necessary to switch on the helipad landing lights so that the helicopter pilot knows where to land. Switching on the landing lights is the job of the PSAs. Communication within the Emergency Department, and between the Emergency Department and outside agencies, had become so dysfunctional that sometimes it was only when the PSA told the Shift Coordinator that he or she had been asked to switch on the landing lights, that the floor managers become aware that a seriously ill patient was about to arrive.

In that and many other ways, the variety and importance of the PSAs work was a revelation to many of the other staff who worked there.

Triage

It is almost impossible to describe the overall complexity that unfolded as the mapping proceeded, but Figure 20.1 is my attempt at capturing what emerged.

Initially, we thought the mapping would be concluded in one 2-hour session. In reality, it took three sessions of more than 2 hours each, partly because this was our first Big Picture Map, and partly because of the sheer complexity of the departmental practices.

Many of the problems that emerged had their origins in one of the first steps that we examined. When a patient arrives at the Emergency Department, the first clinical step is a review by a Triage nurse at the Triage desk (unless a forewarned Emergency Physician is waiting in the air-lock to get a first look). The processes at Triage had become so complex and convoluted that we all cheered when, toward the end of the second session, we finally "got out of Triage."

On arrival at an Emergency Department, each patient is allocated a Triage score by an experienced Emergency Department nurse, working as the Triage nurse for that shift. Triaging was initially a battlefield concept. Dressing stations triaged wounded soldiers into "will not survive; don't waste precious time and effort" and "might survive, treat as soon as possible."

Triaging in Emergency Departments has been extended into the more general task of identifying how safe it might be to allow patients to wait before commencing treatment. The Triage categories in use in Australia are shown in Table 20.1. They are similar to systems commonly in use in Canada. European Triage systems such as the Manchester Triage systems are also very similar, except that Category 3 in Australia is 30 minutes, while the Manchester Triage Category 3 has a 60-minute window, and Category 5, 240 minutes, rather than the 120 minutes in the Australian system. There are no America-wide Triage systems in everyday use, although many American hospitals use systems such as the Emergency Severity Index which is a 5-level severity measure but without specific time criteria.

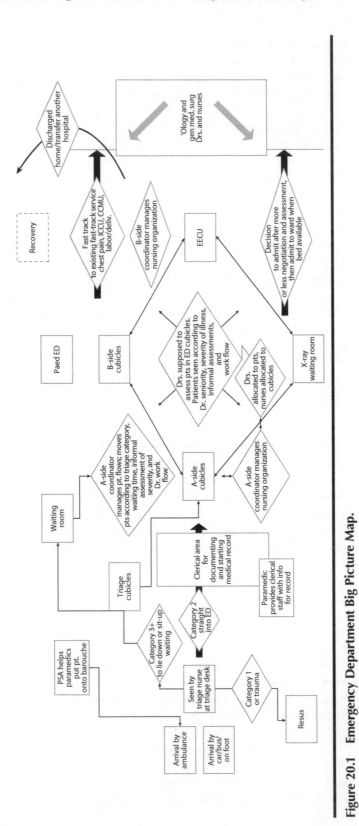

Figure 20.1 Emergency Department Big Picture Map.

Table 20.1 The Australasian Triage Scale

Description	Should be Seen by the Provider and Definitive Care Commenced Within (minutes)
Resuscitation	0
Emergency	10
Urgent	30
Semi-urgent	60
Routine	120

Australian Emergency Departments have to report the degree to which they meet the Triage category timelines. It is assumed that the more a department adheres to Triage times, the safer it is likely to be.

While urgency and complexity are not identical in Health Care, the overall distribution of Triage scores of patients treated in a department (2% Category 1, 10% Category 2, 20% Category 3, etc.) is commonly used as a measure of the complexity of that department's workload. Hospitals with many patients in high Triage categories are assumed to have complex case loads of seriously ill patients.

Triaging is intended to provide a rapid assessment only. That assessment is then followed by the initiation of definitive care in the main body of the Emergency Department. In Australia in general, and in the Flinders Emergency Department in particular, Triage categories had also become a way of organizing the order in which the staff in the body of the department saw patients. Mapping made it clear that every effort was made to see patients in a FIFO order within Triage categories. Patients in higher categories were seen in preference to any patient already waiting in the Emergency Department who had been allocated to a lower Triage category, no matter how long the lower category patients had already been waiting. All Category 1 patients had to be seen before any other patients, all Category 2 patients before all other patients, except Category 1 patients, and so on. If you, as a patient, had been allocated to Category 4, you were not supposed to be seen by a doctor or nurse within the body of the department if there were any Category 1, Category 2, or Category 3 patients in the department, no matter how recently those patients have arrived, and however long you have already waited. Technically, this practice is known as pre-emption. The more recently arrived more urgent category patient pre-empts the spot the less urgent patients has in the queue to be seen, and no credit is given for time already spent waiting.

It quickly became clear that if you were a Category 4 or Category 5 patient, you were continually pushed down the queue by new patients allocated to higher Triage categories and you could wait hours and hours to be seen. Angry patients, who had been waiting for hours on end and had watched a stream of newly arrived patients being seen before them, would ask the nearest nurse or Clerical Officer "How long am I going to wait?" The answer would truthfully be "I do not know." As an Emergency Physician put it, every assessment with a new Category 3, Category 4, or Category 5 patient began with an apology for how long the patients had waited to be seen.

The mapping also made it clear that the Emergency Department Shift Coordinators, who were the floor bosses of the department, went through extraordinary contortions to try to deal with the ever-rising tide of low Triage category patients who accumulated as the day wore on.

Figure 20.1 is complicated, and yet it does not begin to cover many of the issues that emerged, such as different processes for different times of day. Exhausted by getting the basics down, we decided to leave for another day. However, it did become clear that queuing was not the only issue.

Doctors Are Allocated to Patients, Nurses to Cubicles

Emergency Departments are generally laid out as a series of more or less complete oval "race-tracks." The patients are in cubicles around the race track itself. An observation area (a complex of desks with computer terminals, forms, etc.) is commonly placed in the middle of the track area. Patients cannot see each other but can be seen from the observation point. There may be various small pods of cubicles off the race track, but the basic principle holds.

The Flinders Emergency Department was laid out as two partial race tracks, each with an observation area (or "fish-bowl," as it was locally known) in the center, plus a couple of pods off the main track. One of these pods was the Resus area—two rooms that were fully equipped as small Intensive Care facilities, complete with inbuilt X-ray capabilities. The Resus rooms were used for the initial management of critically ill or injured patients (essentially all Triage Category 1 patients and many Triage Category 2 patients).

While the Emergency Department had a fixed number of cubicles, the mapping confirmed that there were commonly more patients than cubicles. Various strategies were used to accommodate the extra load. Wall areas and some waiting areas had become designated as de facto cubicle spaces, with patients being kept on moveable stretchers called barouches. There were also a series of chairs that made up a de facto multi-occupancy cubicle. And when all those spaces were full, patients were housed, outside the Emergency Department, in the main Recovery area attached to the operating theaters.

Just to add to the difficulties, doctors were linked to patients, and nurses to cubicles. Being a busy place that was open 24 hours a day, each 24-hour period was divided into three shifts, with staff changing over between shifts. On each shift, the Emergency Department was staffed by a group of doctors at various levels of seniority. The senior medical staff on the floor had the notional authority to allocate more junior doctors to cases. In practice the various doctors kept an eye on the Emergency Department computer screens, and when they were free, attended to patients who needed to be seen, based on patients' Triage categories. That doctor then followed that patient through until the patient's Emergency Department care was completed, or until the doctor's shift ended. As the shift went on, patients would be at various stages of their treatment and the doctors would be juggling their time, moving from patient to patient wherever they were as their care progressed.

Meanwhile the shift coordinators on the floor have to keep moving patients around to try and create spaces for incoming patients at various levels of urgency. If patients were moved to accommodate the needs of the department as a whole, the nursing care had to be handed over to the nurses assigned to the new cubicles. But doctors stayed with their patients. On top of all this, there was a need for groups of staff to drop everything to respond to the arrival of Triage Category 1 or Category 2 patients.

The resulting problems of communication and challenges to working as a care team were compounded by staff members being allocated individually on each shift. There was no team structure. Any nurse could work in any cubicle, next to any other nurse, on any given day. The advantage was that if you did not like the people you were working with, you did not have to worry, because you would be working with a different group the next day. The disadvantages in terms of building up an ethos of teamwork were also clear. And the complexities went on. There were issues to do with the range of experience of doctors and nurses, the roles of enrolled versus registered nurses, the need to supervise doctors in training, and more besides.

Do Not Use Mapping to Talk about Solutions

This was our first attempt at mapping. While it was a bit chaotic, the amount of new information that was emerging kept everyone engaged. Over three sessions, the numbers participating in the mapping increased, and staff at every level became increasingly comfortable with speaking out. We rapidly learned not to try and use the mapping to talk about solutions to problems that emerged. Once or twice, when something seemed especially crazy, we would begin to explore what the alternatives might be. Those conversations quickly deteriorated into bickering, as people pointed out the flaws in whatever was being proposed as a solution. It was one of the Emergency Physicians who reminded us that the sessions were supposed to be about understanding, not looking for quick-fix solutions.

The Oxygen Cylinders

At the very end of the mapping session, an interchange occurred that summed up the whole experience. Gwynn (not his real name) is a senior PSA in the Emergency Department. As the mapping sessions were drawing to a close, he said, "And then there is the issue of the oxygen bottles." Someone replied, "What about the oxygen bottles?"

There is a certain tolerant but slightly incredulous look that practical people get when they confront the ignorance of those in positions of power and authority. Gwynn gave us all a minute of that look, then good-humouredly took us through the issue.

"Is this an Emergency Department?" he asked.

"Of course it is—what do you think we have been doing these past few days?" came the reply.

"Do Emergency Department patients need oxygen?"

"Of course they do."

"Where does the oxygen come from?"

"We don't really know how it is produced, but it comes in big trucks and is stored under pressure in a big container somewhere. It then comes out of taps on the wall in the department. We hook people up to an oxygen tap in the Department, and there you are."

Gwynn said, "Yes. The oxygen taps are in the walls of the cubicles. But do we have patients who need oxygen, who are on barouches in corridors, not in cubicles? And do we keep them on those barouches for long periods?"

We started to see where Gwynn was going, and everyone started to listen very carefully. "Yes," someone said.

"How do those patients get oxygen?" Gwynn asked.

"From oxygen cylinders; we have got special cylinder holders on our barouches that hold the oxygen bottles in place," a nurse said.

"Exactly," said Gwynn. "Oxygen," he went on, "comes in two kinds of cylinders; big brown ones and little red ones. The big brown ones hold lots of oxygen under very high pressure. They are never put on barouches. They are heavy and if they fall over, the tap can get blown off and do terrible things. We have the small red oxygen cylinders to put on the barouches. Does anyone know how long a red oxygen bottle will last?" asked Gwynn.

There was a bit of blustering, and "it all depends on flow rates," but basically it became clear that no one really knew. "Yes, it depends on how high the flow is turned up, but generally, it's a couple of hours," said Gwynn, "and patients are often in the Emergency Department for hours on end."

This was met with silence, and finally someone asked, "Gwynn, who changes the bottles when they run out?"

"I do," said Gwynn.

"So who changes them when you are not there?" was the next question.

"I don't know," said Gwynn. "It is not a job that has been allocated." And we had a sudden, terrible, vision of people lying on barouches, with oxygen masks strapped to their faces, slowly turning blue because nothing was coming out of the mask.

"I have been trying to get someone to pay attention to this for years. Diving shops sell cheap alarms that go on to oxygen cylinders to let you know when they are running out, but I don't think we use them," said Gwynn. Then, trying to be reassuring, "I think people do look out for the cylinders, though I can't be sure."

We realized that for years, people like Gwynn had seen all sorts of problems that could easily be sorted out and that put patients at risk. But the way hospitals worked did not give them a setting where they can be listened to, and heard.

The Real Problem

The mapping helped everyone involved to see the real problem. The Emergency Department staff had started with the assumption that the chaos in the department was not of their making. They felt themselves to be the victims of other people's bad behavior. Emergency got their own work done, but then patients stayed in the department taking up precious cubicle space, but because the medical and surgical staff in the body of the hospital were too idle to discharge people, no beds could be found for their patients. And even when a bed did become available, the wards would still not take patients but kept the patient hanging around in the Emergency Department while they did other things. "Give us back our cubicles, and everything will be all right," was the Emergency Department's cry.

By the end of the mapping, it was clear to everyone that, while prompt patient exit from the department was an issue, the most important immediate problems were in the Emergency Department itself. In particular, sticking rigidly to using Triage categories as a way of organizing which patient to see next was a major source of delay and confusion. The patients who spent hours waiting to get to the head of their particular Triage queue mostly just sat, and waited, although at its worst, about 1 in 10 left the department without completing their treatment. Those did-not-wait patients did not just go home; they often went to find a doctor or a hospital that would see them. The patients who stayed became increasingly frustrated as they waited in a waiting room in a department that got more and more crowded as the day wore on.

Intervention

At this point, we had identified a problem that was within the sphere of influence of the Emergency Department itself, rather than requiring better behavior by others. What to do about it?

Emergency Departments all over the world have a problem of identity. They are filled with highly trained staff who need to be able to deal promptly and effectively with fast-moving medical crises, and who get a professional buzz from the resultant drama. But the vast majority of the patients they actually have to look after have less than life-threatening problems. In Australia, far more patients are allocated to Triage Category 3, Category 4, and Category 5, than Category 1 and Category 2. At Flinders, Category 4 was usually the most common Triage category allocated (around 40% of all patients), and Category 3 and Category 4 together added up to around 80% of patients. And most patients who come to Emergency Departments come under their own steam. Only a minority come by ambulance or are referred by a doctor working in a general practice, and even fewer have life-threatening problems.

Emergency Department staff can easily start to resent the lower Triage category patients, and, consciously or not, feel that getting them to wait will teach them a lesson about not wasting the Emergency Department's time. This latent hostility became increasingly obvious as the mapping sessions went on. But about 60% of all Flinders Emergency Department patients go home directly from the Emergency Department. In many Emergency Departments across Australia, 70% or more patients go straight home, and in the United Kingdom, because of differences in Primary care provision, there are departments where 80% of patients (or more) go home directly.

But whichever country you are in, the vast majority of patients make their own judgment about needing to go to Emergency. They do not have any medical training. They just worry that they have a problem, and they want something done about it. They do not know how Emergency Department staff are trained or how they think.

After the Flinders mapping, Dr. Di King, then the head of the Emergency Department, made an important statement about the work of the department. A very well regarded Emergency Physician, and a great leader, Dr. King said that it was not up to the department to judge people's motives in coming to the department. No patient came to an Emergency Department to have a good time. The department was there to provide the best care possible, and everyone was entitled to that care. Caring was the work the department should be concentrating on, not judging. The challenge was how to turn that basic statement of values into better care.

The National Health Service Modernization Agency

I presented our mapping work to the Hospital Board and the hospital's senior management group. Everyone could see there was a problem but no one knew what to do next. The United Kingdom's then newly elected Labour government had made it mandatory for hospitals to reorganize their Accident and Emergency (A & E) Departments so that 95% or more patients spent no more than 4 hours in total in A & E. Fortunately, Helen Bevan, then a senior staff member from the English Modernization Agency was in Australia, and came briefly to Adelaide. The Modernization Agency (which was to be disbanded a couple of years later) was leading the work around implementing the 4-hour rule in the National Health Service (NHS). Helen Bevan put us in touch with her Modernization Agency colleagues doing the Emergency Department work. With the support of our Hospital Board, a small group of us were able to spend a week, hosted by the Modernization Agency, visiting hospitals across London, talking to staff in the Emergency Departments and in the Modernization Agency itself. This was followed by a visit to Adelaide by Ben Gowland, at that time a Modernization Agency staff member who was playing an important role in the 4-hour rule program.

The group of us was impressed by what we saw in London. There have been all sorts of critiques of the NHS 4-hour rule. Some of them have certainly been justified, but the departments we visited were big frontline departments very much like our own. The staff we talked to made it clear that the departments they worked in had been transformed by the increased speed of patient flow. And importantly, each department had achieved it in a different way. There was no single best way.

Each department had achieved the target using a strategy that worked in their own physical and staffing context. During our visits to the Modernization Agency, we were also given the book *Lean Thinking*. A number of Modernization Agency staff had had some experience using Lean Thinking in other contexts and said it had been very helpful. Importantly, neither Ben Gowland nor any other Modernization Agency staff member told us what to do. They encouraged us to think for ourselves and gave us confidence that we could be successful. And Ben talked to us about the importance of developing a team structure, and getting a governance process in place.

Streaming

When our little group got back, we started a small workgroup. Di King reiterated that we needed "a big hit." The department needed something that would have an impact on the majority of patients, not just a small group. It needed something radical. Di proposed that the Emergency Department should move away from using Triage categories as a way of organizing the order in which patients would be seen, and go to a completely different way of sorting and queuing. Di questioned whether there was really such a difference between Category 3, Category 4, and Category 5 patients. Almost all of these patients would survive, and most would be able to go home. Did we really need to go on with the Triage-induced practice of pre-emption and giving no credit for waiting?

At that moment, only an Emergency Physician as senior and experienced as Di King could put that view forward. The implications would be a substantial departure from current practice, but it was a clinical, not an organizational, matter, so was within Di's sphere of influence.

Di proposed splitting the Emergency Department into two functional areas. Triage nurses would continue to give each patient a Triage score. But they would also predict if patients would be admitted to hospital or go home directly from the department. The Triage nurse would then allocate patients to either the larger A-side of the department (a group of cubicles around fish-bowl A) or the B-side (a group of cubicles around fish-bowl B). The A-side would be for patients who were likely to be admitted to hospital, the B-side for patients who were likely to go home. Triage Category 1 and Category 2 patients would continue to use the Resus Rooms as necessary.

A brief trial demonstrated that the Triage nurses were over 80% accurate in their judgments about who would either eventually be admitted or go home directly from the department, and in practice, if they were wrong, patients could move between sides if required.

Our plan was that each day, nurses and doctors would be allocated to A-side or B-side, and work on that side for their whole shift. Influenced by what we had seen, and our first contact with Lean Thinking, the proposal was that the likely-to-go-home patients on the B-side would be seen in order of arrival, not in Triage order. The B-side patients were also to take their paperwork with them, an issue that is explained in the following sections.

In queuing terms, work on the B-side was to move from a complex five-queue prioritized system with pre-emption, to a single, simple FIFO queue. It was as though numbered tickets were to be printed up, and given out in order to patients assessed as likely to go home, as they arrived. Staff would then work through those patients in ticket order. The process was easy to understand, easy to explain, and easy to implement, provided you were brave enough to swim against the tide of usual practice. The A-side likely-to-be-admitted patients were still to be seen in Triage category order, and absolute precedence was always given to threat to life or limb.

Jane Bassham and I prepared some briefing material that explained what was proposed and why, and we spent about a week talking to doctors, nurses, clerical staff, and the PSAs, explaining what was to be done. Then one morning, the Emergency Department just did it. The new way began.

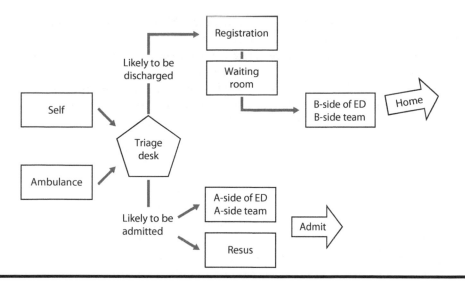

Figure 20.2   Emergency Department redesign: value stream flows.

The First Day

By 5 p.m. on the first day, it was clear that we were on to something. By chance, one of the more skeptical Emergency Physicians was rostered to be on the A-side that day. At the end of his shift, he said there seemed to be something in this change. He said, maybe it had been a quiet day, or maybe things just worked better.

We were monitoring the impact of the experiment on a daily basis, and we knew it had not been a quiet day—it felt quiet because the usual chaos had fallen away almost immediately. Within days, it was clear that things had truly got a lot better. There was no longer any need to manage patients in Recovery, and the operating theaters got their recovery area back. Patients were able to be managed within the Emergency Department, and the Emergency Department started to get back on its feet.

In Process Redesign terms, a 5-queue priority system with pre-emption was transformed into a two-value stream flow pattern, the value streams being likely to go home and likely to be admitted. The patients who were likely to go home were seen in order of arrival. This newer, simpler method of processing meant that that one group of staff concentrated on what was, in redesign terms, a short work stream (Figure 20.2). They got that stream moving and the impact was immediate and transformative. Now queues just did not build up.

ED Works

That was just the beginning. A decision was made to formalize an ongoing program of work and give it a name: "ED Works." The core ED Works Governance Group consisted of the embryonic Redesigning Care Team, Dr. King, the Emergency Department nursing manager, and anyone else who was responsible for whatever was being worked on at the time. For several years, the group met regularly once a week at 8 a.m. in the Chief Executive's office.

There is not enough space to cover the whole range of issues that were worked through during the life of the ED Works program, but our driving ambition was to make the department a safer place for patients. One of the issues that had been pointed out in an earlier review, and that re-emerged as an issue in the mapping, was the extent to which no one was keeping an eye on the overall progress of patients during the day. Doctors worked very much on their own, picking up patients and trying to complete their care before going off-shift. But no single doctor was trying to get an overview, making sure nothing was being missed.

The department moved to having three "ward rounds" a day, when the senior Emergency Physicians on shift on both the A-side and the B-side would go through each patient "on the board" either at the fish-bowl or moving from cubicle to cubicle. The timing of the rounds was not left to the discretion of the physicians but announced by the department administrative staff. Gradually, the rounds helped to transform the role of senior physicians from standalone doctors into supervising consultants.

At a more mundane level, we timed a number of common specific treatment processes to see if we could find a way of developing a takt time processing strategy. The processes proved to be too variable to allow the identification of a specific Emergency Department takt time, but the work helped identify some obvious steps that were pure waste, or just plain dangerous.

Many patients left the Emergency Department on crutches, of which the department had a supply. We spent some time tracking the journey of the crutches. There were lots of stages involved. The department hired out crutches to people in need. But for reasons that presumably had seemed sensible at the time, the stored crutches, along with a variety of other pieces of equipment, were under the control of a Supplies Officer, who was supposed to give out the crutches. The role of the nurses was to be confined to educating patients how to use the crutches.

When a set of crutches needed to be dispensed, the theory was that a nurse would page the Supplies Officer, who in practice was often unavailable. After a variable delay, the nurse would decide to give out a set of crutches once the patient or the patient's family had completed the paperwork around the formalities of hiring crutches. The paperwork pack contained several forms, two or three of which seemed to have little purpose.

We were able to streamline the whole process firstly by cutting out the Supplies Officer as the dispenser of crutches (he had lots of other things to do to keep him busy) and then by simplifying the paperwork and process for patients to return crutches. Hours and hours of cumulative time were saved, staff could get on with what was important, and patients could get home half an hour to an hour sooner.

The crutches were not the only improvement to paperwork. One of the early problems revealed during the mapping was that Emergency Department staff often struggled to find out about a patient's prior hospital treatment because of misidentification at the registration area. Mr. Smith might appear to be Mr. Smyth, Mr. Smeet, or Mr. Smithy, each persona with its own, or no, medical record. While this would eventually get sorted out, important information was often missing at the point that treatment began.

The clerical officers at the registration desk registered each patient, created an Emergency Department case record, and generated the all-important set of tear-off sticky labels on which were printed the patient's name and hospital record number. The labels would be used to identify request forms (and samples, where relevant) for investigations of all types.

The mapping made it clear that notes were commonly mislaid in the chaos. After discussion with the clerical staff, a decision was made that, after registration, the clerks would give the B-side patients their own forms and sticky labels, and the patients would then take them into the department when they were seen.

As the clerical staff gave out the registration paperwork, something unexpected started to happen. Not only was time saved looking for notes but also the number of patients misidentified decreased rapidly. On enquiry, we found out that this was because patients, having been given their own paperwork, were coming back to the registration desk to point out that their names or other details were incorrect and needed changing.

Patients who come to an Emergency Department are worried and in pain. Previously, patients would give their names to a Clerical Officer, who would then find them on the hospital's computer system, and read out the details on the system to confirm that they were correct. Patients were distracted and anxious to begin their treatment and, as we often joked, would agree they were the Pope if they thought that would speed things up.

Now, confronted with the frequent errors of identification, the clerical staff got into the habit of rephrasing their questions to patients. Not "You are Bill Smith, is that right?" but "What is your name? Please spell it." Not "Do you live at 54 Vatican Drive?" but "Please tell me your address." And not "Is your family doctor still Dr. Lozenge?" but "Who is your family doctor?" These small changes had big impacts.

We were fortunate to have a very engaged and creative head of clerical staff, who was intimately involved in the redesign process. She and her colleagues embraced the opportunity to improve with enthusiasm. We did, however, discover that, at that time, it was very difficult to make laser printers completely mobile. Battery packs powerful enough to work the printers were just not available, although we did try. There were also problems with the format of the Emergency Department case record, and a new Emergency Department form was developed. Jane Bassham worked through multiple iterations of the form until all parties were happy with it.

Enhancing Team Work

The movement to streaming made a big impact, Doctors and nurses no longer had to apologize for delays. The waiting room was now just a waiting room, not a holding area for angry and frustrated would-be patients. Patients were completing their treatment, not leaving prematurely. Morale had improved, and staff members were no longer leaving in droves. But staff surveys and hours spent observing the Emergency Department at work made it clear that there were still problems with engagement and teamwork among the staff as a whole.

The nursing managers decided to move from daily allocation of nurses to clinical areas, to a team allocation. A team structure was developed that allowed a team of nurses to be allocated to one area over a period (a month to start with) and then rotate as a team to a different area. The teams could train and rehearse together, and share learning and expertise. Creating a roster that made this possible was a complex business, as Emergency Departments are open 24 hours a day, and the staff have holidays, rostered days off after working at night, and so on. But the nursing managers worked it out. The Emergency Department went from struggling to hold on to staff, to having a waiting list of potential employees. The differences in working hours between doctors and nurses made it difficult to completely align them but some progress was made. Interestingly, at the beginning of the redesign, the fear was that no one would want to work on B-side because they would miss out on the drama. But after a time, many people preferred B-side, saying that they got to see their patients right through.

ED Works was active for several years, and the range and variety of redesign activities over that time was too extensive to be fully described here. Important activities included improving the processes around transferring patients between the Emergency Department and the body of the hospital. When the ED Works program began, patients were accompanied by a nurse who provided a detailed handover in person to nurses in the receiving ward. The problem was that it was often difficult to release nurses with detailed knowledge of a specific patient at the moment that the receiving ward was ready to take that patient, and delays often occurred while the transfer process was put on hold until the nurse involved could be made available. Extensive work was done on safe handover protocols over the phone, so that patients could be moved promptly.

One interesting program of work related to the processes around what is called "decision to admit." Patients who may require admission are worked up by Emergency Department staff but are then reviewed by staff from the in-patient teams who make the final decision to admit. Emergency Department Physicians regularly complained about delays and indecision by in-patient teams, and felt that patients would be moved much more promptly if they had the authority to admit themselves. This was an important boundary issue, and prolonged discussion went on at various levels of the medical staff.

Eventually, a decision was made to allow the full-time specialist Emergency Physicians the authority to admit in-patients, who would then be looked after by the in-patient teams. Despite extensive preparation, and the development of an Acute Emergency receiving unit within the body of the hospital, the Emergency Physicians made only limited use of their admitting rights. The problems around moving between the Emergency Department and the body of the hospital were not simply a matter of who had the authority but were complex issues around skills, capacity and, integration between services.

Communication

At the very beginning of the Redesigning Care program, I had a series of arguments with Ms. Penny Gunner who was then the head of our corporate communications program. Penny Gunner insisted that we needed to tell people about what we were planning to do, name it, and communicate about it, using as many different channels of communication as possible, including hold launch events, and generally "flipping the switch to redesign rock 'n roll'." Coming from a medical and clinical research background, I was much more cautious. I wanted to say as little as possible until it was clear that what we were doing was going to work.

Penny Gunner was right and I was wrong. I have apologized to her for disagreeing with her. Communication is vital. When the institution says loudly and clearly what it is trying to do, as it does it, it is clear that the institution is serious about the work. And names provide identity. What we are doing here is Process Redesign. It is not clinical work. Going public means you cannot hide. You have to name the work and see it through. And crucially, give it your own name, not 'the Flinders Method', but The St. Elsewhere Redesign Program (or something a bit more catchy). People want to be leaders, not followers.

However, rhetoric is not enough, however. Hospitals are filled with people who understand numbers and are used to seeing numbers being used to assess the success of interventions of all kinds. When talking about the Redesigning Care program, we need to use a language of numbers as well as stories.

At the very beginning of the ED Works program, we developed some simple metrics, and then kept an eye on them throughout the program. We identified the length of stay of every patient in the Emergency Department and produced weekly averages for both admitted and discharged patients. We reviewed the lengths of stay every week at the ED Works meeting. One out of the set of charts we generated is provided in Figure 20.3. This is an exponentially waited moving average (EWMA) chart. The daily counts make up the jagged up and down lines, and the line that runs through them is the underlying trend line, calculated by a formula that gives more weight to recent than more distant days.

Crucially, we expanded the metrics to include a set of key statistics for hospital-wide outcomes— matters such as total hospital occupancy, surgical cancellations, numbers of hospital outliers, and a range of key safety and quality measures including hospital mortality outcomes, almost all presented as EWMAs. We began an open hospital-wide meeting at 8 a.m. on a Friday. Any staff

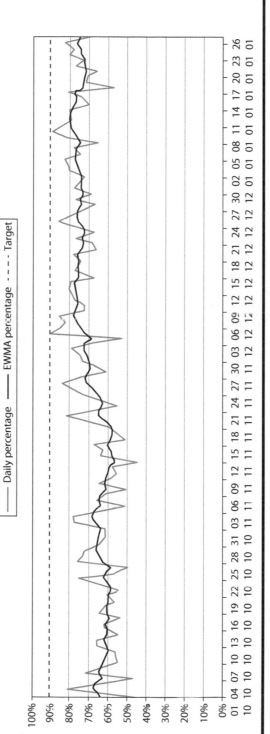

Figure 20.3 Percentage of dischargeable patients in and out of Emergency Department in less than 4 hours.

member could attend. We provided coffee, doughnuts at the insistence of the then CEO, and yoghurt. We began with short presentations on a current work program being delivered by the people involved and concluded with a review of hospital-wide metrics. Senior managers attended, as did a wide variety of clinicians from all the discipline groups across the hospital.

Process Redesign in hospitals presents an interesting problem. When we began, I thought about using a blog to document what was happening and making it available to the staff on a hospital web site. But hospitals are complicated places, and notionally private, but potentially public, written communications about work in process can find their way into all sorts of environments where they could be misinterpreted. We could only maintain trust in our Redesign Program if it was clear that it was not being used simply to advance the careers of the Redesigners, that it would be safe to describe experiments that did not work out as predicted, and that personal and institutional confidentiality could be maintained. The Friday morning face-to-face meetings enabled us to achieve those goals, and they continued for a number of years.

Embedding and Sustaining

In 2003, patient flows in the Emergency Department at the Flinders Medical Centre were transformed from an extremely complex system, depicted in Figure 20.1, to the basic system, depicted in Figure 20.2. Seeing patients in order of arrival was initially trialed in the B-side of the Emergency Department. From then until now, that has been how those patients have been managed. After a few months, it became the norm on the A-side as well, except for Category 1 and Category 2 patients or any obvious threat to life and limb. As a student nurse put it, during a review session some years after the program began, when asked how patients were called in from the waiting room, "They are seen in the order they arrive. How else would you do it?" Nurses have continued to work in teams, and practices like regular ward rounds and Emergency Physicians supervising the work of teams, rather than just functioning as solo practitioners, are now "how we do it round here."

Large Emergency Departments are never static. There are always fresh challenges to deal with, and the ever increasing numbers of patients presenting to the Flinders Department has been a constant challenge. When the Process Redesign work started, 150 patients arriving in one day was a big day in the Emergency Department. Soon 200 arrivals were commonplace, and 250 patients busy. But the basic redesign changes remained in place, because they worked.

Evaluation

At the end of the first year's work, we evaluated the whole program, and wrote it up for a peer-reviewed journal (King et al. 2006). Here, I am able to present a 6-year evaluation of a stable system. Six years is a substantial period within which to review the outcome of Health Care interventions, and as it happened, 6 years after the ED Works program began in earnest, there was a long period of disruption as the unit was rebuilt, and new processes had to be developed. So this 6-year evaluation could concentrate on process issues, uncontaminated by the interruptions due to rebuilding. In the analysis that follows, Year 1 is the year before the ED Works program began. Year 2 is the year during which the streaming program was established, and Years 3–8 are years when the department was physically unchanged, and the senior staff were relatively stable. So the evaluation carries across a reasonably stable external environment. In Year 6, Year 7, and Year 8, external pressures of various kinds, including increasing numbers of admissions leading to the hospital regularly working at 105% of its bed capacity, led to increases in the time that admitted patients spent in the department. So, the periods from Year 1 onward provide two natural experiments: first, before and after the redesign of basic patient flows, and second, with new flows in place, before and during an increase in overall hospital occupancy. The Flinders Emergency Department, like many other large hospital Emergency Departments, has a well-established computer system that automatically time stamps a number of discrete activities. Many of the tables presented in this chapter were generated using that system.

Table 20.2 shows the number of patients presenting to the Emergency Department to begin meaningful treatment in the body of the department. The department caters for both children and adults, and because the management of the two groups is rather different, a number of the tables focus on the work with adults. Children's work is extremely seasonal (winter coughs and colds) and the clinical and process sequences to get children into the Children's Ward was quite different from adult work. Table 20.2 shows a 25% increase in presentations over the whole 8-year period, with the most marked increase occurring in Year 6.

Table 20.3 shows the time taken from arrival at the Emergency Department to beginning meaningful treatment in the body of the department. Across Australia, the assumption is that all Category 1 patients will be seen on arrival, so the initiation of meaningful treatment time stamp for Category 1 patients always set to the arrival time. The table shows that while the time taken to initiate treatment increased slightly for Triage Category 2 and Category 3 patients, it fell substantially for those in Triage Category 4 and Category 5. Overall, the time taken to initiate treatment became much more even across Triage Category 3, Category 4, and Category 5.

Table 20.4 puts this in terms of compliance with Triage times in each category. While compliance had not been the major focus of the ED Works program, it was one of the major indicators that we were judged on by others. The decline in adherence to Triage category times in Category 2 (and to a lesser extent Category 3) is counterbalanced by the improvements in Category 4 and Category 5. Indeed we became one of the best performers in the country in that area.

Table 20.2　Presentations to the Emergency Department

	Total Presents	Pediatric N	Adult N	PAED (%)	Adult (%)
Yr 1	49,762	11,716	38,005	24	76
Yr 2	49,131	10,394	38,717	21	79
Yr 3	50,547	11,003	39,534	22	78
Yr 4	54,397	11,870	42,495	22	78
Yr 5	57,869	12,809	45,025	22	78
Yr 6	62,084	13,526	48,522	22	78
Yr 7	60,342	12,757	47,550	21	79
Yr 8	62,251	13,651	48,549	22	78

Table 20.3 Time in Minutes to Initiation of Meaningful Treatment

	Triage Cat. 1	Triage Cat. 2	Triage Cat. 3	Triage Cat. 4	Triage Cat. 5
Yr 1	0	8.7	33.1	69.3	99.9
		(±16.3)	(±41.7)	(±70.1)	(±125.2)
Yr 2	0	9.8	35.9	63.4	68.9
		(±14.0)	(±40.9)	(±64.1)	(±98.7)
Yr 3	0	11.1	40.3	48.8	44.6
		(±16.7)	(±42.7)	(±46.4)	(±47.9)
Yr 4	0	10.7	35.4	44.1	47.9
		(±15.0)	(±40.2)	(±44.9)	(±52.6)
Yr 5	0	11.6	36.9	45	46.5
		(±18.1)	(±42.8)	(±46.3)	(±51.1)
Yr 6	0	11.6	36	42.3	43.5
		(±17.4)	(±40.6)	(±42.5)	(±43.0)
Yr 7	0	13.3	41.7	46.4	47.1
		(±19.9)	(±50.7)	(±51.5)	(±46.5)
Yr 8	0	12.8	36.9	45.1	49.3
		(±19.3)	(±44.7)	(±475)	(±53.8)

Table 20.4 Compliance with Triage Times

	Seen within Triage Category Benchmark Time—All				
	Triage Cat. 1 (%)	Triage Cat. 2 (%)	Triage Cat. 3 (%)	Triage Cat. 4 (%)	Triage Cat. 5 (%)
Yr 1	100	78	66	59	70
Yr 2	100	73	62	62	81
Yr 3	100	67	56	70	93
Yr 4	100	69	62	74	90
Yr 5	100	68	62	73	91
Yr 6	100	67	62	76	94
Yr 7	100	62	59	73	92
Yr 8	100	63	63	74	91

Table 20.5 shows the percentages of patients in each Triage category (percentages are rounded down, so numbers do not necessarily add up to 100%). While the distribution across categories is reasonably stable, there is a drift toward increasing numbers of patients in the lower Triage categories (from Category 2 to Category 3, and from Category 4 to Category 5). It is possible that the kinds of patient who came to the Emergency Department changed over the years. But a much more likely explanation is that as the processing of patients in lower Triage categories improved, the Triage nurses became more willing to use them, because they did not condemn patients to endless waits.

Table 20.6 shows the problem of the increasing congestion in the department; it shows the number of patients who spent 8 hours or more in the Emergency Department. It is clear how the percentage of patients with longer stays rose suddenly in 2008 and 2009. It has to be noted that the vast majority of the patients spending 8 hours or longer were adults. No more than 2% of children ever spent a prolonged time in the Emergency Department.

Table 20.5   Percentages per Triage Category

	Cat. 1 (%)	Cat. 2 (%)	Cat. 3 (%)	Cat. 4 (%)	Cat. 5 (%)
Yr 1	2	16	37	42	1
Yr 2	2	16	37	43	2
Yr 3	2	14	38	44	2
Yr 4	1	14	41	40	4
Yr 5	3	13	41	38	5
Yr 6	3	13	43	42	6
Yr 7	3	13	40	39	6
Yr 8	3	12	41	37	7

Table 20.6   Patients Spending 8 Hours or Longer in the Emergency Department

	Presentations	N	%
Yr 1	49,762	7398	15
Yr 2	49,131	8549	17
Yr 3	50,547	7077	14
Yr 4	54,397	7424	14
Yr 5	57,869	8664	15
Yr 6	62,084	10,174	16
Yr 7	60,342	12,768	21
Yr 8	62,251	13,564	22

Table 20.7 shows the overall mean or average time patients spent in the department, plus the standard deviation, a measure of the variability of lengths of stay in the department. The table is for adult patients only. It shows how, for the discharged patients, the average time spent fell after Year 3, but went back to pre-redesign levels in Year 7 and Year 8, although the variation in time spent narrowed after Year 3, and remained at that narrowed level. For the admitted patient, the average time fell in Year 3 but increased to pre-redesign level in Year 7 and Year 8.

The actual time taken to treat patients who were discharged did not change very much through the redesign process. Much more time was spent waiting for each of their treatment steps than in actual treatment. The decline in times and variation mostly reflects the decline in time waiting to begin treatment, with a smaller contribution from improvements in processing once meaningful treatment began.

Tables of data do not tell the whole story, but one further table is really important. We had changed the way patients were processed, from using Triage categories as the basis of a queuing process, to a value stream approach. Because this was quite different from existing processes, it was important to demonstrate that no harm was being done in the process. Table 20.8 confirms that patients treated more quickly did not bounce back to the Emergency Department more frequently, and that the percentage of patients who did not wait to complete their treatment was halved by the streaming process, and then stayed low despite the increase in presentations.

One more piece of data is even more indicative of the changes that took place. Australians are quite willing to seek compensation when things go badly wrong in a hospital. The hospital has in-house staff who spend time dealing with potential claims for compensation if and when the delivery of care goes badly wrong. Notifying a case to our insurers means that the insurers "open a file" and the process of attempting to resolve the complaint becomes more formal. In Year 1, in the period leading up to the changes described here, 13 Emergency Department cases were notified to our insurers. A disturbing number of those cases involved patients who died in the Emergency Department, and whose families felt that their deaths could have been avoided.

Table 20.7 Average Times Adult Patients Spent in the Emergency Department

	Admitted		Discharged	
	Mean	Std. Dev.	Mean	Std. Dev.
Yr 1	8.5	7.9	4.1	3.5
Yr 2	9.5	7.9	4.1	2.8
Yr 3	7.8	6.2	3.7	2.5
Yr 4	7.6	5.8	3.7	2.4
Yr 5	8.2	6.4	3.8	2.7
Yr 6	9	7.3	3.8	2.5
Yr 7	10.3	7.6	4.1	2.9
Yr 8	10.7	8.1	4.2	2.9

Table 20.8 Percentage Who Did Not Wait or Returned within 24 Hours

	Presentations	DNW (%)	No. returned within 24 hours	%
Yr 1	49,762	6	512	1
Yr 2	49,131	5	463	0.9
Yr 3	50,547	3	475	0.9
Yr 4	54,397	3	572	1.1
Yr 5	57,869	3	647	1.1
Yr 6	62,084	3	729	1.2
Yr 7	60,342	4	614	1
Yr 8	62,251	4	641	1

The next year, the number of notifications fell to five, and stayed at that level until Year 7 and Year 8, when there were eight notifications, and in 2009, when there were nine. Thankfully, from Year 3 onward, very few notifications involved patient deaths. Apart from the human costs for everyone involved, there is a direct cost. A reasonable estimate of the average cost of settling a notification is about $50,000 Australian dollars. If the number of notifications had continued at 2003 levels, even without adjusting for the increased number of Emergency Department arrivals, at least 100 extra notifications would have been made. This is a saving of least $5 million Australian dollars, considerably more than the total cost of the Redesigning Care program over that period.

Short and Long

The Emergency Department work taught us about being bold, and being prepared to "make a big hit" by changing the processes of care. It also became the model for dividing up work into short and long value streams. As clinicians, we had always been focused on the safety and quality of the clinical content of the work we were involved in. As Redesigners, the Emergency Department program got us into drawing back from the clinical content of a process, and starting to think about the process steps. From then on, we started to look for short work value streams and long work value streams, and to separate them out wherever we could.

Short is short because of the limited number of process steps. Short work is certainly not simple work, and the Emergency Department work reinforced the importance of using the concepts of short and long, rather than simple and complex. As the Emergency Physicians ruefully agreed, keeping patients waiting for hours did half their work for them because by the time they were seen, the clinical conditions involved had either resolved or had fully declared themselves. Seeing B-side patients quickly meant that more skilled judgments were required, not less. At the start of the redesign, the clinical staff had said that it would be boring to work on B-side because the short work involved would be less satisfying than the long work of the A-side patient. But the clinical challenges of getting the short work right, and the sense of movement that came with improved flows, soon won the staff over and, if anything, they came to prefer the B-side work.

Summary

The redesign of patient flows pulled the Flinders Emergency Department back from the brink.

The department had gone from a dangerous place for both patients and staff, to a merely busy, overcrowded, and at times a bit chaotic, Emergency Department. Business was now as usual.

We did not ask patients themselves what they thought about the changes, and that is clearly a weakness. However, there is no more powerful rejection of the services on an Emergency Department than to leave before completing treatment within it. Figure 20.4 was produced for a presentation to a hospital management group. It demonstrates that, for the patients at least, the Process Redesign program made the care more acceptable. In the years before the redesign program, the Emergency Department's DNW rates had reached over 6% per month (and at times, the rates climbed to almost 10%). After the redesign of patient flows, the rate halved, and the monthly averages gradually declined over the next few years, despite the monthly number of patient attendances increasing from around 4000 per month to around 6000. In later years, as the hospital became more congested, the DNW crept up as bit, but never to previous levels.

The impact of ED Works was a consequence of changing the internal flow of patients and altering the existing queue disciplines. Unlike the strategies that had been tried before the program of Process Redesign, the changes were effective and sustained. To the extent that an Emergency Department can ever be calm, calm was restored. The frequency of severe adverse events dramatically reduced. One of the senior nurses who worked through this whole period put it this way: "we have never been busier, but we have never been safer."

As participants, the important elements in creating a sustainable improvement seemed to be the extent to which the scale of the crisis meant that "something had to be done," so that authorization and ongoing support was readily available. We stumbled into the strategy we later came to

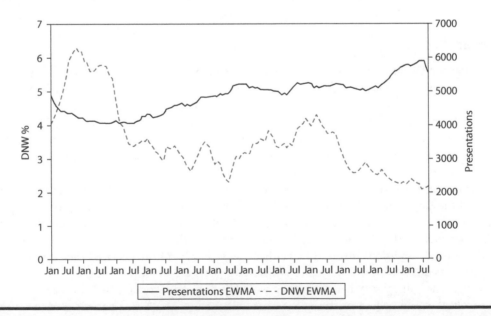

Figure 20.4 Exponentially weighted moving averages of monthly Emergency Department presentations and percentage of did not waits.

name as Big Picture Mapping. The Big Picture Mapping sessions built permission from the staff involved, who developed, and then implemented, a radical redesign of patient flows. The redesign had, at its heart, an ethical imperative. As Dr. Di King said, "it was not up to the hospital to judge patient's motives in presenting to the Emergency Department, and decide their worthiness for care. Our task was to provide safe care to everyone who sought it." A fairer process had been developed and implemented, and that process of streaming, as it is known, has become the norm in many hospitals throughout Australia.

Chapter 21

The Care after Hours Program: Case Study

We learned an enormous amount from the Emergency Department work. It helped us understand what a value stream is in Health Care and the impact that redesigning processes along value streams can make. It demonstrated the central role played by effective governance, and how governance provides authorization for Process Redesign. It demonstrated how mapping and tracking builds permission, and how any one improvement is merely a platform for the next. This case study used all of that learning, and more besides. It is presented at some length, because it was an important evolutionary step in the development of a Lean understandings of basic hospital functions and activities. It is also a further example of a major program initiated in response to a safety concern.

Locally, the care after hours program was known as "Safer Care after Hours." While the focus remained on safer care after hours, the program reached so many areas that a more generic label is appropriate. From here on, the program is described as the Care after Hours (CAH) Program.

The Problem

I was the Director of both the Clinical Governance and Redesigning Care Program when the Redesigning Care program began at Flinders, but 3 years on, formal safety and quality management had become independent of the Redesigning Care Program. Nevertheless, the two program continued to work closely together, and it was the Clinical Governance group who identified after hours care as a problem. They had investigated a series of severe adverse events that had occurred after hours. Their analysis of the events indicated that the variety of problems they uncovered were linked and that, together, the problems posed a systemic risk to patient safety after hours. The identified problems included:

- Problems of communication between nurses and doctors after hours which led to delays in patient reviews
- Responses that varied when a patient review was delayed

■ Uneven distribution of workload between medical staff after hours made managing complex workloads challenging
■ Access to expert clinical support varied when problems occurred during after hours
■ Handover processes varied across disciplines and over time

Authorization and Permission

What followed was a powerful lesson in the difference between authorization and permission. The hospital executive was convinced by the concerns raised by Clinical Governance. It authorized a program of Process Redesign overseen by a Program Governance Group chaired by the Director of Nursing, with participation from Clinical Governance, Redesigning Care, and senior clinicians and managers from relevant services.

A modest amount of extra information was gathered and the available information, including the analysis of various adverse events, was presented at a large meeting whose participants included both senior medical and nursing staff, and a number of the more junior medical and nursing staff who regularly worked after hours. The meeting was designed both to provide information about the issues and generate support for the program of work. In redesign terms, the purpose of the meeting was to generate permission from the senior staff across the institution. The meeting began with a presentation of data rather than a more participatory process, and the discussion that followed demonstrated that work processes after hours were a prickly issue, particularly in relation to medical practices.

Historically, junior doctors worked long hours, up to 100 hours per week or longer, when I was a junior medical officer in the 1970s. Long working hours for junior doctors are still the norm, although such extreme hours are no longer acceptable. Nevertheless, there are continued debates about appropriate working hours for junior doctors (Smith 2013).

There are a variety of reasons why junior doctors' working hours should come into line with the hours of work of the general work force. There was only one occasion when, as a surgical intern, I had been on duty for 60 hours straight, that I actually fell asleep while talking to a patient, but the basic argument for shorter working hours for doctors is that tired doctors make bad decisions. That argument has been ongoing in South Australia, where a series of industrial decisions over a 20-year period have progressively limited medical working hours for junior doctors to a conventional working week, with extra pay for overtime and stringent regulations about adequate breaks between shifts.

An industrial tribunal can award a group of doctors a 37.5-hour working week, and public-sector agencies must implement such an award. But shorter working hours mean that less medical time is available, and doctors take a long time to train. In South Australia, the changes to working hours had been brought in without ensuring the availability of large numbers of extra doctors or of funds to pay for extra doctors, even if doctors had been available.

Returning to the CAH "permission' meeting with the staff, it became clear that the major clinical services had spent a considerable amount of time developing rosters that fitted in with the "Award," as it was known. The unit heads were reluctant to change the arrangements and were not convinced by the data that were presented. Senior clinical staff pointed out that since after hours covered a great deal of each 24-hour period, incidents could not be confined to in-hours, so too much was being made of the adverse event information. Maybe things were actually not that bad. Those views were contested by strongly worded contributions from the junior medical and nursing workforces who actually provided the bulk of care after hours. Eventually, it was agreed that more information was needed and that the results of a more detailed investigation would be fed back to the larger group. Only then would a decision be made as to whether to embark on an intervention program.

Whatever the concerns of the hospital executive or the hospital board, the program could not proceed until it had obtained permission from the senior staff of the units that would be most involved. It was also clear that some further work on defining the scope of CAH was needed before detailed diagnostic work could begin.

Scoping

Large hospitals are single organisations, but day-by-day they function as if they were a series of semi-autonomous de-facto hospitals. That was certainly the case at the Flinders Medical Centre where there was a large adult medical–surgical elective and emergency de-facto hospital; a small children's de-facto emergency hospital mainly devoted to the management of common pediatric emergency conditions, and; a de-facto emergency elective women's hospital, with a substantial obstetrics and gynecology workload.

In all acute-care hospitals, the Emergency Department is the major gateway to all the de-facto hospitals. No matter what the staffing issues, the "lights are always on" in an Emergency Department, which at Flinders was open and fully staffed for the whole 24-hour cycle, with its own complicated rosters and ways of working (as described in the Chapter 20), as was the hospital's large Intensive and Critical Care Unit (ICCU). Despite the best efforts of the medical profession, babies still arrive at all hours of the day and night. The Women's Hospital had worked through a staffing roster that was in line with the relevant national guidelines for staffing obstetrics departments, and there was limited cross-over between that roster and the rest of the hospital. Finally small children get very ill very quickly, but thankfully also recover very quickly. The Pediatric Department had worked out its own arrangements to deal with their workload, and again, the department was generally self-sufficient.

From the beginning of the program, the focus of the CAH work was on the organization of work in the medical and surgical wards that made up the de-facto adult elective emergency hospital. In those wards, many of the lights went out at night, so that those patients who were able to, could sleep.

Bearing those considerations in mind, the basic scope of work for CAH was agreed as "the organization of all patient-care work after hours (6 p.m.–8 a.m.), from patient arrival through to discharge, with the focus on medical and surgical work in the adult medical–surgical wards." This remained the scope throughout the life of the CAH, with the proviso that the scope did not extend to the way the medical and surgical consultant staff worked after hours. Their work practices were deemed out of scope. Whatever the issues that might be involved, taking on the consultant staff over their out-of-hours rosters was deemed counter-productive.

Model of Care

Despite Health Care's supposed basis in science, Health Care practitioners are as subject to fashion as any other group. In recent years, the term "model of care" has crept into Health Care management-speak. Redesigning Care programs were not immune from the model of care infection. While there is no clear definition for what a model of care actually is, the term is best used as shorthand for separating out who, where, what, from how.

Health Care is knowledge work. The details of how a Health Care knowledge worker, in contact with an individual patient, deploys his or her explicit (learned from texts and authorities) and implicit (learned by experience) knowledge is best left to that knowledge worker, in concert with the experts with whom the knowledge worker works, and the fellow knowledge worker to whom he or she reports.

Process Redesign is not about getting in the way of the technical "how" of work (how to do a laparoscopic appendectomy, how to treat a heart attack). That needs to be left to the knowledge worker, and that knowledge workers knowledge work supervisor. Once corporate managers or redesigners without the relevant expert knowledge try to tell knowledge workers about the technical aspects of their knowledge work, they quickly lose those people's cooperation. Just a few days before writing this, I watched a Medical Director, embarking on an important corporate program of redesign, start to lose the support of a key physician by getting into an argument about how many minutes it should take that physician (and her clinical colleagues) to assess a new patient.

How a knowledge worker performs his or her particular knowledge work tasks was out of the scope of this, and most of the other Process Redesign for Healthcare programs I have been involved in. But who, out of a range of appropriately skilled knowledge workers, might potentially do a particular step in the transformative sequence; where that work will be done; and what nontechnical or other steps, after study, may be safely left out or done in a different and more standardized way—these are very much the province of Process Redesign as a cooperative activity, leaving the 'how' to the knowledge work community.

There is nothing intrinsically problematic about bundling together who, what, and where, into a model of care. What is demoralizing is using the model of care concept to impose a top-down model, rather than identifying the problem to be solved, setting the goals or the outcomes for the improved model, and then supporting the people involved to work out how best to reach them. Even if the imposed model is a good one, the fact that it is imposed will lead to resistance, reluctance, and bad behavior in general.

Using model of care in its constructive sense, the scope of the CAH Program was agreed as improving the model of care after hours to make care safer and to provide a safe, satisfying, and sustainable working environment for the people who do the bulk of the work. On reflection, this was more of a goal than a scope of work, but it made it clear that the CAH focus was to be on the adult medical and surgical services.

What followed was almost 11 months of diagnostic work, delving ever deeper into the organization of daily work to understand what the real problem was and build permission for a CAH Process Redesign Intervention.

Diagnosis

The first step was to gather some basic information about the demand for care, and the staff available to respond to those demands.

Figure 21.1 presents an overview of the basic patient information. It is a synthesis of data over a 12-month period. The data made it clear that the times of arrival of patients to the Emergency Department varied sharply from the times patients were admitted to the medical and surgical wards.

The graphs begin at midnight. Figure 21.1 makes it clear that there were low rates of transfer of patients to the wards in the hours immediately after midnight. Admission numbers then increased

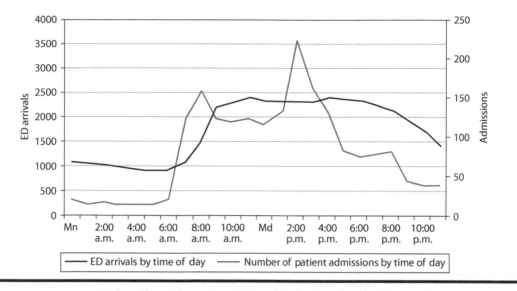

Figure 21.1   ED arrivals and numbers of patient admissions by time of day.

sharply at around 7 a.m., when patients held in the Emergency Department overnight started to move to the wards. Numbers then continued to rise as elective patients started to arrive and get admitted to the wards. The mid-afternoon peak in admission in Figure 21.1 was the consequence of the combined impact of emergency and continuing elective admissions. Importantly, a sizeable number of patients were still admitted up until around 10 p.m., being mainly patients who had arrived as emergencies during the day.

Patients need to be looked after. Figure 21.2 contrasts the number of patients being admitted to the medical–surgical wards with the numbers of junior doctors and nurses available to look after them at each hour of the day.

Nursing numbers remained relatively stable over 24 hours, but there was a dramatic change in the number of junior doctors working in the hospital providing care for the medical and surgical in-patients. The numbers of doctors from 160 during working hours to 11 on the evening shift and 7 overnight. The circled area in Figure 21.2 corresponds to a period of dramatic decline in the number of available doctors without a corresponding fall in the number patients being admitted to the wards.

The graphs do not tell the whole story. There were senior doctors who could be called in as needed who supplemented the staff on the ground. These more senior doctors were called in when the staff on the ground needed a more senior opinion. They were not usually called to do the more routine, immediate management of patients. Not all senior doctors were equally enthusiastic about being called, let alone called in, but, as previously indicated, consultant work practices were out of scope for CAH.

Tracking

The next step was to try and understand more about work patterns and practices, and whether work patterns and practices for junior doctors and nurses differed over 24 hours. We got some clues by asking doctors and nurses to self-track; that is, to fill in diary-type worksheets for stipulated

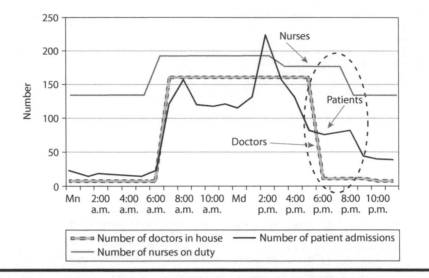

Figure 21.2 Numbers of nurses, doctors, and after hours patient admissions.

periods of time. The self-tracking alerted us to the issues that needed to be focused on, but the CAH Governance Group felt that self-tracking would not convince the undecided. Direct evidence was what was needed. To provide it, CAH supported an extensive program of tracking staff as they went about their business. In a program that spread over a number of months, the whole 24-hour cycle was tracked for various groups of staff. The aim was to build up an accurate picture of who, what, and where.

With the support of the governance group, all sorts of medical and nursing managers and senior staff spent time tracking nurses and doctors. This had some unexpected spin-offs. It had been a number of years since many of the nursing managers had spent time directly at the coalface. Of course, they walked around and talked to nursing staff, but that did not involve the close scrutiny of how daily work was actually done that tracking provides. Sometimes, the senior nurse managers did not much like what they saw, but it gave them a great deal of insight into what was actually happening on the wards. And by getting doctors to track nurses, and nurses to track doctors, everyone developed a more rounded picture of what was happening after hours.

While specialists are very important for developing treatment plans, treating out-patients, and, in surgery, performing operations, day-by-day patient-related medical work in a teaching hospital is mostly undertaken by groups of doctors at various stages of training. The tracking demonstrated that there were marked differences in clinical roles and activities, depending on how far doctors had progresses in the post-graduate training.

The most junior doctors were interns who had only recently graduated. During the day, the interns spent a lot of time shadowing their more senior colleagues, doing a variety of fairly, in medical terms at least, menial tasks such as arranging for tests to be done and writing up case notes and prescriptions. Although in the evenings and late at night they spent more time in direct patient contact, their time was still dominated by relatively general tasks such as taking blood, putting up drips, or writing up prescriptions that had been reviewed. Only about 15% of their time was spent on assessing clinical issues that needed more specific medical expertise.

Next were second- and third-year general medical officers doing further years of general clinical training. They spent about 15% of their time on routine tasks, 30% of their time reviewing and assessing existing patients, and 30% of their time on new patients (and the remaining 25% on communication and administrative activities). The most senior among junior doctors were registrars enrolled in training programs to become specialists. They spent up to 50% of their time on new patients and 30% on existing patients. When they were on duty after hours, they spent the majority of their time in the Emergency Departments seeing new patients who were identified as being likely to require admission.

The nursing work pattern was much more consistent over the 24 hours. Overall, ward nurses spent 20% and 30% of their time in face-to-face direct patient care and about 10% of their time preparing what would be needed later for direct patient care (setting up trolleys, preparing medications, etc.). They spent about 10% of their time communicating with each other at formal and informal handovers; about 10% documenting their activities; between 5 and 10% moving around the ward, looking for things; and about 10% on breaks. The remaining 20–35% or so of their time was spent doing the 101 other things that needed to be done to keep everything going. The major difference between daytime and after hours was that, after hours, there was more time to plan out what needed to be done.

After hours, to a much greater extent than during the day, the nursing and medical staff lived in parallel universes, inefficiently linked by a paging system.

Front-of-House and Back-of-House

The tracking also made it clear that for medical staff, the hospital at night was a different work environment from the hospital during the day. During the day, doctors worked in specific specialist-led teams of interns, RMOs, and registrars, caring for a cohort of patients located in their home wards or as outliers in other teams' wards. After hours, individual daytime medical teams were merged into larger divisional groupings. The work was divided between small teams of "front-of-house" staff in Emergency Departments and other settings where the lights were always on, and "back-of-house" staff working in the wards where most patients were trying to sleep, and the lights were out. The "front-of-house" staff were up from small numbers of medical and surgical registrars and RMOs, operationally based in the hospital's Emergency Department seeing new patients. The "back-of-house" staff were medical and surgical interns, and other more junior medical staff, who were responsible for the ongoing care required by medical and surgical patients in wards spread throughout the hospital. When interns had a problem, they could call for assistance from their seniors, but otherwise, each group got on with its work in a fairly autonomous fashion.

The tracking information was informative, but it needed a more discriminating inner structure if it was to serve as a basis for focused redesign. We had lots of data, but we were struggling to turn it into information.

Four Major Work Streams

It was during a data review session attended by the whole CAH workgroup of redesigners, clinicians, and managers that the breakthrough was made. Up until that point, we had been thinking about the work in relation to discipline groups, and/or value streams, based on clinical structures such as medicine or surgery, on geography (e.g. Ward 12A, Ward 1B, the Emergency Department), or on short patient care or long patient care. None of these did justice to the various role-related work patterns and the in-hours/after hours changes in those work patterns that could be seen in the tracking data. We needed to separate doctor and nursing work, and think about the doctor work in a quite different way.

We realized that the medical work tracking data started to make sense if we divided up the medical work into four discrete functions: new patients, ongoing care, patient maintenance, and responding to instability. We could then allocate specific activities across those functions, to form function-related work streams. We named the four work streams as the following:

1. New patient work
2. Care progression
3. Maintenance work
4. Unstable patient

New Patient Work

New patient work is the clinical and organizational work that has to be done when a patient is seen and assessed as a potential or actual admission. In a public hospital such as Flinders, patients who arrive as an emergency are seen and assessed by the Emergency Department staff, and then the Emergency Department medical team puts the patient "on offer" to an admitting clinical team. After some negotiation, an admitting officer, usually a registrar, agrees to assess the patient. The admitting officer takes a clinical history, makes a physical examination, and orders and reviews a range of diagnostic tests. Once it is clear that admission is required, the admitting doctor will usually make at least a provisional diagnosis of the clinical problems involved, formulate an initial investigation and treatment plan, and order medication or other treatment. If the patient requires an immediate operation, the admitting doctor may alert the relevant staff and put the wheels in motion to book an operating theater.

Once a bed has been found for the patient and all the relevant paperwork has been completed, the patient moves to a ward, where a nurse will be allocated to orientate the patient to the ward, physically settle the patient in, and begin whatever regime of observation and treatment is required.

At some point, the patient will be reviewed by the full medical team, including the consultant in charge of the case. Occasionally, the admitting doctor will seek advice from a consultant at the point of admission, and very occasionally the consultant will have to come into the hospital after hours to review a particularly difficult case or perform an operation. While new patient work in a private hospital has the same structure, in all but the largest Australian private hospitals, a substantial amount of the work required by a new patient will be done by the patient's own specialist.

Care Progression

Once a patient has been admitted, a program of care, intended to transform the abnormal or at-risk physical or mental states and conditions underlying the patient's presenting complaint into a valued health outcome, is put into motion. Care progression is the whole range of clinical and administrative work required to progress and complete that program of work. Care progression extends from the moment the new patient work is complete to the point of discharge, and until the follow-up clinical review, if one is required. For patients with complex problems, a whole range of investigational units such as X-ray and pathology, may also be involved. Finding better ways to coordinate the work of the many different clinical groups is explored further in the case study on visual management and Patient Journey Boards.

Maintenance Work

A lot of nonspecific work has to go on to support the care progression. We found it difficult to find the correct term for this work, although once we talked about it, we could all recognize the work stream itself. For want of a better term, we called it "maintenance work."

For the interns and second-year trainee medical officers who did most of the relevant work, maintenance work involved things like inserting or re-siting drips (or "Jelcos" as they are known locally, after a popular brand of needle kit), writing up medication charts, arranging things, and documenting activities.

For nurses, it involves the whole span of work required to care for the daily mental and physical needs of a group of bed-bound individuals, plus managing the supply chain of consumable goods needed to support the care progression and everyday care. Maintenance work by its nature does not require detailed knowledge of the patient's clinical condition, but face-to-face maintenance work with a patient is an opportunity to get an impression of the patient's physical and mental state.

Unstable Patient

Patients are in various states of clinical stability that may or may not need specific resources. Very unstable patients with hyper-acute conditions that can change very quickly will generally be managed in Intensive Care Units, where the nurse patient ratio is 1:1, medical expertise is always on hand, and the patient's clinical state is intensively monitored by a variety of techniques. Many of the patients involved will need their breathing supported by various means, but that is not the case universally.

Then there are settings such as operating theater recovery rooms, surgical high-dependency units, and coronary care units, where patients who need intensive monitoring for relatively short periods of time are observed and managed. Such units have higher staff–patient ratios than the wards, plus access to various kinds of specialized equipment.

The rest of the patients cared for in hospitals are managed in the in-patient wards. While the patients in the wards are under observation by the nursing and medical staff, most remain relatively stable. But there is always the possibility that a patient's clinical state will suddenly deteriorate, and their vital signs become unstable. Identifying and responding to instability is a crucial activity for nurses and doctors alike, and hospitals have various protocols for responding to clinical deterioration. Outside Intensive Care units, the clinical staff who are asked to respond when a patient suddenly deteriorates may differ from the staff undertaking care progression or maintenance work, because the skills involved in stabilizing deteriorating patients are often rather different from those in progressing that patient's care.

Equipped with the organizing concepts of the varying work streams staff might be involved in, we could now make sense of who did what kind of work, and when; and we could use the diagnostic process to identify the real problem and build permission for a program of Process Redesign work.

Distribution of Work Streams over 24 Hours

New patient work was essentially the same 24 hours a day, with new patient work in evening and night almost exclusively the province of the most senior among junior doctors rostered for that

Table 21.1 The Distribution of Tasks in Work Streams over a 24-Hour Period

Type of Work	Day	Evening	Night
New patient work	++	+++	+
Care progress	+++ (team)	+ (individual)	–
Maintenance	++	++	+++
Unstable patient	++	++	++

task, for example, the on-duty medical registrar, the surgical registrar, or the cardiology fellow on call. The evening shift was particularly busy. Emergency Department processing of patients who arrived from lunchtime on ward often spread into the early evening, leaving the evening staff (some of whom might have also worked during the day) to assess many of these patients.

Care progression work was the primary responsibility of the clinical teams based in the wards and the clinical unit that only functioned as full teams in normal working hours, 8 a.m. to 6 p.m. During the day, clinical decision-making was usually undertaken by the more senior members of the clinical team, with the more junior members making the necessary arrangements to move care along. Some care progression work was still being done in the evening but by individual doctors rather than the whole team. Sometimes care progression work was done by a team member who had been on at some point during the day, and who was working an evening shift, but often it was passed on to doctors on an evening shift who were not otherwise involved with that patient during the day. Very little care progression work was done during the night shift. Table 21.1 summarizes the distribution of work across the work streams over a 24-hour period.

While maintenance work goes on all day, in-hours each medical or surgical team did its own maintenance work. After hours, the more junior medical staff spent most of their time on the night shift undertaking maintenance care work across the institution. As a result, after hours nurses on several wards would only have access to one cover doctor, and there were clearly problems of communication, and overburdening of some junior medical staff.

Unstable patient work could occur at any time of day or night, and identifying clinical deterioration relied heavily on observations by ward nurses. At night, the nurses first port of call if they were concerned about a patient was the Junior Medical Officer covering their ward. While the cover doctors tried to be responsive, it was clear from the tracking data that making clinical assessments on patients about whom nurses were concerned, but who were not critically ill, could struggle to stay a priority in the face of competing demands on a doctor's time. If the deterioration was severe, then any nurse or doctor could ask a special medical team to attend.

The Real Problem

We were now able to see the real problems and present the tracking data and our formulation of the real problems to the clinical managers whose permission we needed if we were to go on and redesign the work streams. The real problems were identified as follows:

■ There was a lack of a team structure to support the work after hours, and people operated in their professional/departmental silos ignoring the needs of other areas.

- Resources were not deployed to match work streams or variations in demand.
- There was no flexibility to respond rapidly to the changing demands of a given shift, particularly during night duty where manpower was lowest.
- Work left over from the day that still needed to be done created more queues as the evening progressed and resources reduced and admissions increased.

In our presentations, we summarized the diagnostic information, documented the extent to which the hospital changed its focus over the 24 hours, and described the four work streams. Figure 21.3 is a modified version of the analysis taken from one of the A3s we used to summarize the work to date. The presentations made sense to everyone involved, and we gained permission to move on to the intervention phase.

Discussion/Analysis:

Across 24 hours the hospital experiences 3 different time zones. The day hospital (8 a.m.–5 p.m.), the evening hospital (5 p.m.–10 p.m.), and the night hospital (10 p.m.–8 a.m.). 4 value streams of work have been identified that cross all time zones—new patient work, maintenance work, care progression work, and unstable patient work. The focus of the required work varies by time zone.

- The day hospital is focused on care progression work (typified by decision-making and consultation).
- The evening hospital is focused on managing new patient work (ED based).
- The night hospital is focused on maintenance work (ward based).

Unstable patient work is present across the 24 hours interrupting the other streams of work that may be the focus for a variety of staff groups. Management after hours is commonly initiated by interns and relies on multiple "pull" systems from nurses to interns, and interns to more senior medical staff. There is a risk that urgency may be lost in the mass of maintenance and new patient work.

For nursing unstable patient, work can interrupt the provision of fundamental care to whole groups of patients.

Care progression work is conducted by the team during the day; however, in the evening individual doctors may continue care progression work as a priority to maintenance work required by other patients.

New patient work is managed in the same way over the 24 hours with the RMO/Registrar being given responsibility for this after hours.

Maintenance work is a lower priority as medical staff attempt to finish off their care progression work when rostered for evening shifts.

In the current state, resources are not deployed to match the value streams, nor is there flexibility to respond rapidly to the changing demands of a given shift. Work left over from the day creates more queues as the evening progresses, resources reduce, and admissions increase.

Nursing work changes little over 24 hours, but the ratio of doctors to nurses changes between time zones, from 1:1 to 16:1 in the evenings and at night. The number of senior nurses, Level 3 and above, changes from 100+ during the day to single Hospital Coordinator in the evening and at night

Hypothesis: If work was complete in the allocated time zone and not rolled over from the previous time zone the demand could be managed by current staffing resources with systems improvement to reduce variability, improve visual management and communication systems.

Figure 21.3 The CAH real problem analysis.

Most crucially, the clear problems with work organization made it obvious that the primary task was to improve work practices within the existing resources, not to try and turn the clock back or look for additional resources.

Intervention

As a first step, the hospital executive agreed to support an improvement event involving 40 junior medical and nursing staff from across the medical and surgical services. The Redesigning Care Team facilitated the event and members of the hospital executive also participated. In many Lean "playbooks," kaizen, or improvement, events take up 5 days, focus on a particular issue, and are intended to go from analyzing a problem to an implementable solution over the 5-day period. We never had the luxury of taking large numbers of staff off the floor for 5 days. Apart from anything else, to make our events possible, it was necessary to backfill clinical participants. That meant paying overtime or hiring agency staff to fill gaps, which could be expensive. So improvement events had to focus on major problems and the events had to be brief and designed to kick-start programs of intervention work, rather than develop a complete future state. An evening and two complete days was usually the most we could expect. We got into the practice of calling such activities "rapid improvement events." These events were an opportunity to work together on understanding and finding solutions, not to work out how best to impose predetermined strategies.

The format for the CAH Rapid Improvement Event, and many other similar events that followed, was that the cross-functional group of invitees gathered in the evening of day one (food provided). The evening session was taken up with presenting the diagnostic information gathered to that point and generating a sense of engagement. In this case, to deepen both the understanding and the engagement, the Redesigning Care team used the strategy of breaking the participants into cross-functional (doctors and nurses) teams and asking them to go on a "Gemba walk."

Gemba is a Japanese word that means "real place." In Lean parlance, a Gemba walk is going to whatever makes up the shop floor—that is, the place where the real work of value creation is undertaken—and once there, trying to understand the value-producing activity that occurs, while also looking for waste and opportunities for improvement. So doctors and nurses were asked to go in pairs, follow staff on the evening shift, look at the work, and report back with their observations. Over the next 2 days, participants broke up into smaller workgroups, and at workgroup and large group sessions, they developed a plan of action. As is common, the problem was too many good ideas, not too few.

Do Today's Work Today

Day shifts are the periods when the whole team looking after a patient is present and available for work. Part of the CAH diagnostic work had included asking doctors who were doing evening and night shifts across the hospital to assess the extent to which tasks they were doing at that time of day could have been undertaken during an earlier shift. Certainly, the doctors' observations were based on potentially biased perceptions and could have been exaggerated. Nevertheless, the doctors assessed that overall, 40% of the work they were asked to do were tasks left over from the day shift. Even if the real figure was closer to 20%, that still was still a lot of work. Leftover tasks were mainly maintenance and care progression work: there were many reasons that work was left over, but an obvious issue was that as the day wore on, there was no simple way for nurses (or fellow doctors) to notify the most junior doctors, each one of whom covered a number of wards, that a task needed doing; other, that is, from a chance meeting on the ward or paging the doctor concerned. Paging interrupted both the nurse and the doctor, and even after being paged, there was no indication that the needed work was then always done.

A simple visual management strategy was developed and implemented across the wards. Each ward identified (or erected) a whiteboard, in a suitable location, and called it the medical task board. Nurses wrote up routine tasks that needed to be completed. At a "check-out" process at around 3–4 p.m. the nurse Shift Coordinator and the junior doctors concerned would ensure that maintenance and new patient tasks were completed before the end of the shift. Because the tasks were on a whiteboard, wiping them off as they were completed indicated that the tasks had been done; leaving them on made it clear that routine work was being left for the next shift.

Reducing Overburden and Handover

The tracking had also made it clear that while the actual workloads of the most junior doctors working overnight varied considerably between the medical and surgical rotations, the actual work was very similar across the divisions. Most of it was maintenance activity for patients with whom the doctors on duty were not familiar: the ward nurses identified the task that had to be performed, and the junior doctor did it. The medical and surgical interns were therefore encouraged to see themselves as members of a single night team and share the work out in a load leveling fashion, rather than adopting the attitude "I am the surgical intern, so it's not my job to put up a drip on a medical patient."

The tracking and discussion at the rapid improvement event also made it clear that there needed to be a formal handover from the evening team to the night medical staff when they came on shift. Providing a regular, timed delivery of pizzas to the junior doctor lounge where the junior medical staff otherwise spent free time was an effective incentive to be on time for the handover. The doctors soon found that working as a team was more fun than sticking to a silo, and this helped even up the workloads.

The overall responsibility for CAH interventions that were to be implemented across the hospital was delegated to the unit managers. But formal workgroups were established to progress the unstable patient work and the maintenance work. A senior member of the nursing staff (Damon Williams) was seconded to the CAH Program to keep the program of work on track. His formal title was Project Facilitator, but his real title should have been "CAH supernatural being," given the miracles he was asked to perform.

The tracking had made it clear that the registrars doing the new patient work after hours were already working very efficiently, and there was limited scope for improving how they did the direct patient care work. The main body of work for this and all the other medical groups working after hours focused around communication between nurses and doctors, and increasing the sustainability of the night shifts for the more junior doctors working back-of-house.

Unstable Patient Work

Unstable patient work was primarily technical in nature. Ensuring that doctors had the time to respond promptly to concerns about unstable patients would be an outcome of successful process redesign of the other components of medical work after hours, in that it released time for unstable patient work. The specific unstable patient issue that came through at the rapid improvement event was, however, the problem of resuscitation status.

Flinders, like many other hospitals, uses a Medical Emergency Team or "MET" process for responding to seriously unstable patients. Hospitals have long had cardiac arrest teams that respond when a patient goes into cardiac arrest. A MET is a team of senior clinical staff with relevant expertise in the management of rapidly deteriorating patients, who can provide intensive on-the-spot clinical treatment in an effort to prevent the deterioration processing to the point of cardiac arrest. In the face of a patient whose vital signs are deteriorating, protocols have been developed to help nurses or doctors determine if they should summon assistance from a more specialized MET.

As the population ages, more and more acute hospital care is taken up with the management of frail elderly patients with complex and comorbid conditions. Many patients (and their families) have definite views about what should happen when and if their hearts do stop beating. Not everyone wants the intrusive and not necessarily dignified process of attempts to resuscitate them. The colloquial term for the general decision whether or not to vigorously intervene in the face of deterioration is "resus status." For instance, in the event of cardiac arrest, should nature be allowed to take its course (i.e. if the patient is not to be resuscitated, NTBR) or should energetic efforts be made to get the heart beating again? As the MET process has developed, the dilemma has become more complex. Should the MET process be initiated, or should nature be allowed to take its course? Once a MET has been summoned, if it fails to stabilize a patient's condition, should an arrest procedure be initiated in the event of a cardiac arrest? How long to go on with attempts at resuscitation? Discussions about these kinds of issues need to initiated, and their results documented, well before the events that precipitate the interventions.

The problem that was identified at the improvement event was that even when resus status had been discussed with the patient and family, and preferences identified, resus status was documented in nonstandard ways, and the documentation was hard to find. This was particularly important when, late at night, a nurse made a MET call, and neither the nurse nor the members of the MET had detailed prior knowledge of the patient they were trying to stabilize, and there was no one easily available who knew the patient. A Resuscitation workgroup was formed whose scope of work was to focus on improved identification of patient preferences and, once they had been obtained, clearer documentation of those preferences, so that they could be adhered to in the event of clinical deterioration.

Documentation of Resuscitation status had not previously been a senior management concern; it had been managed within clinical teams and issues around it had not previously surfaced. The Resuscitation workgroup was important both because of the problem itself, and because it was evidence that the concerns of the people on the ground were being taken seriously even if they intruded into areas that had previously been left to team managers.

The Resuscitation group was primarily supported by the staff from the Clinical Governance team, while the Maintenance Care and other work were supported by the Redesigning Care Team, with Damon Williams working across both.

The Resuscitation work group (and a Maintenance Care work group described in more detail later) reported regularly to the CAH Governance Group, which in turn reported to the overall Redesigning Care Governance Group, and to the hospital's Management Executive. Both workgroups met regularly for more than 18 months.

Problem and Scope of Work

The Resuscitation status work was a new kind of program in the Redesign program of work. It needed a clear problem definition, a scope of work, and a diagnostic phase all of its own, before embarking on an intervention.

The problem was fairly clear. In an early A3, the Resuscitation Governance Group defined the problem in these terms: "The opportunity for patients to discuss their wishes and convey these to the right staff [and have them documented and acted on] ... is highly variable and largely dependent on the experience and confidence of staff across different disciplines."

The diagnostic work that followed had a number of components, including:

- Case note review to determine where information on resus status was held
- Focus group session with medical, nursing, and Allied Health staff (hospital and community representation)
- Participation of facilitator in a related-issue training program in an adjacent hospital
- Scan of national and international literature
- Review of current systems and processes used at sister hospitals, and scan of international literature

Real Problem

At the end of the diagnostic process, the real problem started to become clear: variation. It is possible to think of the resus process as a sequence of steps. Patient admitted → the possible need to discuss resuscitation status and end-of-life care options with patient and family is identified → discussion is held → outcomes of discussion are documented → documentation can be readily located when or if clinical condition deteriorates.

There are many patients for whom discussions of resuscitation and options for end-of-life care are clearly inappropriate. But there are an increasing number for whom it is of great relevance. The need to discuss resuscitation status was not being identified consistently, and junior medical staff sometimes lacked the interpersonal skills and maturity necessary to manage difficult conversations, and they did not necessarily have access to good role models for such tasks. When discussions were held, the results were documented in variable ways, in many different places. That made it difficult to access patient preferences when decisions had to be made rapidly by clinicians who were unfamiliar with the patient. Under circumstances of uncertainty, the only ethical thing to do was to make every effort to resuscitate a patient. In medicine, not doing what is possible without a good and clear justification lays you open to much more criticism than doing the possible, even if what follows is intrusive and potentially distressing to all concerned.

Intervention

Try as you might, young doctors cannot be more mature people than they already are. Discussing resuscitation status and end-of-life care is never going to be easy for them. But the work processes could be standardized, so that there was clear guidance as to what needed to be talked about, and where to document the results. The Resuscitation workgroup developed a form that structured the conversation and a method for displaying the form in an easy-to-find location. Figure 21.4 shows the most important component of what became known as the RSR (Resuscitation Status Record), a format for identifying that a conversation has taken place, and recording its outcome.

The RSR also contained a visual management component: a prominent green border on the right-hand side. The RSR and any advanced directives were inserted at the front of notes in a commercially available green-backed plastic sleeve.

Date and Time	Summary of Discussion	Outcome	
Dr. Signature Print Name/Pager No.		☐ MET Call and CPR (for full active resus) ☐ MET Call but no CPR ☐ No MET Call No CPR	Retain

Figure 21.4 Resuscitation status record.

A series of small PDSA experiments were undertaken to assess the use in practice of the RSR form and the green sleeve. The first PDSA experiment involved two medical wards that volunteered to adopt the RSR form and the plastic sleeve. An audit of the outcomes of the trial indicated that while the green sleeve was well used, the documentation of the resus discussion itself remained variable. Some medical staff used the RSR. Others documented the resus discussion in the follow-up notes in the medical record, and extracts from the record were photocopied and placed in the sleeve.

A number of modifications were then made to the form in an attempt to reduce variation and increase the use of the form, rather than an information note in the medical record.

The improved form and the sleeve, plus some in-service education about using the form, was reassessed in a second PDSA experiment which involved four wards. The analysis of the outcome of the experiment showed that the resuscitation status was easily found 100% of the time when the RSR was in the sleeve in the notes and 73% of the time when resuscitation status was documented in the follow-up notes or elsewhere in the medical record. When the RSR form was used, the record of the discussion with the patient and family always included MET responses, as opposed to being included only around 50% of the time when the discussion was recorded in the body of the medical notes.

The most important conclusion from the experiments was that improving communication of resuscitation status was clearly a hospital-wide issue. Since that was the case, a decision was made that the best way to ensure hospital-wide participation was to develop a regional policy on resuscitation, endorsed by the Regional Executive. That policy came into operation in 2010, incorporating not only the RSR form and the sleeve but also a proposed flow chart for determining and documenting the resuscitation policy developed within the CAH Program.

Maintenance Work

Maintenance work made up the bulk of the work after hours for the more junior of the medical officers on call. The maintenance tasks were relatively standardized. The problem was that, after hours, a small number of doctors had to complete a large number of these relatively standard tasks in many locations across the hospital. The tracking and the rapid improvement event made it clear that it was not possible to predict in advance what nurse, in what ward, would flag the need for the next maintenance task, and the communication methods used to "order" the tasks were not standardized. The equipment required to perform the most common maintenance tasks was stored and organized in many different ways, and often, the person who had ordered the task was not immediately available when a doctor arrived to perform it, resulting in the doctor probably spending many minutes trying to establish what was required.

The rapid improvement event prioritized the need to standardize the "who" and "where" of communication between doctors and nurses after hours, given that, after hours, they were not necessarily familiar with one another. Another issue related to the interns becoming able to "see" all the maintenance work that needed to be done, not just the work generated by their notional divisional group. The task list for the maintenance workgroup generated by the rapid improvement event included the following, and three major interventions were worked on over the next few months:

- Implement visual management to easily identify the ward Shift Coordinator
- Develop rounding across areas/patients
- Formalize and support the role of Shift Coordinator as primary liaison with doctor
- Visualize intern work—make it visible to all on-ward team
- Formalize ordering of diagnostics by accredited ward nurses

Shift Coordinator Identification

In recent years, nurses have made a major effort to move away from the traditional ways of organizing themselves. Historically, a nursing sister sat at a desk in the centre of the ward and, amongst other things, sent nurses out to do tasks such as checking the temperature of all the patients. Nowadays, nurses are allocated a group of patients when they come on shift and each nurse tries to provide as much as possible of the care their patients need. As a result, authority and oversight are necessarily more decentralized. But someone still needs to keep an eye on what is going on and coordinate the various activities that are involved in running a ward over a shift. At Flinders, on each shift, one nurse is identified as the Shift Coordinator.

One of the roles of the Shift Coordinator is to be the interface between the ward and the various people that come to a ward to provide a service to any one of the patients. Nowadays, nursing roles are not identified by uniform. When I was a junior doctor, ward sisters were instantly identifiable by their imposing dark blue uniforms. Those days are long gone, and on any particular shift it could be hard to identify the Shift Coordinator. Some kind of visual identifier was necessary and Damon Williams took on the task of developing one.

Arriving at an agreed solution needed a number of PDSA cycles. The first attempt was a slip-on sleeveless overjacket in a distinctive color, as it was thought that the visual signal "I am the Shift Coordinator" needed to be visible from all angles.

A number of nurses felt the vests were not very professional and they reminded them of "hi-vis" jackets used on building sites and other public settings. The next attempt was a broad, colored arm band with "Shift Coordinator" written on it. There were difficulties finding a supplier who could produce armbands in a material which could be printed with the correct logo, was easy to take on and off, was economical to produce, and could be sterilized. But even when those hurdles had been overcome, a number of nurses reported that, for various reasons, wearing a wide wrap-around armband did not enhance their self-esteem.

Finally, Damon hit on the idea of a printed, distinctive label (red with a red lanyard at Flinders) on a wide, colored lanyard that would be worn round the neck over the nursing uniform, as shown in Figure 21.5.

The shift coordinator identifiers were quickly embraced. They were taken up throughout the hospital, and for all shifts. They continue to be used, and their use has spread to regional partners. Shortly before writing this, I was at a meeting with some staff from an aged care agency. The staff

Figure 21.5   Shift coordinator identification.

said how nice it was to go to Flinders, because simply by looking for the red label, they knew who to talk to.

Standardizing IV Equipment

Tracking of maintenance activities revealed that 27% of maintenance tasks involved changing, re-siting, or putting up, intravenous (IV) therapy equipment of some kind. A survey of 23 interns confirmed that the equipment was stored in different places and in different ways on every ward and that 100% had problems with finding IV equipment. The majority of the interns surveyed wanted the IV equipment stored in the ward treatment room where many other items of frequently used equipment were stored.

Relocating IV equipment across the hospital sounds easy, but doing it involved crossing both divisional and unit geographic boundaries, and related spans of authority. An A3 was prepared, and the standardization of IV storage across the hospital was agreed to by both divisional directors and senior hospital managers.

After a period of experimenting with layout and equipment, a series of brightly colored yellow multi-bin wall storage systems were bought. The contents of each bin were standardized so that the contents could be found by the doctors and the bins refilled by PSAs and nurses in a standard way. Wherever possible, the wall storage systems were placed in a conspicuous place in the treatment rooms.

An audit demonstrated that it took on average 2 minutes 47 seconds to find the IV equipment before the redesign, and 56 seconds afterward. That this released between 30 and 60 minutes each shift for the night interns demonstrated what an important task IV management was for them. The group of interns who were working during the period the wall storage was installed thought it was a brilliant innovation. After that, everyone took it for granted. How else would you store IV equipment?

The Electronic Medical Task Board

Re-siting the IV equipment was a low-tech, but much needed, improvement. The Electronic Medical Task Board (EMTB) was a remarkable example of what a collaborative Process Redesign program can achieve in relation to a more technically sophisticated intervention.

In the *British Medical Journal* in August 2013, a long article (Hoeksma 2013) noted that one of the important reasons for the failure of a £12.7 billion IT initiative in the NHS (yes, almost £13 billion wasted) was that it did not secure local support. The article discussed the potential value of turning doctors and nurses into coders who could write computer applications that would fit their actual needs, and so be taken up and used. The EMTB demonstrates the force of those observations.

The EMTB was a response to a problem identified during the tracking, and confirmed at the rapid improvement event described earlier. The problem, as summed up in one of the documents drafted after the event, was that the "after hours the JMOs (junior medical officers) receive an overwhelming number of multi-channelled requests, leading to constant interruptions that affect their ability to safely manage, plan and coordinate the after hours in-patient workload."

A common scenario would be that a nurse would identify a task to be done, page the JMO using the text paging system, get no response, wait a while, then page again but asking for a return phone call to the ward phone. The JMO, interrupted in what he or she was doing, would make a note of the call and phone back when it was convenient, by which point the nurse, having waited for a reply that did not come, had gone elsewhere on the ward, and the person answering the phone did not know what the page was about. Frustrating all round.

One of the participants in the rapid improvement event was Dr. Nick Kennedy, one of the new breed of doctors who are both fine clinicians and highly computer-literate. Dr. Kennedy and his colleagues thought there must be a better way of dealing with nurse–doctor communication, and Dr. Kennedy took the lead in finding a better way. The result was the EMTB.

The EMTB extended the concept of a whiteboard to the Internet. The basic idea was simple. The EMTB is a web application that, when a user logs on to it, presents the user with a simple form for "logging a job." The form is formatted as rows in a table (see Table 21.2). The user inserts a job, location details, clinical team details, and task details. Time and job number (for the log-on session) are automatically inserted by the program. Crucially, there is a box the doctors tick when they complete a task. The program that lies behind the task board knows which intern is responsible for the ward and is "on" for the relevant team, as the program has a look up table derived from the existing medical staff electronic rosters.

The clever trick is that the task board can be looked at in three views: in a ward view that shows all the outstanding jobs for each ward; in a team view that shows the job list for the clinical teams; and as a "cover" view that allows each intern (designated by role) to see his or her outstanding tasks. Once developed, the EMTB was placed on the hospital's intranet where it could be accessed from any computer connected to the intranet.

Table 21.2 Logging a Job Using EMTB Form

Job No.	Ward	Bed No.	Team	Task Description	Create on	Create by	Edit	Completed
1	9d	12	hemo	D/c med	08/05 22.46	9d nurse		

The EMTB was trialed in three wards for a 2-week period. No technical problems were found with the Board. It was clear and simple to use, detailed information could be written on it, it could be accessed from any terminal, and the after hours medical workload was visible to all users.

The entire nursing staff strongly agreed that the board should be more widely used, although one RMO felt that looking at the screen was an extra task, and that he would have preferred a larger display.

The trial was clearly very successful, and the EMTB was released for use between 5 p.m. and 8 a.m. throughout the hospital. Its use was intended for after hours only, to minimize the complexity of the cover views (although in time it began to be used in daytime too). The final format for the EMTB made it clear that it was only intended to be used for routine tasks and the release was monitored carefully to ensure that the EMTB was used only for such tasks, rather than unstable patient reports. No adverse events were reported due to inappropriate use of the EMTB. At the time of writing, the EMTB had been in use for many years without interruption and without needing major changes to its format or operation. The number of tasks logged on the EMTB increased rapidly after it was released, and after hours paging of junior medical staff dropped by 50%. No adverse events occurred as a result of any initial incidents of inappropriate use. Figure 21.6 shows how rapidly the EMTB had an impact on text paging after hours.

The nurses liked the EMTB because they could see the workloads of the interns and get a feel of how long the intern might take to get to the work. The interns and other junior doctors liked it because, as one said, "I can look at my tasks, and work out how to organise my time so that I am not wasting time walking round and round from job to job." A number of other initiatives were undertaken as part of the further development of the Task Board concept, but they are not presented here.

Early on in the life of the CAH Program, there was some discussion around the development of a role for a nurse "task scheduler" who would take calls from nurses needing tasks to be completed, and then liaise with the junior doctors to get the tasks done. There was even a brief trial of the role, but the EMTB rendered it redundant. In Lean terms, we had thought that a task scheduler might be necessary to create kanban cards for the medical staff (kanban cards are work schedule cards that Toyota developed). The EMTB turned out to be a kind of "self-help" kanban that was rapidly accepted. Because it used generic programs that the hospital already had access to, there was no cost (other than a large Christmas basket for Dr. Kennedy).

Evaluation of the CAH Program

Many of the specific programs of the CAH work were evaluated as they were implemented. Overall, evaluation of such a broad-based program is difficult. Anecdotally, the program was very successful. The medical staff found night work much less stressful and did not resign to avoid it. The nurses found communication much more straightforward. A good indication of the overall acceptability of the work came sometime after the program was formally wound up. Following a further change to the industrial award, the rosters for registrars, interns, and second-year trainees changed, so that a night team would now not work as a team throughout a roster period. But the doctors could vote to change their roster arrangements to stay working in teams, which they did, even though doing so was not in their immediate self-interest.

Formally, we tried to evaluate the overall impact in several ways. First, we periodically asked junior doctors to indicate what percentage of their after hours tasks could have been accomplished

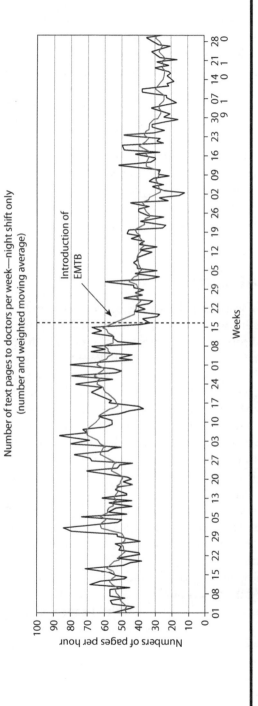

Figure 21.6   The impact of the EMTB on text pages to doctors on night shift.

during the day. We found that after the CAH program, the percentage dropped from 60% to around 20%, and this was confirmed by an analysis of tasks posted on the after hours task board.

But CAH had been prompted by a concern over safety. The CAH Program did not change the number of staff available after hours, the hypothesis being that work reorganization would increase the time available for activities such as managing unstable patients. Reassuringly, as the overall activity increased, the percentage of people dying after hours decreased, but the decrease in deaths was a trend that was already established when the CAH Program began.

Gross mortality is a very difficult measure to change, because many different factors will impact on the exact time of death in a hospital. However, the number of MET calls (calls from nurses to doctors to provide urgent assistance for a patient who has suddenly deteriorated) after hours fell as the CAH program progressed, indicating that the time released for more systematic care was decreasing crises.

CAH had been launched after an analysis of a series of hospital adverse events. Fortunately, severe hospital adverse events are relatively rare data, and confidentiality concerns related to linking a death to a time of day, means that it is not possible to show the actual numbers involved. But it was clear that the overall adverse event data mirrored the MET call data, with number of events after hours falling during the course of the CAH Program.

Embedding and Sustaining

CAH was a large program of work. Initially, we misjudged the extent to which senior medical staff were committed to the existing ways of working. We needed much more evidence about the real problem before we obtained permission for a program of Process Redesign. The extended diagnostic period laid a strong foundation for the work that followed.

Dividing the patient-related workup into four major functions was a turning point in the program. Using that structure, we were able to see and then redesign key processes in both the unstable patient and maintenance functions. The resuscitation status work was widely applied, and the whole hospital continued to use the Shift Coordinator lanyards with essentially 100% compliance. The EMTB became an accepted element in how the hospital works, and no one remembers when IV equipment was stored any other way than in the yellow bins. We have also found that the four stream structure—new patient work, care progression, maintenance, and unstable patient work—holds in many different settings.

The end-product of a successful program of Process Redesign is changed behavior on the ground and, ultimately, that was what CAH delivered. Doctors and nurses want to do good work. The changes that were made were sustained because they made it easier for doctors and nurses to spend more time doing what was important for them and they spent less time on wasteful activities. The interventions made it safer for patients and easier for the staff as well. The creativity of the staff drove the program, and the opportunity to use that creativity kept the participants engaged.

The CAH Program was able to deliver sustainable change because care was taken to ensure that authorization was obtained for each strand of the program at the point that strand of work got going. Authorization was "refreshed" when there was sufficient information to identify the real problem, and again at the conclusion of the PDSA trials. Authorization was built step by step. But authorization without permission is of no value, and our initial failure to build permission took many months of work to overcome. There was no doubt that the expertise and support provided by Susan O'Neill, who chaired the Program Governance Group, was instrumental in keeping the work on track.

Did the CAH Program save any money in direct costs? Probably not. But, it reduced the costs of recruitment for people who left because of impending night duty, and it improved the quality of care. The CAH program also highlighted a much bigger problem.

Continuity of Information

When the Redesigning Care Program began, the medical and nursing staff in the most senior positions still came from generations in which doctors had worked very long hours. We had all worked in hospitals where the same groups of doctors worked in medical teams that, apart from the consultant, stayed together day and night. Teams would work a one-in-two or one-in-three roster, in that the teams would be on overnight every second or third night. There was no shift work involved in a one-in-two or one-in-three roster. When the team was "on," the whole team worked all day, stayed on into the evening and overnight, and then worked the next day before having the evening off, and so on. There were no "night shift" doctors. The team stayed together.

Because hospitals were generally less crowded, patients were usually managed in their home wards, so nurse–doctor teams got to know one another well, and because patients stayed longer than nowadays, it was easier to get to know the basic facts about the other patients on the ward. This provided a continuity of care for all the patients, with much of the knowledge being shared, but undocumented.

Some years ago, it became the norm across Australia for physicians in large hospitals to adopt a "ward-service." When I was a medical student and an intern, physicians such as Dr. Slater or Dr. Nabarro ran their own teams. Day-to-day decisions were often taken by the most senior among junior doctors in training, but when they were away on leave, the consultants did regular teaching and business ward rounds on their "firms." That was what they did, and they were always available to give advice. They were a constant presence.

Over the years, as the length of stay of patients has shortened and hospitals have started to run at almost 100% occupation much of the time, the pace of in-patient care has speeded up. Hospitals have also developed large ambulatory and out-patient services where highly specialized care is provided. Many physicians have moved from running their in-patient service all year round, to fixed periods of "ward service," taking it in turn to run an in-patient service for defined periods (2 weeks, 4 weeks, etc.) over a rotating roster that runs throughout the year. They spend the rest of their time on a variety of other responsibilities. Continuity of care in the public sector has been in retreat for many years; industrial decisions to limit working hours for junior medical staff simply extended that process.

Do these restrictions provide for optimal care? As one of the senior physicians put it, without appreciating the irony of his remarks, "I hate the loss of continuity of care from the reduction in working hours. For the two months of the year I am on ward service, I really hate how we have lost continuity." In a large public hospital, for the majority of patients, continuity of medical care based on the extended personal knowledge of team members no longer exists. It has to be replaced by continuity of information, and existing resources such as the medical record, in its current form, are a poor vehicle for that (and there is limited information as to whether electronic medical records will be an improvement). The resuscitation order problem was just one manifestation of a larger problem of continuity of information that had to be tackled over and again in the programs of Process Redesign. When junior doctors brought up in the current ways of working get into positions of authority, all this will be second nature to them, and no doubt they will extend the ingenuity shown in the development of the EMTB to other means of communication. In the meantime, the rest of us struggle to catch up.

Chapter 22

Visual Management: Case Study

Over and again, making it visual makes it work. Visual management systems (O'Brien et al. 2014) have been part of almost all the Process Redesign programs I have been involved with that have made a real difference. Chapter 17 described some of the theory behind visual management systems, and Chapter 21 provides a number of examples of the development of visual management systems. This chapter expands on that, describing the development of a very successful Visual Management tool, the Patient Journey Boards, and how the existence of a visual language opened the door to a whole new way of looking at, and responding to, a major problem in patient care.

The Patient Journey Boards

There are several types of problems in the delivery of Health Care. The first type is "What is the best evidence-based treatment for stage 2 cancer of the X?" The second type is how, given the particular mixture of primary and secondary clinical conditions she presents with, should Mrs. Y's stage 2 cancer of the X be best treated, given that she is also the primary carer for her husband who has early stage Alzheimer's disease. The third type is how to coordinate and integrate the many different processes that make up the complicated mixture of services Mrs. Y requires. One day, comprehensive electronic systems will sort out many of the scheduling and coordination problems that occur in a large and busy hospital. That day has not yet arrived.

In the meantime, the Patient Journey Boards were a more accessible response to the problems of who will do what, where, and when, to progress a patient journey.

Background: "The Man Goes to the Work"

Once the Emergency Department work had got under way, and the Redesigning Care Team was assembled, we launched a larger program of work improving the flow of patients through the hospital. The first step was a series of Big Picture Mapping sessions mapping out the basic journeys of medical and surgical patients admitted as emergencies. It immediately became clear that everywhere we looked, we found tortuous, complicated, inefficient, and highly variable processes where queuing had become the norm at every step along the way. It made me think that there was a more general problem underlying all this complexity.

One of the characteristics of craft work is that the craft worker schedules his or her own work, choosing when, and in what order, to undertake the operations involved. Chapter 2 described Henry Ford's breakthrough in relation to the production of the Model T car. Henry Ford transformed large-scale production by taking the work to the worker, rather than maintaining craft work processes in which the workers choose what work to do next.

In mass production, the work comes to the worker (or to the complex machines that replace the craft worker), prompting the worker both as to the task involved, and how to perform it. Scheduling of the workflow is predetermined in the layout of the production line and is embedded in the design of work processes.

In general, in Health Care, the patient lies still in bed; sits in the consulting room; or sits, lies, or stands in the investigation or intervention area. If you took a time-elapsed photograph of a patient in a hospital bed, you would see the patients mostly lying in the bed, and an array of people coming in and out of the ward in various numbers and configurations, going up to a patient, briefly interacting with that patient, then moving on to another patient. The more complicated the patient care involved, the greater the variety of teams and individuals that would be involved, and the harder it would be to keep track of what was going on, where, and when.

The Problem

Denise Bennett drove the Patient Journey Board work in its early stages, and Lauri O'Brien vigorously pursued it when she joined the team some time later. However, the scale of the work involved meant that all the members of the Redesigning Care Team were involved at various points along the way.

A basic aim in Lean Thinking and Process Redesign for Health Care is flow—the smooth and well-coordinated movement of patients from arrival through to exit. As the Redesigning Care Program got going, it was clear that a major program of work was necessary to improve the flow of patients through all the in-patient services. Queues and delays were pervasive and ever-present, but were either not seen, or ignored, by care providers, so that specific problems that were blocking patient flow were not being identified by them in a timely manner.

Everywhere we looked, we saw a breakdown in communications between the many different staff members involved in providing care to individual patients (Wong et al. 2008). An A3 prepared at the time put the issue in the following terms: "Patient flow information is held but not easily shared by Shift Coordinators and medical staff, and buried in patient notes." The problem was to find the best method for making patient flow information visible.

Scope

A number of wards and units had been experimenting with visual management strategies for improving the visibility of patient flow information. At a large multidisciplinary staff meeting held to identify potential strategies to improve patient flow across the hospital, the need to visualize patient journeys and quickly identify major sources of delay across the medical and surgical in-patient units was agreed upon as an important piece of work. That defined the initial scope for the Patient Journey Board work.

As in every other hospital, many different kinds of whiteboards were already in use in many wards. It made sense to build on the board concept. The scope of work was to produce a format for a Patient Journey Board that would be cheap to produce, be consistent in use across units, yet be flexible enough to accommodate the differences between care processes in different clinical areas. Above all, it needed to be easy to understand. The board needed to be ward-based, not clinical-team-based, as any one ward might be home to several different clinical teams. The aim was to unify, not to further fragment, the information required to manage the care of patients in a ward.

It was recognized that the initial medical and surgical wards would form "model lines," and that if journey boards could be developed and implemented in those wards, they could go on to become the templates for journey boards in other areas.

Tracking

The initial Big Picture Mappings provided the context for the work. The traditional methods of communication in hospitals are writing or word of mouth. Historically, ward rounds, the major medical method of organizing care, follow a military model. Once or twice a week, the senior officer (the consultant) plus his (and historically, medical consultants were almost always men) staff officers (junior doctors of various grades) plus the warrant officer (the ward sister) and various discipline-based privates would walk around from bed to bed, reviewing the field of battle (the patient) and the progress of the battle (against disease).

Most of the information about the progress of the battle would be provided by a subaltern/junior doctor and/or the warrant office/ward sister, who would have been briefed by their troops (junior doctors and bedside nurses) at morning handovers. In the ward round, discussion would occur, and commands (instructions related to action items, things that needed to be done) would be issued by the commanders (the senior medical and nursing staff). The commands (instructions) were written down in the patient's notes during the battlefield review (the ward round) and would also be conveyed by the nursing sister to the ward nurses after the ward round. The more junior subaltern/junior doctors who had to implement the commands (instructions) were usually present during the ward round, and they were then expected to actually carry out the medical aspect of the orders. The most important design feature of the white coats that doctors used to wear, and that have largely been abandoned because they are a potential source of cross-infection, was the need to have pockets large enough to carry the handheld devices (notebooks in which the tasks were listed plus small reference books) that were vital for daily work. While notebooks still have a part to play, they have largely been rendered obsolete by handheld electronic devices.

While that description is something of a caricature, it is striking how often military metaphors are used in Health Care: winning or losing the battle against cancer, she won't surrender, she is a fighter, and so on, and many of the elements of the ward round I have described continue to be important. But there are problems. Substantial numbers of patients treated in modern general hospitals fall into one of two contrasting groups. There are "short work" patients who have single conditions requiring well-understood and clearly documented interventions, and there are "long work" patients who have multiple clinical comorbidities, with or without complicated social and environmental issues. Long work patients are often older and frailer than short work patients; stay in hospital longer; and require complicated, multidisciplinary programs of care. As people live longer, and have increasing expectations of health services, long work patients will make up an increasingly important part of the work of a modern hospital.

Military-style ward rounds are a successful strategy for managing short work patients. What needs to be done is reasonably standardized, and once the relevant decisions are made, the work can proceed relatively autonomously, although the shortened length of stay of those patients means that ward rounds need to be conducted very frequently, and the patients need to be managed in settings where the nurses are familiar with the tasks involved.

But the ward round is a poor way of managing the day-to-day work of long-stay patients. Each long work patient has his or her own particular combination of problems that needs a personalized combination of clinical and support services; therefore, a dedicated work group has to form around each patient. The roles and responsibilities of the work group participants will vary from patient to patient. Tracking of both patients and staff, and further direct observation of ward work, made it clear that it was neither time-efficient nor effective to bring together all the varied participants from all the teams and disciplines involved in the care of a team's caseload for ward rounds. At most, this was only possible once or twice a week, and even then, a large number of people spent time listening to patient problems that were not within their remit. And the infrequency of the rounds meant that many decisions were batched, rather than being taken when they were needed.

Given the need to keep care progression moving, decision-making had commonly become decentralized, but this was informal in nature, and it worked in an ad-hoc fashion. Since existing methods of inter-staff communication were fragmented, when plans were, or needed to be, developed and decisions needed to be implemented, finding out who was doing what, and what had already been decided or implemented, was very difficult.

When we observed groups of nurses, junior doctors, and Allied Health staff at work, the question they most frequently asked each other was variants of "Where are we up to with Mr. X?" The relevant information was scattered throughout case notes, handover sheets, computerized spreadsheets, the records of multidisciplinary meetings of various kinds, including formal discharge planning meetings, and in the heads of many people. Even if the relevant information was in the patient notes, the notes were not kept where they were needed for bedside or conference room decision-making. Considerable time was spent looking either for the notes or for the person who might know about the issue in question. If the notes were available, the required information was neither easy to locate nor in a format that answered the question in hand, and the person who was assumed to know might not be available or be fully briefed.

Wards had put informal visual management systems in place to deal with these problems. They usually involved some kind of table-like format of rows and columns, with the rows being specific patients, and the columns being information or actions relevant to the patients. But there was considerable variation in what was recorded, the manner in which it was recorded, and how consistently the record was kept up to date.

The Real Problem

The diagnostic work made it clear that the real problem was continuity of information. Many people were involved in the care of individual patients, and many of those individual staff members worked across medical or nursing teams. As a consequence of rostering, shift, and training requirements, team membership varied from day to day and week to week. The real problem was that there was no way to visualize key patient-related information at a glance. Any system that was developed would need to be standardized enough so that the visual language system involved did not have to be relearned from ward to ward. It would also need to be flexible enough so that the tool could be relevant to the needs of each ward, and yet still be easily understood by an occasional user, with the relevant information being presented in an easily accessible manner. It was relevance that would motivate the staff to keep it up to date.

Intervention

A rapid improvement event was held. Participants included nurses, ward clerks, Allied Health and medical staff from medical and surgical in-patient wards, and senior managers, including the Chief Executive, the Directors of Nursing and Allied Health, and line managers. The participants tried out various formats and reached an agreement on some key issues.

It was agreed that the format of the Patient Journey Boards needed to be table-like. The rows were to be ordered by bed number (a symbol that stood for a physical location) and the columns were signs and symbols related to actions and information about the person who was in a particular bed at a moment in time.

When a patient was admitted to a bed, the patient's surname and prefix (Mr., Ms., or Mrs.), but no initial, was entered in the column for name, and the shortened name of the medical team involved was entered in the column for team (see Table 22.1).

Some wards liked to have a column, to the left of the bed number, indicating which nurse was tasked with looking after which group of patients on a particular shift (Table 22.2). That was acceptable, provided the patient name and medical team columns were always present.

The next standard element was a column labeled pre-hospital profile (Table 22.3). This was a signal both about the degree of independence of the patient and the capacity of the environment at the point of discharge. A series of written codes indicated the status of the patient and the environment, and indicated whether the patient lived in supported accommodation If they were in supported accommodation, the codes indicated whether they were in receipt of high or low care, and whether they got any support from community-based services.

Table 22.1 Patient Journey Board Table

Bed	Patient name	Medical Team
2	Mr. Smith	Onco

Table 22.2 Patient Journey Board Table Variation

Nurse	Patient Name	Medical Team
Jackie	Mr. Smith	Onco
	Mr. Jones	Gastro
	Ms. Hardy	Onco

Table 22.3 Patient Journey Board Table—Pre-Hospital Profile

Nurse	Patient Name	Bed	Pre-Hospital Status
George	Mr. Smith	5	H A
George	Ms. Jones	12	HWC

Referrals

A key standardization strategy related to internal referrals to Allied Health staff members (see Table 22.4). The major Allied Health disciplines working across the wards were occupational therapy, social work, physiotherapy, dietetics, and speech therapy. Individual Allied Health staff would work across clinical teams, and across wards. Each group had its own column. Allied health expertise was not required for every patient, and the long-standing practice was to request such assistance by way of a referral (request for assessment and treatment) to the relevant practitioner. Who could make the referral? Any authorized member of the home clinical team could make the referral.

In Table 22.4, the initials were PT (physiotherapy), OT (occupational therapy), SW (social work), and DN (dietetics and nutrition). Having created the columns, the next step was to decide what to enter in them?

A system of symbols was developed to indicate the status of referrals to each Allied Health discipline. The symbols needed to indicate more than that a referral had been requested. They needed to provide, at a glance, information about the progress of the work generated by the referral. The symbol structure was based on a symbol system we had seen in various industrial settings. The symbol system was based on completing a triangle, as seen in Figure 22.1.

Table 22.4   Journey Board Table—Columns for Referrals for Allied Health Disciplines

Nurse	Patient Name	Bed	Pre-Hospital Status	PT	OT	SW	DN
George	Mr. Smith	5	H A				
George	Ms. Jones	12	HWC				

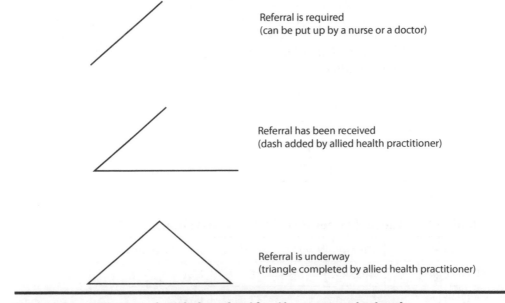

Referral is required
(can be put up by a nurse or a doctor)

Referral has been received
(dash added by allied health practitioner)

Referral is underway
(triangle completed by allied health practitioner)

Figure 22.1   Structure of symbol used to identify progress of referrals.

The sides of the triangle indicated the operational status of the referral: requested, received, underway. What was also needed was an indicator of the outcome of the referral once it was underway; that is, the outcome from the viewpoint of the staff member doing the work and not the functional outcome from the viewpoint of the experience of the patient. The latter viewpoint was of primary importance, but, as will be discussed later, the journey boards were specifically a provider eye-view, not a patient eye-view. Once the practitioner to whom the referral had been made, completed what she or he could do, the referral outcome was indicated by a green, orange, or red colored magnet placed in the centre of the circle (the Redesigning Care Team sourced a provider of colored magnets, and bought them in large numbers!). The outcomes identified by the colors are shown in Figure 22.2.

By the end of the rapid improvement event, the basic format and scope of the Patient Journey Boards had been set. As previously indicated, the boards used a table, or spreadsheet metaphor, with the rows being bed locations (and their accompanying patients) and the columns mainly being taken up by structured communications between the nursing and medical clinical teams caring for a patient. Although the allied health columns were standard across the whole hospital, the same structure could be applied to other disciplines as required. Using bed locations as the main row identifier not only located the patient geographically but also indicated where there was an empty bed, shown as an empty row. Other standard columns referred to the discharge destination of each patient, and a "waiting for" column. There was also a column for the expected length of stay of each patient. The diagnostic work indicated that this was not well used, and the relevant issues are discussed again in the discharge traffic lights section below. It was also agreed that wards could add columns that reflected issues that were particular to, and important for, the kinds of patients managed in that ward.

Location, Privacy, and Confidentiality

The session also featured a discussion on an important ethical issue. The diagnostic work before the rapid improvement session had made it clear that an effective visual management system for inter-staff communication needed to be located in a prominent and discipline-neutral place. A board was never going to be seen as the joint property of all the discipline groups using a clinical area if it was kept in an area that was the "territory" of a specific work group. If a board was in

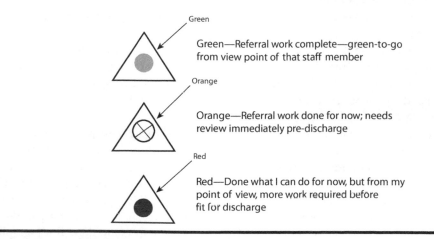

Figure 22.2   Traffic light systems to identify status of referral.

a nursing office, it would be seen as a nursing board; likewise, if it would be seen as in a medical office, it was a medical board. The boards needed to be placed in neutral territory, and easily seen by the many different kinds of professionals who passed through a ward.

The boards identified patients by their surnames. While a surname alone, without an initial or a date of birth, is a fairly "soft" identifier, there is no doubt that displaying a surname where it can be seen by the many different individuals who visit a ward is an intrusion into the privacy of a patient. It raises the possibility of identifying an individual as a patient in a hospital ward. Was this an acceptable thing to do? The important issue here is the difference between privacy and confidentiality.

Australian hospitals, like hospitals all over the world, are covered by legislation related to maintaining individuals' rights to privacy and confidentiality. Privacy and confidentiality are related, but not identical, concepts. Privacy is essentially to do with ownership: a private thought or action is a thought or action that is mine alone, and under most circumstances, only I am entitled to decide whether, and with whom, to share it. Confidentiality relates to transactions where I have provided information to a second party, on the condition that that information will not be provided to others. I have a pain in my chest. Someone asks me, "Do you have a pain in your chest?" If I respond, "That is my business," I am making a statement about privacy. If I reply, "Yes, but do not tell my employer," that is a statement about confidentiality.

Patients give us their names, and by placing a surname in an open setting on a ward, we were interfering with that patient's right to decide to whom his or her name should be disclosed. Unfortunately, in a public hospital, given the many different staff members providing services, the open layout of hospital wards, and the many different existing sources of information about the presence of individuals as patients in hospitals, privacy of that kind is already extremely difficult to maintain. And all the relevant legislation makes it clear that privacy legislation is not intended to interfere with the primary purpose of a hospital, the provision of patient care.

Confidentiality is another matter. Patients have the right for their personal information to be kept confidential, except under very specific circumstances, such as when a court orders records to be produced.

The journey boards did not include information that patients provided to the hospital in confidence. They did not contain clinical information about their present or past conditions. The content related to the scheduling and coordination conversations the different groups caring for a particular patient were having with each other. No confidential information provided by the patients was involved.

At least in our context, the Patient Journey Boards fell under the primary purpose provisions within the relevant legislation, and there was general support for locating the boards in places where they could readily be seen by all the relevant groups of hospital staff, as they went about their daily business. If a patient had a concern, he or she could request for his or her surname not be written on the board.

It is worth noting that at the Finders Medical Centre alone, in a 7-year period, more than 400,000 patients have had their names on a Patient Journey Board in the hospital, without, to my knowledge, a complaint or adverse event related to their use. But all staff members needed to remain vigilant to maintain confidentiality in relation to clinical matters. A good example is if a ward had decided to include a "location" column. In a surgical ward, where patients may go for tests and operations, a location column that indicates the location of a patient is important, but saying what is being done would be breaking confidentiality. Radiography suite—OK; MRI of abdomen—not OK.

Spread

We had adopted the practice of a structured, wider managerial, feedback session at the end of each day of a specific event, and at its conclusion. We had learned from past experience that it was important to maintain a positive tone in these feedback sessions, as a session at the end of a long rapid improvement day was too early to place the event under the microscope of critical thinking. The feedback sessions for the boards did not require any stage management. The enthusiasm for the boards was clear among both the participants and their line managers and senior managers.

When the event had concluded, the participants went back to their medical and surgical wards. They mocked up a board with their colleagues and decided on any extra columns they needed. We had sourced a commercial printer who would print an agreed journey board format either directly onto a whiteboard or as an overlay for an existing whiteboard. Very soon, the boards appeared on all the medical and surgical wards that had participated in the rapid improvement event, and quickly spread throughout the hospital, where they remain in universal use. They have also spread to the other hospitals and services in our region, and to various community services. The capacity to add extra columns to the standardized, core components provides the flexibility to meet local demand.

Evaluation

Some months after the rapid improvement event, the Patient Journey Boards that had been implemented were formally evaluated. The evaluation (which Lauri O'Brien conducted) was confined to those wards where a board had been in place for at least 3 months.

A brief survey provided qualitative information about staff views and responses to the boards. The survey form was sent out to 53 staff members, with all staff groups from medical officers to ward clerks and patient services assistants being represented. Forty-five participants (85%) completed and returned the questionnaire. The participants were representative of all the discipline groups providing patient services, but the sampling was informal, rather than rigorous in design.

Of the 45 respondents, 44 agreed or strongly agreed that the boards had improved the visibility of the patient journey, and 41 respondents agreed that they had increased the timeliness of care. There was less agreement as to the extent to which the boards improved the safety and quality of care. Of the 45 respondents, 19 thought that the boards had made an impact, 10 thought they had made no difference, and 16 were unsure. The relevant point made most commonly in comments attached to the survey was that the impact of the boards on safety and quality was indirect via issues such as improved timeliness of care.

Of the 45 respondents, 35 themselves updated the board regularly or sometimes, 5 updated sometimes or occasionally, and 5 never updated. Updating was clearly discipline-specific; the nurses and most of the Allied Health staff were frequent "updaters," whereas the Patient Services Assistants and medical officers updated less frequently.

When asked if the boards had made "their job easier," of the 45 respondents, 36 strongly agreed or agreed, 6 disagreed, no one strongly disagreed, and 3 were unsure. Finally, when asked if they would recommend the boards as a method of improving patient flow and communication, of the 45 respondents, 39 strongly agreed or agreed, 1 disagreed, and 5 were unsure.

Respondents were also given the opportunity to make comments. The majority of comments were very positive, except one or two negative comments.

The evaluation also included an audit of the boards in use, conducted in all the wards where they had been using them for longer than 3 months. Ten boards were reviewed.

The boards were in active use in all the wards audited. Of the 10 wards, 9 were using the columns well, but 3 wards were using the Estimated Date of Discharge column infrequently or not at all, and its use was still patchy in most of the wards that attempted to complete the relevant column. All eight of the standardized columns were used in 7 of the 10 wards, while 3 wards had chosen not to implement one column. The Allied Health columns were being used as intended in all wards.

In 7 of the 10 wards, the board was both mobile and taken to meetings such as discharge planning meetings. In the other three, the board was either not mobile or was not taken to meetings. In one ward, the contents of the board were transcribed into a book for discharge planning meetings, which seemed double handling.

In the majority of cases (6 of 10 wards), the boards were not used for inter-shift nurse-to-nurse handovers. In many of the wards, nurse-to-nurse handover was conducted at the patient's bedside, and the boards were not appropriate for that. In most wards, the boards were used for medical handovers about 50% of the time. There were queries about confidentiality in two cases, usually related to potential overspecific identification of procedures by the addition of codes, and further standards were developed to ensure confidentiality was maintained. Agreed symbols for special precautions were used consistently in 7 of the 10 wards.

Overall, the boards were being used as intended, and had become "how we do it round here." Effective strategies had emerged for keeping them up to date, and unrepresented discipline groups were beginning to lobby to have their own columns. In some wards, junior medical officers were marking up the board themselves, rather than leaving it to ward clerks or nurses: the management group saw this as a breakthrough moment.

Evolving a New Visual Language

One of the most interesting aspects of the Patient Journey Boards story is how they provided the basic building blocks for a symbolic language which enabled communities of Health Care workers to define and improve whole new value streams of care.

In his poem, "The Death of the Hired Man," the American poet Robert Frost wrote:

> Home is the place where, when you have to go there,
> They have to take you in.

A large public hospital with a big Emergency Department as its front door is the place where when you have to go there, they will take you in. Its doors are always open. As a result, there is an ongoing conflict between having enough capacity to manage unpredictable surges of demand and trying to stay within some kind of budget. Because they are expensive to run, and run on the public purse, many public hospitals tend to work at high levels of occupancy, often being at least 95% full much of the time. Is this a false economy? As the Chapter 18 discussion on queuing theory demonstrated, when hospitals are 95% full most of the time, queues will form. But I fear that there is no real likelihood of public hospitals running at 85% capacity any more. Given the realities of high levels of occupancy, the challenge is how best to manage a system under the resultant strain.

The early work of the Redesigning Care Team had brought Flinders back from the brink of disaster in the Emergency Department, but the hospital continued to work at a very high level of occupancy. A number of attempts were made to maintain patient flows and manage the queues that formed, but identifying what needed to be done when journeys were not running to plan was difficult and an ever increasing use was made of a "waiting for" column in the Patient Journey Boards. Entries in the waiting for (or barriers to discharge) column were however regularly reviewed and analyzed. The reviews and reports formed the basis for a hospital-wide report on barriers to discharge, which was reviewed each week at the daily 1 p.m. regional hospital status meeting, attended by senior nursing and clinical managers. It was during a particularly difficult winter period when Flinders was struggling to deal with a more than usually virulent strain of influenza that a decision was made to use the journey boards to provide a better forward look at the state of the hospital. The blue dot work came out of that concern.

Discharge Traffic Lights and Blue Dots

Hospitals are so complicated that it is often easier to be reactive to bed capacity crises as they arise than to look ahead and try to manage prospectively. The major challenge, highlighted by the winter crisis, was to find a way to look ahead and see what might happen in a few days' time, so that efforts could be made to prevent, rather than manage, bed crises. The Patient Journey Boards included an Expected Date of Discharge column for each patient. Aggregating those expected days might have provided a clue to upcoming bottlenecks, but the audit, described earlier, demonstrated that the column was only completed sporadically, at best. A basic redesign philosophy was that the customer was always right. When something that managers think ought to be done is not done, there may be a good reason. We needed to find another way to look ahead, not just complain about lack of cooperation.

Diagnosis

At the point that an emergency patient arrives in hospital, asking a doctor to predict exactly how long that patient will stay in hospital turned out to be an uphill task. The complex mixture of clinical and care needs of many patients made the doctors reluctant to look too far into the future.

At the time the blue dot program was developed, niche software providers had installed very expensive computerized predictive software in some local hospitals. The software was usually loaded with several years of previous hospital data, and a proprietary analytic "black box" then used that data to make predictions of numbers of patients in beds in the short-term and long-term future.

A great deal of work was needed to set up and maintain such software, and once installed, the software provider "captured" the hospital, and fees for annual maintenance and updating were substantial. For those, and other reasons, that kind of proprietary software had not been installed in Flinders.

Intervention

At a whole of hospital meeting convened by Susan O'Neill, who was then the acting CEO, it was decided that rather than expecting doctors to predict an expected date of discharge, a discharge traffic light system would be adopted for the Patient Journey Boards. The discharge traffic lights were an extension of earlier work standardizing responses to various levels of hospital congestion, undertaken by Jane Bassham and Margaret Martin from the Redesigning Care team, and drew on similar work in other centers using Lean Thinking in Health Care.

The problem with the expected date of discharge system in a hospital with a substantial emergency, or unplanned work load, is the uncertainty around the outcome of such patients, especially if they are older with a degree of frailty. The traffic light strategy replaced a prediction at the point of admission with a clinical judgment related to the likely time of discharge made during care progression.

The traffic light system had a specific task; to inform patient flow. It asked clinicians to allocate their patients to defined categories; red—those who would stay at least 3 more days; orange—likely to stay 2 to 3 more days; dark green—likely to stay 24 hours; light green—to be discharged today. The judgments were made by the treating medical team and updated on a daily basis. They were judgments doctors were comfortable with making, and the basic traffic light system mirrored similar processes used elsewhere. But one more sign was added that was particular to the traffic light system at Flinders: a blue dot on a green background. The blue dot stood for patients who were medically stable and, from a medical point of view, were ready to leave, but who, for other reasons, were not able to be discharged. Figure 22.3 shows the discharge traffic light metric.

In practice, the medical staff identified the status of each ward patient during the daily patient reviews, and then an appropriate colored magnet was placed in the predicted discharge column of the Patient journey board.

The predicted discharge traffic light column provided a very effective visual signal as to the status of a ward. A board filled with red indicated at one glance that things were going to be difficult. A board with lots of dark and light green was a ward where lots of movements were likely to occur. The lighter the green, the greater the resources that would be required for the discharges and the consequential flow of admissions. Shift coordinators and nurse unit managers quickly became familiar with the implications of the board's various configurations.

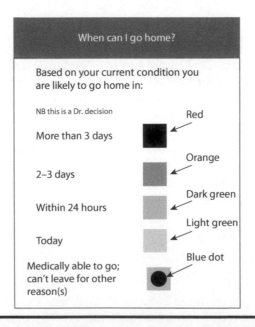

Figure 22.3   Definitions for predicted likely time of discharge, including blue dot status.

Something unexpected also happened. The decision to create a "blue dot" status reflected a long-standing awareness of the extent to which a minority of long-stay patients could take up a disproportionate percentage of the hospital's capacity. The Australian system for classifying hospital activity divides the length of stay of patients into three components:

1. A patient group whose stay is of the usual or predicted length
2. Short-stay outlier: a patient whose stay is very brief
3. Long-stay outlier: a patient whose stay is more than two-and-a-half times the usual length for that type of patient

Well before the Redesigning Care Program began, our Clinical Epidemiology group had been monitoring the extent to which a small number of long- and very-long-staying patients were influencing available hospital capacity. In one such analysis, long-stay outliers accounted for 4.6% of the total number of patients treated that month, but 29.2% of the available bed capacity. Various strategies had been used to try and contain and reduce the lengths of stay of such patients, but considerable problems remained.

The term long-stay outlier simply refers to the length of stay. It provides no information as to the underlying causes of that prolonged stay, which could vary from a prolonged severe illness that was not responding to treatment, to a patient with a problem that from the moment of admission, was clearly a problem of lack of community support, and that needed only minimal medical expertise. Now, the blue dot system created a term for a class of patients for whom the primary task of providing acute hospital care had been concluded, but whose discharge was delayed significantly by dysfunctional interactions between the acute-care sector and the many other hospital and nonhospital systems devoted to longer term patient care and support.

Blue dots made such problems visible and their contribution to capacity problems and hospital congestion easier to identify. The blue dot also made it much easier to separate out longer staying patients who were still in hospital because of the severity of their illness from patients who had got stuck in the gaps between noncomplementary systems. The blue dot patient entered into the conceptual and spoken language of the hospital, and a long program of work followed. Jane Bassham, Lisa Gilbert from the Social Work Department at Flinders, and Pamela Everingham from the hospital management provided the engagement and commitment necessary to progress what turned out to be a very complex program of work.

Blue dot patients were not a homogeneous group of patients. They had become stuck because their delayed journey presented a combination of personal and contextual challenges. Progressing the journeys required collaboration between the multiple organizations that together make up a Health Care system (i.e. acute and sub-acute Health Care services, and disability, community, and residential care services). In the Australian social welfare system, the "owners" of these varied services included the state health system, the Commonwealth Government, and a range of community and institutionally based not-for-profit and for-profit services. Sometimes, the owners acted as service purchasers, purchasing care from each other, sometimes as providers, and sometimes as both. Inter-service suspicion was pervasive and quasi-competitive bidding for service contracts (and individual clients) between providers made them reluctant to share information with each other or the purchaser. There was no forum for conflict resolution and no overarching authority.

Here are just three examples of the problems, chosen at random, from the many kinds of problems and issues involved.

■ A 77-year-old man with severe dementia and aggressive behavior was admitted after an incident in his nursing home. During the admission, the nursing home made it clear that they would not retain his nursing home place, due to concern for safety of other patients. Despite multiple meetings with placement officers, various funding problems, cross-jurisdictional resistances, and the need for a setting his wife could access led to a lengthy hospital stay, despite his clinical state rapidly stabilizing.

■ A 54-year-old man with a neurological condition, previously living alone, was admitted following a concern that his physical state was worsening. It quickly became clear his increasing frailty meant that he required access to a residential facility with high-level care capacity and specialist physical management skills. While formal approvals were in place, and funding had been identified, difficulties in finding an appropriate placement led to long delays in transfer.

■ An 84-year-old woman was admitted with a fractured Neck of Femur (NOF), language problems, aggressive behavior, and cognitive decline. She was clearly in need of High-Level Care in a nursing home. While the family could not provide the required care themselves, multiple meetings were needed before the family was ready to accept placement and allow listing.

There are no simple answers to improving journeys across such complicated systems, but at least the blue dot terminology provided a btase from which to identify the scale and nature of the problems, and a lengthy program of collaborative work was initiated during which a range of sources of delay were identified, and new strategies for improving inter-sector cooperation were developed.

Evaluation

What was the impact of the blue dot program? Figure 22.4 combines the relevant information over a 3-year period. It shows that monthly number of blue dot patients was halved at periods of

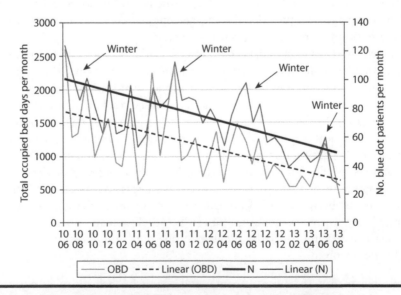

Figure 22.4 Monthly number and total beds used by blue dot patients.

peak demand in the winter, with a saving of up to 1500 beds per month over the winter months. If we assume an overall hospital average length of stay, for adults, of 5 days (and the exact figure is somewhat less than that), that means at least 300 patients more could be admitted and treated per month, with no change in bed capacity or human resources, and a much better patient outcome. And Chapter 18, makes it clear how sensitive institutions running at high levels of occupancy are to small changes in capacity.

Interdependency and Interoperability

Hopefully, the case study of the evolution of the patient journey boards, and the discharge traffic lights, give a flavor of how a Process Redesign program works, and how continuous improvement leads to unexpected new opportunities. The case study also illuminates one of the key ways in which visual management supports a key task: increasing interoperability within Health Care systems.

Some years ago, I started a new job as the Director of a Clinical Service. I sat down in the imposing high-backed chair bequeathed to me by my predecessor, and surveyed my new domain. As I did so, I gradually sank from view. The back of the chair was broken, and it became horizontal when I put any weight on the chair back. Clearly, this was undignified, and I spoke to the hospital stores, requesting another chair. "No worries doc, we will send someone over from maintenance to fix it up." A man duly came over and cheerfully put new bolts through the frame back into the back of the chair. As soon as I sat down, the bolts snapped and I became horizontal again. Obviously, this would not do, and I phoned the stores to get another chair. "No worries doc, just put in a chit, and we will get you another chair." "Great. About how long will that take, as I really need another chair." "No worries doc, we should be able to get that for you within twelve months at least." Hmm! I recounted this sorry story to the Ward Sister, who just laughed. "They are having a bit of a go, aren't they?" She made a phone call, and a new chair arrived that afternoon.

Hospitals, and indeed any large organization, are filled with informal networks developed by people who work together, and who use those relationships to work around formal and unwieldy systems to get the work done.

Technically, this is called interdependency: a quality of a system in which elements link together and communicate by nonstandard, or nonpublic (and therefore nonaccessible), protocols, and where certain kinds of communication are restricted to specific partners. The elements can range from specific components up to complete stations in a product value stream.

There is nothing intrinsically wrong with interdependency. In institutions, when formal systems are not good enough (i.e. formal systems for requisitioning new items of furniture), interdependency allows for rapid improvements to be made in the functioning of the system. New strategies can be tried out and adopted, or abandoned, without having to be formalized, with a considerable saving of time and effort.

However, that informality and lack of defined, public structures for predictable and effective communication is also a weakness in certain contexts.

System designers identify interoperability as an important characteristic of systems that have to be able to respond predictably and effectively in contexts where many different working groups (each of whom may be more or less interdependent in their internal functioning) have to work together to complete complicated end-to-end transformative processes. On any ward in a modern general hospital, especially one that accepts a substantial number of unplanned, or emergency, admissions, patients will present with an extraordinary combination of clinical, social, and personal care requirements. Relying on personal relationships, or face-to-face allocation of tasks in meetings where the members of the various discipline groups involved are all present, is cumbersome and unwieldly. Because of the difficulties of getting such groups together with any frequency, batching is inevitable.

The patient journey boards structured communication between key discipline groups in such a way that overall care processes became interoperable. Groups could link and communicate key information on the status of interactions using a visual language that was formalized, consistent, easy to understand and maintain, immediate, and available to all at a glance.

Over time, the journey board concept has been adapted to a wide variety of hospital and community functions. At the time of writing, they have been in use at Flinders for over 10 years. They remain a key tool for managing everyday work in a variety of institutions across Australia (Clark et al. 2014), and inevitably have begun to be digitized.

Chapter 23

Redesigning Podiatry Care: Case Study

Podiatrists care for feet. More accurately, in Australia, podiatric medicine is described as a branch of medicine that is devoted to the study of the diagnosis and treatment of disorders of the foot, ankle, and lower extremities.

Podiatrists care for patients of all ages, from children needing orthotic implants for gait problems through to the frail elderly who are unable to care for their own feet. In a large general hospital such as the Flinders Medical Centre, podiatrists are heavily involved in the management and care of patients with problems due to poor circulation to their feet. They are also very much involved with patients who sustain damage to their feet and lower extremities because of loss of sensation following sensory nerve damage. Patients with diabetes can have both sensory and vascular problems, and the diabetic foot is a well-recognized and very disabling complication of diabetes, with which podiatrists are much involved.

Organizationally, podiatrists are part of the Allied Health workforce. Podiatrists are important care providers, but Podiatry Units in hospitals are often small in size, and work out of self-contained units that include both clinic space and laboratory/workshop areas where orthotics and other aids are produced.

As the Redesigning Care program became established, the head of Allied Health Services at Flinders took an experienced Allied Health practitioner, Brenda Crane, "off-line" to support a program of Process Redesign across the hospital's Allied Health services. After an initial 2-day workshop in which redesign principles were introduced to representative groups of Allied Health practitioners, a number of specific programs of work were developed. The redesign of Podiatry Services was one such program. It provides a case study of redesign in a small unit focused on clinic-type services, that is, of the redesign of a service where most of the work comes to the practitioner, rather than the practitioner going to the work. But in the case of the podiatrists, the service was complicated by the fact that practitioners also provided a limited range of services to current in-patients, who either were brought to the Podiatry Unit or required the podiatrists to go to them in the ward area.

The Problem

Podiatry at the Flinders Medical Centre was based in a suite of rooms in a clinic and administrative area. The unit staff consisted of a small group of trained podiatrists and a nonclinical support worker who provided a range of clerical and administrative services. The 2-day Allied Health workshop had made it clear that the staff in the Podiatry Unit felt overburdened. Waiting times for appointments were increasing, clinics did not run to time, and when the in-patient services asked for a podiatry review, there were often delays in being able to undertake the review.

Evidence

The podiatry group was a case study in frustrated enthusiasm. The staff were deeply committed to their work and its importance but were under strain because of the challenges in providing the kind of timely service they felt their patients deserved.

Diagnosis

Big Picture Mapping

A Big Picture Mapping was held with the whole Podiatry Unit, including both professional staff and the clerical administrative officer. The major functions of the unit were identified as processing a referral, triaging those referrals, booking patient appointments, providing treatment and rebooking, or going through the relevant procedures when care has been completed. As expected, the processes were very complicated. What became clear was that referrals were being received from a wide variety of sources, both internal to the hospital, and external. Referrals were triaged into urgent, nonurgent, or not able to be seen, with the "urgent" category generally relating to wound care issues, and the "not able to be seen" category to preventative care in low-risk patients. There was considerable complexity around both the acquisition of referrals and triaging, but it was at the booking step that things really got difficult.

There were only a small number of professional podiatrists working in the unit, and each podiatrist was trained to undertake the whole range of podiatric care. But the Podiatry Service as a whole was provided through a variety of named clinics that functioned on different days of the week, with criteria and booking templates varying across the clinics. The named clinics included the General, Pediatric, Vascular, and Diabetic Patient Clinics. While each clinic had its own predetermined (and different) times for new and repeat appointments, and each had its own waiting list, there was in practice considerable overlap between the kinds of patients treated in each clinic. There were many waiting lists and queues of varying lengths, creating great complexity for the Clerical Officer who did the booking, and a lack of transparency for the overall functioning of the unit. The rigid template structure of the computerized booking system meant that a great deal of improvisation was required to keep the clinics running, and problems arose when podiatry staff tried to fit in-patient referrals into their already complex day.

Tracking

Brenda spent time tracking both the professional staff and the Clerical Officer. It was clear that everyone involved worked very hard. The podiatrists spent the majority of their time providing care, but the whole service was dependent on the multitasking activities of the Clerical Officer,

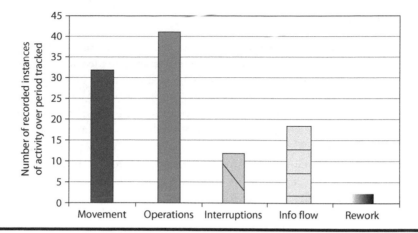

Figure 23.1   Tracking podiatrist activities during a clinic.

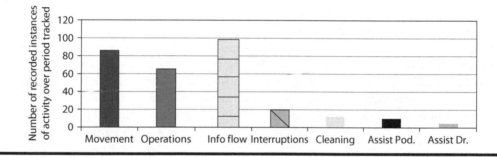

Figure 23.2   Tracking the Patient Management Assistant/Administrative Officer activities during a clinic.

who undertook all the processing of referrals and bookings, while also cleaning and re-stocking the unit, and assisting the podiatrists. Figures 23.1 and 23.2 show the distribution of time of podiatrists and the Patient Management Assistant/Administrative Officer during a typical clinic. It is clear that both professional and support staff spent considerable amounts of time in movement, looking for things and moving backward and forward between clinic and storage areas.

The Real Problem

By the end of the mapping and tracking processes, there was strong support for a radical rethink of the Podiatry Service processes, as it was clear that the internal organization into multiple clinics was a major source of difficulty.

Interventions

A workgroup was formed of the podiatry professional staff and the Patient Management Assistant. The workgroup met at least weekly, usually with Brenda's participation. I was also able to join the workgroup on a number of occasions.

Simplifying Structures

The workgroup decided to radically redesign the clinic structure. The process of designating clinics by name was discontinued. Instead, the professional staff provided morning and afternoon clinics in their own names, and any patient could be booked into a slot in any practitioner's clinic (the one exception was a joint activity with a Vascular Surgery group).

One of the most common sources of interruption was that there was only one computer viewing screen of sufficient quality to view X-rays and other clinically relevant images, which was also the screen the Clerical Officer used. We arranged for the unit to have extra screens in the consulting rooms.

The simplification of the clinic structure immediately reduced waiting lists and provided greater flexibility for the staff, and a more satisfying range of work on a day-by-day basis. It also made it easier to allocate set times during which the podiatry staff were available for in-patient work, as the professional staff's working day became both more predictable and more flexible.

Booking

The next step was to examine the booking process. Up to that point, the clinic bookings were made using a computerized booking system with fixed "slot," or appointment, times for new and repeat bookings. The computerized system also opened the clinic lists one screen at a time, so that although all the bookings for a clinic over a period of time could be seen, screen by screen, the total workload for a day was not visible. This made it hard to balance work across the available staff. In redesign terms, the existing booking system made it hard to load-level the existing workloads.

Despite some initial trepidation, the unit trialed a new approach to the booking process. The computerized system was turned off for a period. The morning and afternoon clinics were divided into fixed but nonspecific time slots (initially 20 minutes, later 10 minutes). Slots were not identified as new patient or follow-up slots, but just as a time period.

Podiatry staff nominated how many slots they wanted for each patient they were due to see. The daily activities for each podiatrist, divided into 10-minute slots, were laid out side by side on a large sheet of paper, one sheet per day, using a large template sheet with each slot filled in by hand. Patients were booked according to the time asked for, treatment room, and podiatrist, and were seen in order of arrival of the referral; a small number of pre-allocated slots were ruled off for emergencies.

There were regular cycles for review and planning of the interventions as they were undertaken, and the clinic processes were refined over a 4-month period.

It quickly became apparent that the clinic time was being more effectively used. Appointment times came closer to the actual time required to see a patient so that small gaps in the clinic schedule were used more effectively. Adjustments were needed to fit in with joint activities with vascular surgeons, and slotting clinics together was sometimes challenging. And for those patients who were "regulars" (needing frequent appointments to manage chronic and disabling conditions), some adjustment was needed as they lost the familiarity of fixed days and fixed clinics. But once refined, the system worked well and the handwritten templates were computerized.

Evaluation

Brenda undertook an evaluation of the interventions 6 months after the work began. She noted that in a period of significant staff instability, with one of the podiatrists leaving on promotion and not being replaced during the period of the evaluation, the number of patients seen slightly increased, representing a substantial increase in productivity of professional staff. The department's rate of booked patients who did not attend their appointment fell steadily over time (from 7.4% before redesign to 4.2% after redesign), which appeared to relate to easier access due to early referral. A greater percentage of patients who were referred were now offered appointments (70% before redesign, 88% after redesign). Many new referrals were now seen within 1 week, and the average waiting time for an appointment fell from 15 to 10 working days. The range of wait times was also decreased, from 2–27 days to 5–16 days.

It was clear that the more flexible booking system led to shorter, and more consistent, waiting times for appointments.

The staff feedback was that the new Booking Templates were easier to use and more flexible, and the added flexibility in the new clinic structure made life easier. Emergency slots had been added to the templates, and they provided useful buffers to prevent clinic overruns, and it was easier to get to the wards to see referrals. Importantly, because every podiatrist saw every type of patient, specialist skills were not lost from the team if staff left.

The final step in this phase of work was a 5S program to reorganize storage of podiatry equipment in the unit's laboratory, reducing time spent in movement during the clinic.

Summary

The new system enabled the staff to increase their productivity substantially. There was a 12% increase in the number of referred patients who were offered an appointment; waiting times for appointments were reduced; and in-patients were now seen on the day of referral. And these improvements were maintained despite a loss of professional staff when a podiatrist was successful in obtaining a promotion to a different unit, leading to a 20% reduction in full-time equivalent staff during the protracted period taken to recruit a new staff member.

The podiatry staff were very enthusiastic about the work, presenting the program at national professional meetings, and continuing both to evolve and adapt their own work, and contribute to the broader program of redesign in the Allied Health area.

Chapter 24

Process Redesign for Health Care Using Lean Thinking

This book has been based on a decade-long set of experiments redesigning hospital and health service processes across Australia and other parts of the world. Over that period, the Flinders Medical Centre, where I was based, was caught up in a ceaseless vortex of health service restructuring. The health system that it is part of was substantially restructured five times. The Redesigning Care Program itself reported directly to at least six chief executives and general managers, and indirectly to a somewhat larger group of regional or supra-regional managers. Under those circumstances, it is just not possible to work to clear goals and strategic plans: they do not exist. That is not exceptional for public health services. On the contrary, it is the new normal. But what we discovered was that Process Redesign for Health Care using Lean Thinking is resilient. Whatever the broader organizational context, gains in Patient Flow and improvements in Safety and Quality of Care can be produced and maintained, provided the work of Process Redesign has the permission of the managers in place at the time, and, crucially, the permission and engagement of the staff who do the work.

There is much that has not been covered in this text, and the case studies offered here are only a small selection of the work that has been done. The Redesign examples that have been provided are based on Process Redesign in a hospital setting, but as the years have gone on, the methodology has proved equally effective for community-based services, as well as other human service locations. Wherever there are problems with work flows, waste, scheduling, and coordination, the principles and methodology remain the same.

It continues to be difficult to identify how much money Process Redesign saves the health services involved. In many Health Care settings, especially those in the public sector, improved productivity as a result of Process Redesign is not cashed in and handed back to the Treasury. It is used to improve the care of existing patients, to enhance access to care, or to develop new services. Is that a good use for potential savings? That is for others to decide.

I was recently at a meeting of Health Care redesign and improvement practitioners from hospitals and health services across Australia. As we were talking, it became clear that one of the common threads was the use of the A3 as a basis for documenting and developing specific programs of redesign and Lean work. I asked the group where the practice began. Many of the participants said that this was the practice that was in place when they joined the Redesign group in the organization they worked for. One of the participants said their group had picked up the idea from the training program a colleague and I had delivered several years ago at the beginning of their major, state-wide, Redesigning Care Program. That program had in turn influenced the programs that many of the other participants worked in.

The most certain indicator of success of a program of Process Redesign is when the origin of a redesigned process is lost sight of, and the new and improved process becomes "the way it's done around here." I very much hope that Process Redesign for Health Care Using Lean Thinking can further extend that support and influence, so that a Lean Thinking approach just becomes a usual part of the way work is done around here.

Over the years, being involved in Process Redesign for Health Care Using Lean Thinking has made one thing crystal clear—99% of the Health Care work force come to work to do a good job. When their creativity is allowed to blossom, miracles can happen, and it is those that make it all worthwhile.

References

Bagian, J., Lee, C., Gosbee, J., et al. 2001. Developing and deploying a patient safety program in a large health care delivery system: You can't fix what you don't know about. *Joint Commission Journal on Quality and Patient Safety* 27: 522–32.

Ben-Tovim, D., Bassham, J., Bolch, D., et al. 2007. Lean thinking across a hospital: Redesigning care at the flinders medical centre. *Australian Health Review* 31: 10–15.

Bentley, T., & Wilsdon, J. (eds.). 2003. *The Adaptive State: Strategies for Personalising the Public Realm*. London: Demos.

Bohmer, R.M.J. 2009. *Designing Care Aligning the Nature and Management of Health Care*. Boston, MA: Harvard Business School.

Brennan, T.R., Leape, L.L., Laird, N.M., et al. 1991. Incidence of adverse events and negligence in hospitalised patients: Results of the Harvard Medical Practice Study. *New England Journal of Medicine* 324: 370–6.

Brockmeyer, E., Halstrom, H.L., & Jensen, A. 1948. *The Life and Works of A.K. Erlang*. Copenhagen: The Copenhagen Telephone Company.

Chandler, A. 1988. Historical determinants of managerial hierarchies: A response to Perrow. In: McCraw, T.K. (ed.), *Essential Alfred Chandler*, pp. 451–58. Boston, MA: Harvard Business School Press.

Clark, K.W., Moller, S., & O'Brien, L. 2014. Electronic patient journey boards a vital piece of the puzzle in patient flow. *Australian Health Review* 38: 259–64.

Davis, P., Lay-Yee, R., Briant, R., et al. 2002. Adverse events in New Zealand public hospitals; 1 occurrence and impact. *New Zealand Medical Journal* 115: U271.

Deming, W.E. 1986. *Out of the Crisis*. Cambridge, MA: MIT Press.

Drucker, P.F. 2008. *Management Challenges for the 21st Century*. Oxford: Butterworth-Heinemann.

Galsworthy, G. 1997. *Visual Systems: Harnessing the Power of a Visual Workplace*. New York: AMACOM.

Gibson, J.J. 1979. *The Ecological Approach to Visual Perception*. Boston, MA: Houghton Mifflin.

Goodney, P.R., Dzebisashvili, N., Goodman, D.C., et al. 2014. *Variation in the Care of Surgical Conditions*. http://www.dartmouthatlas.org/publications/reports.aspx, accessed 20 September 2016.

Greenhalgh, T. 2008. Role of routines in collaborative work in health care organisations. *British Medical Journal* 337: a2448.

Heifitz, R.A. 1994. *Leadership without Easy Answers* Cambridge, MA: Harvard University Press.

Hoeksma, J. 2013. Turning doctors into coders. *British Medical Journal* 347: f5142.

Holweg, M. 2007. The genealogy of lean production. *Journal of Operations Management* 25: 4204–37.

King, D.L., Ben-Tovim, D.I., & Bassham, J. 2006. Redesigning emergency department patient flows: Application of Lean Thinking to health care. *Emergency Medicine Australasia* 18: 391–7.

Lazonick, W.H. 1981. Production relations, labour productivity, and choice of technique: British and US cotton spinning. *Journal of Economic History* 41: 491–516.

Little, J.D.C. 1961. A proof for the queuing formula: $L = \lambda W$. *Operations Research* 9: 383–7.

Long, J.C. 2003. *Health care lean. Michigan Health and Hospitals* 39: 54–5.

Marr, D. 1976. Early processing of visual information. *Philosophical Transactions of the Royal Society London* 275: 483–519.

Menzies, I.E.P. 1959. The functioning of a social systems as a defence against anxiety: A report on a study of the nursing service of a general hospital. *Human Relations* 13: 95–121.

Norman, D. 2013. *The Design of Everyday Things.* Revised and Expanded Edition. Philadelphia, PA: Basic Books.

O'Brien, L., Bassham, J., & Lewis, M. 2014. Whiteboards and discharge traffic lights: Visual management in acute care. *Australian Health Review* 39: 160–4. doi: 10.1071/AH14131.

O'Neill, S., Jones, T., Bennett, D., & Lewis, M. 2011. Nursing Works: The Application of Lean Thinking to Nursing Process. *Journal of Nursing Administration* 41: 546–52.

Ohno, T. 1998. *Toyota Production System Beyond Large-Scale Production.* Portland, OR: Productivity Press.

Plsek, P.E., & Greenhalgh, T. 2001. The challenge of complexity in health care. *British Medical Journal* 323: 625.

Reinstaller, A. 2007. The division of labor in the firm: Agency, near-decomposability and the Babbage principle. *Journal of Institutional Economics* 3: 293–322.

Rother, M., & Shook, J. 2003. *Learning to See: Value Stream Mapping to Add Value and Eliminate MUDA.* Cambridge, MA: Lean Enterprise Institute.

Smith, R. 2013. *Patients at risk from junior doctors working 100 hour weeks: GMC.* http://www.telegraph. co.uk/news/health/news/9869932/Patients-at-risk-from-junior-doctors-working-100-hour-weeks-GMC.html, accessed 15 September 2016.

Terdiman, D. 2011. Boeing's 787 Dreamliner: A legacy of delays'. *CNET,* 19 January 2011. http://news.cnet. com/83011–3772_32–00288545–2.html#ixzz1Z1kEClBk, accessed 26 September 2016.

Trist, E.L., & Bamforth, K.W. 1963. Some social and psychological consequences of the longwall method of coal getting. *Human Relations* 4: 33–8.

Wilson, R.M., Runciman, W.B., Gibberd, R.W., et al. 1995. The quality in Australian health care study. *Medical Journal of Australia* 163: 4584–71.

Womack, J.P., & Jones, D.T. 2003. *Lean Thinking: Banish Waste and Create Wealth in Your Corporation.* New York: Free Press.

Womack, J.P., Jones, D.T., & Roos, D. 1990. *The Machine that Changed the World: The Story of Lean Production.* New York: Rawson Associates.

Wong, M.C., Yee, K.C., & Turner, P. 2008. *Clinical Handover Literature Review.* Sydney: Australian Commission on Safety and Quality in Healthcare.

Index